# Teaching Fractions and Ratios for Understanding

## Third Edition

# Teaching Fractions and Ratios for Understanding

## Essential Content Knowledge and Instructional Strategies for Teachers

## Third Edition

*Susan J. Lamon*

Routledge
Taylor & Francis Group

NEW YORK AND LONDON

First published 2012
by Routledge
711 Third Avenue, New York, NY 10017

Simultaneously published in the UK
by Routledge
2 Park Square, Milton Park, Abingdon, Oxon OX14 4RN

*Routledge is an imprint of the Taylor & Francis Group, an informa business*

*Library of Congress Cataloging in Publication Data*
Lamon, Susan J., 1949-
Teaching fractions and ratios for understanding : essential content knowledge and instructional strategies for
teachers / Susan J. Lamon. – 3rd ed.
p. cm.
Includes index.
1. Fractions–Study and teaching (Elementary) 2. Ratio and proportion–Study and teaching (Elementary) I. Title.
QA137.L36 2011
372.7'2–dc23
2011019888

ISBN: 978-0-415-88612-3 (pbk)

ISBN: 978-0-203-80316-5 (ebk)

Typeset in Aldine401BT
by Exeter Premedia Services Private Limited

Printed and bound in Canada

*For Sydney, Kylie and Grant*

# Contents

# Preface

Understanding fractions marks only the beginning of the journey toward rational number understanding. By the end of the middle school years, as a result of maturation, experience, and fraction instruction, it is assumed that students are capable of a formal thought process called *proportional reasoning*. This form of reasoning opens the door to high-school mathematics and science, and eventually, to careers in the mathematical sciences. The losses that occur because of the gaps in conceptual understanding about fractions, ratios, and related topics are incalculable. The consequences of *doing*, rather than understanding, directly or indirectly affect a person's attitudes toward mathematics, enjoyment and motivation in learning, course selection in mathematics and science, achievement, career flexibility, and even the ability to fully appreciate some of the simplest phenomena in everyday life.

For this reason the National Council of Teachers of Mathematics asserted in their Curriculum and Evaluation Standards (1989) that proportional reasoning "is of such great importance that it merits whatever time and effort must be expended to assure its careful development" (p. 82). By the middle school years, mathematics and human cognition are sufficiently complex that studying the development of understanding in fractions, ratios, and rational numbers presented a challenging research site. Without a research base to inform decision-making about the important conceptual components of proportional reasoning, textbook approaches unintentionally encouraged simplistic, mechanical treatment of ratios and proportions, highlighting the algebraic representation of a proportion and the manipulation of symbols. The rules for solving problems using proportions were indelibly printed into our memories: put like term over like term, cross multiply, and then divide. For most people, this mantra is a proxy for reasoning about quantities and their relationships.

In 1999, the first edition of this book translated the author's longitudinal research into usable ideas for the classroom. Since then, teachers from all around the world, who have been using the book to design fraction and ratio instruction for their students, have found that, not only is this material faithful to the ways in which real children think and solve problems, but that teachers' and students' understanding is enhanced by its new perspectives on the subject matter. Over the last 12 years, I have visited and taught in hundreds of mathematics classrooms where changes are occurring, where fractions fuel deep thought and discussion among teachers and students, and are not merely exercises that wear down pencils and erasers. The task of changing fraction instruction is now a world-wide action research project.

Recognizing that the work of teachers and students is complex, this book crosses traditional boundaries to include many topics that have been dissected into little bits and packaged separately. It includes all of the elements that are integrated in a genuine teaching–learning enterprise: mathematics content, the nature of conceptual development in the domain, connections to students' prior learning, teaching/reasoning techniques, classroom activities, connections to other content, and applications to everyday life. The material used in the book has already been used with students, and their work is presented so that you can see the brilliance of their insights as well as the issues that challenge their understanding.

This book is intended for researchers and curriculum developers in mathematics education, for pre-service and in-service teachers of mathematics, and for those involved in the mathematical and pedagogical preparation of mathematics teachers. In particular, for graduate students who are considering research in any area of multiplicative thinking, it provides an introduction to the content and issues in that exciting research domain.

This is real math, but it is written in a user-friendly, conversational style. This book answers the questions: If we were to take away all of the rules for fraction operations, what should we teach and what should our students understand? You may find it difficult to abandon fraction rules and procedures that you have relied on all of your life, but forcing yourself to work without them will unleash powerful ways of thinking. After solving problems yourself, discuss your solution with others and compare it with alternative solutions they may have produced. In adults' work, as well as in children's work, you meet diverse reasoning that affords a broad and deep experience and understanding of the mathematics. After you have worked out misconceptions, disagreements, and alternative solutions with your colleagues or fellow students, you will be better prepared to orchestrate discussion in your classroom.

In this edition, material has been expanded and reorganized in order to make the connectivity of topics more transparent. Several features that were introduced in the previous editions of this book have been retained, while some new features have been added.

- *Children's Strategies*. Samples of student work are provided in every chapter. This edition incorporates even more student work than did earlier editions.
- *Activities*. A good collection of activities is provided so that you can try for yourself the thinking strategies explained in the chapter. All are to be solved without rules or algorithms, using reasoning alone. In this edition, the activities in every chapter have been expanded and more real-world applications have been included.
- *MORE! Teaching Fractions and Ratios for Understanding*. This book containing in-depth discussions of selected problems is a valuable complement to *Teaching Fractions and Ratios*. When a person is deprived of the rules on which they have always relied, it is difficult to begin reasoning. Very often, the inclination is to describe step-by-step the computations that should be performed to solve the problem, rather than engaging in reasoning. *MORE* provides some scaffolding for this difficult process. This edition includes an expanded set of supplementary

activities for which solutions are not provided and a collection of challenging problems involving fractions. A new feature in this edition is a set of Praxis preparation questions related to the material in each chapter of *Teaching Fractions and Ratios*. More student work has been added for teacher analysis, and templates for key manipulatives have been included.

• *On-line Resources for Instructors.* Web resources provide a syllabus, including chapters, pacing, and homework assignments suitable for a 14-week college/university semester course, as well as discussion of the ideas that need emphasis in pre-service teacher classes. For the instructor's convenience, the website also includes many graphics that may be copied and resized for use in instruction and in constructing exams. See www.routledge.com/9780415886123.

I am grateful to all of the principals, teachers, and parents who have worked with me over the years to change fraction instruction. Their dissatisfaction with outdated, ineffective teaching methods and their determination to make a difference in mathematics instruction were inspirational. I remember most vividly the limitless energy and enthusiasm of the many students, now adults, who participated for four years in my initial study. A recent email update from one of them said:

Our fate was sealed by all of your mathematical reasoning. My brother and I are still 'pushing the envelope.' We graduated with degrees in mathematics and computer science and are now developing futuristic technologies at [a huge internet corporation].

Stepping out of one's personal comfort zone is initially difficult, but ultimately rewarding. I sincerely hope that this book serves as a comfortable companion as you begin your journey into the world of fractions and ratios.

# CHAPTER 1

# Proportional Reasoning: An Overview

## STUDENT STRATEGIES: GRADE 6

Some middle school children discussed the tree house problem and the responses from students A, B, C, D, and E are given here.

First, solve the problem yourself and explain your reasoning to someone else, then rank the student responses according to the sophistication of their mathematical reasoning.

These people disagree on the height of the tree house. How high do you think it is? Explain your reasoning.

**A**

15 feet

If the tower was in front of me and I looked up it would look near 15 feet tall.

**B**

9ft Tall

Mrs pechiki said the gold part of our pencil is a inch so I kept adding the inches and I got nine.

**C**

It about 18 feet. I figured out that it takes about 3 people the size of that man to be as tall as the tower. I found that out by counting the ___ I knew that every 8 of those would be 6 feet. So I just count every eight.

**D**

I thank its about 30 feet because one man said it ten feet. It cant be because the other man is feet and the tower is more than 10 feet so I think its 30 feet.

**E**

It is 24 feet. I took my thumb and pointer finger measured the man 3 times.

# INTRODUCTION

For too long, *proportional reasoning* has been an umbrella term, a catch-all phrase that refers to a certain facility with rational number concepts and contexts. The term is ill-defined and researchers have been better at determining when a student or an adult does *not* reason proportionally rather than defining the characteristics of one who does. Without appropriate instructional goals, purposeful teaching of the topic was impossible, and proportional reasoning remained an elusive by-product of instruction in fractions. Because elementary and middle school mathematics curricula provide no more than a cursory treatment of rational number ideas, the emergence of proportional reasoning is left to chance. Yet, the fact that most adults do not reason proportionally—my estimate well exceeds 90%—presents compelling evidence that this reasoning process entails more than developmental processes and that instruction must play an active role in its emergence.

Proportional reasoning is one of the best indicators that a student has attained understanding of rational numbers and related multiplicative concepts. While, on one hand, it is a measure of one's understanding of elementary mathematical ideas, it is, on the other, part of the foundation for more complex concepts. For this reason, I find it useful to distinguish proportional reasoning from the larger, more encompassing, concept of proportionality. Proportionality plays a role in applications dominated by physical principles—topics such as mechanical advantage, force, the physics of lenses, the physics of sound, just to name a few. Proportional reasoning, as this book uses the term, is a prerequisite for understanding contexts and applications based on proportionality.

Clearly, many people who have not developed their proportional reasoning ability have been able to compensate by using rules in algebra, geometry, and trigonometry courses, but, in the end, the rules are a poor substitute for sense-making. They are unprepared for real applications in statistics, biology, geography, or physics, where important, foundational principles rely on proportionality. This is unfortunate at a time when an ever-increasing number of professions rely on mathematics directly or use mathematical modeling to increase efficiency, to save lives, to save money, or to make important decisions.

For the purposes of this book, proportional reasoning will refer to the ability to scale up and down in appropriate situations and to supply justifications for assertions made about relationships in situations involving simple direct proportions and inverse proportions. In colloquial terms, proportional reasoning is *reasoning up and down* in situations in which there exists an invariant (constant) relationship between two quantities that are linked and varying together. As the word *reasoning* implies, it requires argumentation and explanation beyond the use of symbols $\frac{a}{b} = \frac{c}{d}$.

In this chapter, we will examine some problems to get a sense of what it means to reason proportionally. We will also look at a framework that was used to facilitate proportional reasoning in four-year longitudinal studies with children from the time they began fraction instruction in grade 3 until they finished grade 6.

## THE CONSTANT OF PROPORTIONALITY

The mathematical model for directly proportional relationships is a linear function of the form $y = kx$, where $k$ is called the constant of proportionality. Thus, $y$ is a constant multiple of $x$. Equivalently, two quantities are proportional when they vary in such a way that they maintain a constant ratio: $\frac{y}{x} = k$. The constant $k$ plays an essential role in understanding inversely proportional relationships as well. In the mathematical model for inverse proportions, $k = xy$. In spite of its importance, $k$ is sorely neglected in instruction.

Pedagogically speaking, $k$ is a slippery character, because it changes its guise in each particular context and representation involving proportional relationships. It frequently does not appear explicitly in the problem context, but rather, is a structural element lying beneath the obvious details. In symbols, it is a constant. In a graph, it is the slope. In a tabular representation, it may be the difference between any entry and the one before it,

| # of stacked wooden cubes | 1 | 2 | 3 | 4 | 5 | 6 |
|---|---|---|---|---|---|---|
| Height of the stack in inches | 3 | 6 | 9 | 12 | 15 | 18 |

or, equivalently, it may be the rate at which one quantity changes with respect to the other expressed as a unit rate,

| # of stacked wooden cubes | 2 | 5 | 9 | 12 | 15 |
|---|---|---|---|---|---|
| Height of the stack in inches | 6 | 15 | 27 | 36 | 45 |

In general, in rate situations, it is the constant rate. In reading maps, it is the scale. In shrinking/enlarging contexts, or in similar figures, it is the scale factor. It may be a percentage if you are discussing sales tax, or a theoretical probability if you are rolling dice. These examples suggest the need to visit many different contexts, to analyze quantitative relationships in context, and to represent those relationships in symbols, tables, and graphs. We simply cannot perform operations without thinking about which quantities are related, how they are changing together (or co-varying), what the constant of proportionality is, and what that constant of proportionality means.

## REASONING: BEYOND MECHANIZATION

Proportional *reasoning* refers to detecting, expressing, analyzing, explaining, and providing evidence in support of assertions about proportional relationships. The word *reasoning* further suggests that we use common sense, good judgment, and a thoughtful approach to problem-solving, rather than plucking numbers from word problems and blindly applying rules and operations. We typically do not associate reasoning with rule-driven or mechanized procedures, but rather, with mental, free-flowing processes that require conscious analysis of the relationships among quantities. Consider these problems and an eighth grader's approach to them:

a.  If a bag of topsoil weighs 40 pounds, how much will 3 identical bags weigh?
b.  If a football player weighs 225 pounds, how much will 3 players weigh?
c.  If Ed can paint the bedroom by himself in 3 hours, and his friend, Jake, works at the same pace as Ed does, how long will it take to paint the room if the boys work together?

d.  I was charged $1.20 for sales tax when I spent $20. How much sales tax would I pay on a purchase of $50?

e.  Bob and Marty like to run laps together because they run at the same pace. Today, Marty started running before Bob came out of the locker room. Marty had run 7 laps by the time that Bob ran 3. How many laps had Marty run by the time that Bob had run 12?

Mason

a.  $\dfrac{1 \text{ bag}}{40 \text{ p.}} = \dfrac{3 \text{ b.}}{? \text{ p.}}$    $3 \times 40 = 120 \text{ p.}$

b.  $\dfrac{1 \text{ f}}{225 \text{ p.}} = \dfrac{3 \text{ f}}{? \text{ p.}}$    $3 \times 225 = 675 \text{ p.}$

c.  $\dfrac{1 \text{ man}}{3 \text{ hrs}} = \dfrac{2 \text{ men}}{? \text{ hrs}}$    $2 \times 3 = 6 \text{ hrs}$

d.  $\dfrac{\$ 1.20 \text{ tax}}{\$ 20} = \dfrac{?}{\$ 50}$    $\$ 1.20 \times 50 = 60$
$60 \div 20 = \$ 3$

e.  $\overset{M}{\dfrac{7 \text{ laps}}{? \text{ laps}}} = \overset{B}{\dfrac{3 \text{ laps}}{12 \text{ laps}}}$    $7 \times 12 = 84$
$84 \div 3 = 28$

Certainly, part of understanding a concept is knowing what it is *not* and when it does *not* apply. Two quantities may be unrelated (as in problem b); one quantity may be related in an inversely proportional way to another quantity, as in problem c (increasing the number of people decreases the time needed to do a job), or it may be that the *change* in one quantity is proportional to the *change* in the other quantity, as in problem e. Many other important relationships do not entail proportional relationships at all and it is important to recognize the difference.

## INVARIANCE AND COVARIANCE

One of the most useful ways of thinking and operating in mathematics entails the transformation of quantities or equations in such a way that some underlying structure remains invariant (unchanged). Proportional relationships involve some of the simplest forms of covariation. That is, two quantities are linked to each other in such a way that when one changes, the other one also changes in a precise way with the first quantity, and there exists a third quantity that remains invariant (i.e., it doesn't change). The quantity that doesn't change is called the *constant of proportionality*.

In a direct proportion, the direction of change in the related quantities is the same; both increase or both decrease. As you analyze a situation, you might write this as ↑↑ or ↓↓ . But a critical aspect of direct proportion is that both quantities increase by the same factor. That is, if one doubles, the other doubles. If one becomes five times as great, the other becomes five times as great. Then we say that "*y* is directly proportional to *x*" or that "*y* varies as *x*." Just because two related quantities both increase or both decrease does not mean that they are directly proportional. For example, as a person's age increases, his height increases ↑↑, but age and height are not directly proportional because they do not increase by the same factor.

Here is a problem involving quantities that are directly proportional:

- If a box of detergent contains 80 cups of powder and your washing machine recommends $1\frac{1}{4}$ cups per load, how many loads can you do with one box?

    Think: $1\frac{1}{4}$ cups for 1 load. The more loads I do, the more cups of detergent

    I need: ↑↑

    for 4 loads I will need 5 cups
    for 32 loads I will need 40 cups
    for 64 loads I will need 80 cups

We can double both quantities (cups and loads), or quadruple both quantities, or take 8 times both quantities, but the two quantities always maintain the same relationship to each other. Notice that the number of cups (c) is always $1\frac{1}{4}$ times the number of loads (d). Symbolically, $c = 1\frac{1}{4} d$. 5 is $1\frac{1}{4}$ times 4; 40 is $1\frac{1}{4}$ times 30; 80 is $1\frac{1}{4}$ times 64. Another way to think of this relationship is: $\frac{c}{d} = 1\frac{1}{4}$.

In an inverse proportion, one quantity increases and the other decreases (↑↓), but in a connected, synchronized way. One is multiplied by a certain factor and the other one is multiplied by the inverse or reciprocal of that factor. So if one quantity is halved, the other doubles; if one quantity is divided by 5 $\left( \text{same as being multiplied by } \frac{1}{5} \right)$, the other is multiplied by 5. Then we say that "*y* is inversely proportional to *x*" or that "*y* varies inversely as *x*." Again, be careful: just because two related quantities change in opposite directions does not mean that they are necessarily inversely proportional.

- It takes 6 men 4 days to pick the apples in a certain orchard. How long will it take if the owner hires 8 pickers?

Think: 6 men take 4 days.

1 man doing the work of 6 men all by himself will take 24 days.

8 men, dividing up the work that 1 man did, will take 3 days.

We know that increasing the number of people working on the job should mean that the job can be completed in less time. (people ↑, time ↓) Conversely, decreasing the number of people working on the job should increase the number of days needed to complete the job. The number of pickers and the number of days change in a connected way. However, there is another quantity that remains invariant. That quantity is *the number of picker days* that are required to get the job done—regardless of how many men are going to share the work. In this case, it will take 24 picker days to get the apples picked. That invariant quantity is the constant of proportionality and it is given by the product of the two quantities, *number of pickers* ($p$) and *number of days* ($d$). Symbolically, $p \cdot d = k$.

| # men picking | # days | # picker days |
|---------------|--------|---------------|
| 6 | 4 | 24 |
| 8 | 3 | 24 |
| 1 | 24 | 24 |
| 4 | 6 | 24 |
| 2 | 12 | 24 |

Part of what it means to understand proportionality is to recognize valid and invalid transformations, those that preserve the ratio of the two quantities in the case when quantities are directly proportional, or the product of the quantities in the case when the quantities are related in an inversely proportional way.

## SOLVING PROPORTIONS USING *K*

Using the constant of proportionality can help your proportional reasoning. You have to think about what the constant means. One way to keep track of what it means is to label every quantity and "cancel" the quantity labels. For example, if John types 30 words per minute and it takes him 1.25 hours to type a paper, speed and time are both changing quantities. In fact, we have speed ↑, time ↓. What does the constant stand for? $\frac{30 \text{ words}}{\text{minute}} \cdot 75 \text{ \sout{minutes}} = k = 2250$ words. Thus, $k$ is the total number of words in the document. Different numbers of people may share the work, and the more people you have, the less time it will take to do the work, but the total number of words that need to be typed does not change.

- Suppose Joe, who can type 40 words per minute, takes 2.5 hours to type a document. To speed things up, his friend Mack offers to help him. Mack can type 25 words per minute. How long will it take them working together to type the document?

Think: We have typing speed (r) ↑ and time (t) ↓. We know that our answer will be less than 2.5 hours and because Mack works more slowly than Joe does, the total time will be longer than 1.25 hours. (Think: Mack's help won't cut the time in half.)

Let's solve this problem in two ways: (a) using the constant of proportionality and (b) using an inverse proportion.

(a)

What is the constant? $\dfrac{40 \text{ words}}{1 \text{ minute}} \cdot \dfrac{2.5 \text{ hours}}{1} \cdot \dfrac{60 \text{ minutes}}{1 \text{ hour}} = 6000$ words

What is the rate when two people work together? 65 words per minute

$$6000 \text{ words} = \frac{65 \text{ words}}{1 \text{ minute}} \cdot T$$

$$T = \frac{6000 \text{ words}}{1} \cdot \frac{1 \text{ minute}}{65 \text{ words}} = 92.31 \text{ minutes} = 1.54 \text{ hours}$$

Notice that the labels "hours" and "minutes" divide just as numbers do. $\dfrac{\text{hours}}{\text{hours}} = 1$ and $\dfrac{\text{minutes}}{\text{minutes}} = 1$, so we could have done this more simply:

$40 (2.5) = 100$. This means $k = 100$. So $65 \cdot T = 100$ and $T = \dfrac{100}{65} = 1.54$ hours.

(b)

In a directly proportional situation, we would put like quantities over each other:

$$\frac{r_1}{r_2} = \frac{t_1}{t_2}.$$

Because rate and time are inversely proportional, we invert one of the ratios before solving:

$$\frac{r_1}{r_2} = \frac{t_2}{t_1}$$

$$\frac{\dfrac{40 \text{ words}}{1 \text{ minute}}}{\dfrac{65 \text{ words}}{1 \text{ minute}}} = \frac{t_2}{2.5 \text{ hours}}$$

Now solve the proportion as usual: multiply $\dfrac{40 \text{ words}}{1 \text{ minute}}$ by 2.5 hours and divide by $\dfrac{65 \text{ words}}{1 \text{ minute}}$:

$$\frac{40 \text{ words}}{1 \text{ minute}} \cdot \frac{2.5 \text{ hours}}{1} \cdot \frac{1 \text{ minute}}{65 \text{ words}} = \frac{100 \text{ hours}}{65} = 1.54 \text{ hours}$$

# MULTIPLICATIVE THINKING

In the previous problems about laundry detergent and apple picking, why did the transformations consist of *multiplying* (or dividing) both quantities by the same whole number? It takes some degree of mathematical maturity to understand the difference between adding and multiplying and contexts in which each operation is appropriate. One of the most difficult tasks for children is understanding the multiplicative nature of the change in proportional situations. Children who cannot yet tell the difference indiscriminately employ additive transformations simply because they are most comfortable with addition.

The process of addition is associated with situations that entail adding, joining, affixing, subtracting, separating, and removing—actions with which children are familiar because of their experiences with counting and whole number operations. The process of multiplication is associated with situations that involve such processes as shrinking, enlarging, scaling, duplicating, exponentiating, and fair sharing. As students interact with multiplicative situations, analyzing their quantitative relationships, they eventually understand why additive transformations do not work. However, this takes time and experience, and it does not happen until the student can detect certain quantities called *intensive* quantities.

Intensive quantities are new quantities that are formed by comparing two other quantities and they are not always explicit in the wording of a problem. Consider this problem:

- For your party, you planned to purchase 2 pounds of mixed nuts for 8 people, but at the last minute, you realized that 10 people were coming. How many pounds should you purchase?

| # people | Pounds of nuts |
|----------|----------------|
| 8        | 2              |
| 10       | ?              |

It is true that 10 people are 2 more than 8 people, but adding 2 pounds of nuts for 2 more people suggests that we need a whole pound for each additional person, and originally we were not figuring on a pound per person. Hence, an additive transformation changes your original plan for providing $\frac{1}{4}$ pound per party guest. Clearly, a student is not going to be able to analyze this situation until he/she "sees" in it the implicit third quantity *pounds per person*.

# CRITICAL COMPONENTS OF POWERFUL REASONING

The goal of this book is to share some teaching methods and materials that may be used throughout the elementary and middle school years to promote the ways of thinking that contribute to a deep understanding of the rational numbers and to the ability to reason proportionally. The term *proportional reasoning* is used to describe sophisticated mathematical ways of thinking that emerge sometime in the late elementary or middle school years and continue to grow in depth and sophistication throughout the high school and college years. It signifies the attainment of a certain level of mathematical maturity that consolidates many elementary ideas and opens the door to more advanced mathematical and scientific thinking.

But the beginning of the story occurs early in elementary school with fractions. Experiences in many real-world contexts that require *fracturing* or *breaking* a unit provide the basis for the rational number system. Because traditional fraction instruction has not been particularly effective, one of the most compelling tasks for researchers has been to discover how fraction instruction can better facilitate the long-range development of rational number understanding and proportional reasoning. By deeply analyzing mathematical content, children's thinking, and adult thinking, we have begun to identify a number of central or core ideas that must be addressed in instruction. These highly interrelated concepts, contexts, representations, and ways of thinking are shown in the following diagram.

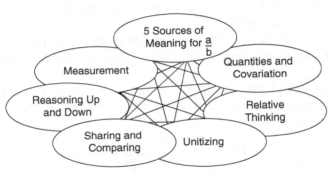

We certainly don't want to underestimate the complexity of the knowledge-building process; these topics comprise a minimal set of essential topics. They develop in a web-like fashion, rather than in a linear order. When students make progress in any one of these areas, there are repercussions throughout the web. They are built up over a long period of time and are called *central* because they constitute part of the very backbone of mathematical and scientific domains—ideas and processes and representations that are recurrent, recursive and of increasing complexity in elementary through advanced studies. We will expand each of these ideas in later chapters.

## GETTING STARTED

To get a sense of what is entailed in proportional reasoning, try the next two problem sets. The first set of 10 questions that may be answered quickly and mentally if you reason proportionally. The second set is composed of more substantial problems whose solutions require proportional reasoning or some way of thinking critical to proportional reasoning. Because you know that many of these problems may be solved using proportions, you may be tempted to use an equation of the form $\dfrac{a}{b} = \dfrac{c}{d}$, but using those symbols is not reasoning. Think about each problem and explain the solution without using rules and symbols.

---

Solve these problems mentally. Use your pen or pencil only to record your answers. Do not perform any computation!

1. Six men can build a house in 3 days. Assuming that all of the men work at the same rate, how many men would it take to build the house in 1 day?

2. If 6 chocolates cost $0.93, how much do 22 cost?

3. Between them, John and Mark have 32 marbles. John has 3 times as many as Mark. How many marbles does each boy have?

4. Mac can mow Mr. Greenway's lawn in 45 minutes. Mac's little brother takes twice as long to do the same lawn. How long will it take them if they each have a mower and they work together?

5. Six students were given 20 minutes to clean up the classroom after an eraser fight. They were angry and named 3 other accomplices. The principal added their friends to the clean-up crew and changed the time limit. How much time did she give them to complete the job?

6. If 1 football player weighs 280 pounds, what is the total weight of the 11 starters?

7. Sandra wants to buy an MP3 player costing $210. Her mother agreed to pay $5 for every $2 Sandra saved. How much will each contribute?

8. A company usually sends 9 men to install a security system in an office building, and they do it in about 96 minutes. Today, they have only three men to do the same size job. How much time should be scheduled to complete the job?

9. A motorbike can run for 10 minutes on $1.30 worth of fuel. How long could it run on $0.91 worth of fuel?

10. Posh Academy boasts a ratio of 150 students to 18 teachers. How can the number of faculty be adjusted so that the academy's student-to-teacher ratio is 15 to1?

---

When you are finished, discuss your reasoning with someone else. As you listen to other explanations, you may discover that there is more than one way to think about each problem. The next set of problems is more challenging. You may need to spend a considerable amount of time on them, so do not give up if you do not have a solution in 5 minutes. Remember that the goal is to support each solution with reasoning. Do not solve any of the problems by applying rules or by using a proportion equation $\left(\text{e.g. } \frac{a}{b} = \frac{c}{d}\right)$.

11. On a sunny day, you and your friend were taking a long walk. You got tired and stopped near a telephone pole for a little rest, but your nervous friend couldn't stand still. He paced out your shadow and discovered that it was 8 feet long even though you are really only 5 feet tall. He paced the long shadow of the telephone pole and found that it was 48 feet long. He wondered how high the telephone pole really is. Can you figure it out?

12. Which is more square, a rectangle that measures 35″ × 39″ or a rectangle that measures 22″ × 25″?

13. Two gears, A and B, are arranged so that the teeth of one gear mesh with the teeth of another. Gear A turns clockwise and has 54 teeth. Gear B turns counterclockwise and has 36 teeth. If gear A makes 5.5 rotations, how many turns will gear B make?

14. Mr. Brown is a bike rider. He considered living in Allentown, Binghamton, and Chester. In the end, he chose Binghamton because, as he put it, "All else being equal, I chose the town where bikes stand the greatest chance on the road against cars." Is Binghamton town A, B, or C?
    A. Area is 15 sq mi; 12,555 cars in town.
    B. Area is 3 sq mi; 2502 cars in town.
    C. Area is 17 sq mi; 14,212 cars in town.

15. Mrs. Cobb makes and sells her own apple-cranberry juice. In pitcher A, she mixed 4 cranberry-flavored cubes and 3 apple-flavored cubes with some water. In pitcher B, she used 3 cranberry and 2 apple-flavored cubes in the same amount of water. If you ask her for the drink that has a stronger cranberry taste, from which pitcher would she pour your drink?

16. Jim's mother asked him to go to her desk and get his dad's picture and its enlargement, but when Jim went into her office, he found five pictures of his dad in various sizes. Which two did she want?
    A. 9 cm × 10 cm    B. 10 cm × 12 cm    C. 8 cm × 9.6 cm
    D. 6 cm × 8 cm    E. 5 cm × 6.5 cm

17. From Lewis Carroll: If 6 cats can kill 6 rats in 6 minutes, how many cats will be needed to kill 100 rats in 50 minutes?

18.  Two identical balance beams are placed on a table and a number of weights are added while the beams are held in place. Would you expect each beam to tip toward the right or toward the left when it is released?

19.  What is the ratio of men to women in a town where $\frac{2}{3}$ of the men are married to $\frac{3}{4}$ of the women?

20.  In a gourmet coffee shop, two types of beans are combined and sold as the house blend. One bean sells for $8.00 per pound and the other for $14.00 per pound. The shop owner mixes up a batch of 50 pounds at a time and sells the house blend for $10.00 a pound. How many pounds of each kind of coffee go into the blend?

Don't worry if you were not able to solve all of problems 11–20 on your first try. These are some of the types of problems that you should be able to explain by the time you are finished with this book. It would be a good idea to return to them periodically to apply new insights. Now that you have some impression of what proportional reasoning entails, let's return to the students' work shown at the beginning of this chapter.

## ANALYZING CHILDREN'S THINKING

Because critical ideas develop and mature over a period of time, children should begin to think about the activities in this book early in elementary school and continue to discuss and write about these ideas all the way through middle school. As you try problems in this book with children in real classrooms, you will find that many elicit a broad range of responses. The tree house problem is one such problem.

Student C used the most sophisticated reasoning to solve the problem. The tree house is 18 feet above the ground. Student A is the only student who indicated no reasoning at all. A said that he or she would just look up at the tower and guess. Student D failed to pick up on any of the clues in the picture and focused only on what the child and the man had to say. Unfortunately, this student used faulty reasoning and assumed that one of the characters had to be correct, arguing that if the child in the tree house is wrong, the man on the ground must be correct. Students B and E both used measurement as the basis for their arguments. Student E, who measured using the man's height, could have gotten a correct answer if he or she has known that $3 \times 6 = 18$, but student B, who measured with the end of a pencil, probably had some misconceptions about measurement and scale. He or she assumed that 1 inch in the picture converted to 1 foot in real distance. On the other hand, student C used three quantities to help discover the missing height: the height of the man, the total number of rungs on the ladder, and the number of rungs corresponding to the man's height. This thinking was closest to proportional reasoning. Based on this analysis, the levels of thinking, ranked from lowest to highest, are A–D–B–E–C.

The tree house problem makes a good assessment item. If you asked children to respond to it in September and again in June, you would see a dramatic change in their thinking. The more you analyze children's work at various stages of development, the better you become at discerning levels of sophistication in their thinking. This information, in turn, can help you to make instructional decisions. But even more important than recognizing good reasoning when it occurs is knowing how to facilitate it. In the following chapters, we will examine activities to promote powerful reasoning.

## ACTIVITIES

1.  Try this famous problem about *Mr. Short and Mr. Tall.*

    Here is a picture of Mr. Short. When you measure his height in paperclips, he is 6 paperclips tall. When you measure his height in buttons, he is 4 buttons tall.

    Mr. Short has a friend named Mr. Tall. When you measure Mr. Tall's height in buttons, he is 6 buttons tall. What would be Mr. Tall's height if you measured it in paperclips?

2.  Mr. Tall's car is 15 paperclips long. How long is his car if we measure it in buttons? His car is $7\frac{1}{2}$ paperclips wide. How wide is it in buttons?

3.  The Bi-Color Egg company has just hired you to fill egg cartons with brown and white eggs. The cartons come in different sizes, and your job is to fill every carton so that the numbers of brown eggs and white eggs are in the same proportions as they are in carton A. Color the eggs in cartons B and C.

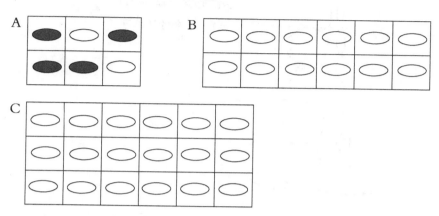

4.  In each case, determine whether or not the pricing is proportional.

    a.  The Green Grocery sells tomato sauce in 6 oz. cans for $0.49 and in 15 oz. cans for $0.69.
    b.  The Town Market sells its store brand sugar in a 4 pound bag for $2.99, a 5 pound bag for $3.75, and a 10-pound bag for $11.74.
    c.  At the farmers' market, strawberries were priced at $2.98 for a pound, and $1.49 for 8 ounces.
    d.  I can buy 25 fabric softener sheets for $1.69, 50 sheets for $2.99, or 100 sheets for $5.99.
    e.  A certain breakfast buffet charges $0.89 for each year of a child's age, up to the age of 12.
    f.  Stop N Shop sells 12-can soft drink boxes for $3.29 each or a bundle of 3 boxes for $10.19.

5.  Josh is a sixth grader. Here is his solution to *Mr. Short and Mr. Tall*. Describe Josh's strategy. Even though he did not express a proportion symbolically, what proportion does he appear to understand?

Josh 6B

Draw it out and
see that Mr. Tall must
be 9 paperclips tall.

6.  What does the speedometer in your car measure? Suppose you are taking a 60-mile trip. Figure out the time your trip would take at various speeds. Is the time for your journey proportional to your speed?

7.  In #6 above, is time inversely proportional to speed? What is $k$, the constant of proportionality?

8.  Write an equation for each situation described.

    a.  The amount of illumination (I) from a light source is inversely proportional to the square of its distance (d) from the source.
    b.  The force $F$ on a mass is directly proportional to the acceleration (a) of the mass.
    c.  The gravitational force ($F$ in Newtons) between two masses is inversely proportional to the square of the distance between them ($d$).
    d.  The resistance ($R$ in ohms) of a wire is directly proportional to the length ($l$) of the wire.
    e.  The mass ($m$) of a liquid in a cylindrical container is proportional to the square of the radius ($r$) of the container.
    f.  The weight of a body ($W$) varies inversely as the square of its distance ($d$) from the center of the earth.

9.  As accurately as you can, describe to someone how to tell when a relationship between two quantities is a direct proportion, an inverse proportion, or not a proportion at all.

10. At our zoo, the number of sardines a fish is fed is proportional to the length of the fish. For example, Long Louie, who measures about 65 cm, gets 30 sardines for lunch. There are two other fish in the tank with Louie: Mighty Mo, who measures 97.5 cm, and Pete the Pip, who measures 32.5 cm. How many sardines are needed to feed all three fish?

11. Two quantities are given in each example. Using arrows and words, show how the quantities change together or write NR when the quantities are not related.

    Example: People working on a project, time to complete the project

    Think: ↓↑ and ↑↓ With fewer people working on the project, it will take more time to complete the project. With more people working, the project can be completed in a shorter time.

    a. Unit cost, total cost
    b. Size of a gas tank, cost to fill your tank
    c. Distance in feet, distance in meters
    d. Diameter of your tires, gas consumption on a given trip
    e. Side length of a square, area of a square
    f. Percentage of discount, discount in dollars
    g. Price paid for an item, sales tax
    h. Population of a town, time in years
    i. Number of hours you drive, average speed over your trip
    j. Number of office colleagues who buy a lottery ticket, share of the winnings
    k. Number of work days in a month, number of vacation days in a month
    l. Price of a candy bar, number of candy bars you buy

12. Which of the pairs in question 11 are related proportionally?

13. Which of the quantities in question 11 are inversely proportional?

14. Sixteen men can complete a building project in 24 days. Name the two variables and the constant. Write a statement in symbols and in words telling how the quantities are related. Make a proportionality statement.

15. Step 1. Using four little sticks, Jim builds this figure.

    Step 2. Using more little sticks, Jim builds this figure.

Step 3. Using even more little sticks, Jim builds this figure.

And so on.

Identify two variables and a constant, and show how they are related using words and symbols. Make a proportionality statement.

16.  When there is a car accident, the police can tell if someone was speeding by examining the length of the skid marks left by that person's car. This is because stopping distance is proportional to the square of the speed of a car. For example, if they find skid marks that are 300 feet long, they can estimate that the car was going about 77.46 mph. Suppose a car left skid marks about 120 feet in length in a 50 mph zone. Should this person receive a speeding ticket?

17.  Charlie is a translator who has been asked to translate a 350-page book. It will take him 70 hours to complete the work. His wife Elaine can translate at the rate of 4 pages per hour. If she helps Charlie with this book, how long will it take to complete the translation?

18.  Fill in the blanks.

   a.  An object is traveling at a constant speed. The distance traveled is proportional to _____ and the constant of proportionality is _____.
   b.  The circumference of a circle (distance around the circle) is given by the rule $C = \pi d$. _____ is proportional to _____ and _____ is the constant of proportionality.
   c.  When you fill up your car's gas tank, _____ is proportional to _____ and _____ is the constant of proportionality.
   d.  You work at a grocery store. The amount you are paid is proportional to _____, and _____ is the constant of proportionality.
   e.  If you buy several identical candy bars, _____ is proportional to _____ and _____ is the constant of proportionality.
   f.  When you convert centimeters to meters, _____ is proportional to _____ and _____ is the constant of proportionality.
   g.  When you read a map and figure out the distance between two cities, _____ is proportional to _____ and _____ is the constant of proportionality.

19.  Jim is a cyclist who participated in a 72 km ride to benefit cancer. His progress over the journey is given in the following chart:

| Distance in km | 12 | 24 | 36 | 48 | 60 | 72 |
|---|---|---|---|---|---|---|
| Time in hours | 1 | 2 | 3 | 4 | 5 | 6 |

Were his distance and time proportional? What is the constant of proportionality and what does it mean?

20.  A high school student provided this explanation of direct and inversely proportional quantities. Do you think his explanation is helpful?

If you pick apples and put them in a basket, then the number of apples you have picked varies directly with the number of baskets you have. The inverse relationship is a little less obvious. An inverse relationship means as one thing gets bigger the other gets smaller. Think of fractions. If the denominator gets bigger then the quantity gets smaller.

# CHAPTER 2

# Fractions and Rational Numbers

## STUDENT STRATEGIES: GRADE 4

Think about the division of whole numbers and discuss the ways it might have influenced student thinking as they solved this problem:

There are 15 students in your class, including you. On your birthday, your mom made 5 pounds of cookies for the students to share. How much will each person get?

Eva.    15/5 = 3 pounds per person

Mary Elizabeth
5 pounds isn't big enough so I changed it to oz.   16 oz. = 1 lb.

16 oz. × 5 = 80 oz. in 5 pounds

$$15 \overline{)80} \quad \begin{array}{c} 5 \\ \underline{75} \\ 5 \end{array}$$

Give everybody 5 oz. and give the other 5 cookies to the teacher.

Many people have a fear of mathematics. In high school, they were reluctant to take more than the minimum required courses. They had feelings of "being lost" or 'in the dark' when it came to mathematics. For most of these people, their relationship with mathematics started downhill early in elementary school, right after they were introduced to fractions. They may have been able to pass courses—perhaps even get good grades—beyond the third and fourth grades by memorizing much of what they were expected to know, but they can remember the anxiety of not understanding what was going on in their mathematics classes. This chapter looks at some of the reasons why fractions present such a big mathematical and psychological stumbling block.

## NEW UNITS AND A NEW NOTATIONAL SYSTEM

As one encounters fractions, mathematical content takes a qualitative leap in sophistication. Suddenly, meanings and models and symbols that worked when adding, subtracting, multiplying, and dividing whole numbers are not as useful.

Several very large conceptual jumps contribute to the children's difficulty in learning fractions. In the preschool years, a child learned to count by matching one number name to each object in the set being counted. The unit "one" always referred to a single object. In fractions, however, the unit may consist of more than one object or it might be a composite unit, that is, it may consist of several objects packaged as one. Furthermore, the new unit is partitioned (divided up into equal parts) and a new kind of number is used to refer to parts of that unit.

$$\bigcirc\bigcirc\bigcirc \quad = 1 \text{ unit}$$

$$\bigcirc \quad = \frac{1}{3} \text{ unit}$$

$$\bigcirc \quad = \frac{1}{2} \text{ unit}$$

Furthermore, in each new situation, the unit may be something different.

$$\bigcirc\bigcirc \quad = 1 \text{ unit}$$

$$\bigcirc \quad = \frac{1}{2} \text{ unit}$$

$$\bigcirc \quad = \frac{1}{3} \text{ unit}$$

Even perceptual clues are no longer reliable. What *looks* like the same amount may not always have the same name. For example:

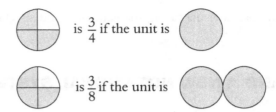

Finally, there is not a unique symbol to refer to part of a unit. The same amount can be referenced by different names.

For example, $\frac{1}{2}, \frac{2}{4}, \frac{6}{12}$, and $\frac{9}{18}$ of the same unit are all the same amount of stuff.

## THE PSYCHOLOGY OF UNITS

There are many different types of units with which one can study fractions. If the unit is a single pizza and you buy more than one pizza, say three of them, then you have purchased 3 one-units or 3 (pizzas). If you purchase a package containing 3 frozen pizzas, then you have purchased one unit that is a composite unit. You have purchased 1 (3-pack). You may argue that, in the end, it is all the same amount of pizza, but in early fraction instruction, when you are using concrete examples to help children understand meanings, notations, and operations, the phenomena that give rise to fractions are diverse. Children attend to such differences and ignoring them often causes confusion and miscommunication.

Here are some examples:

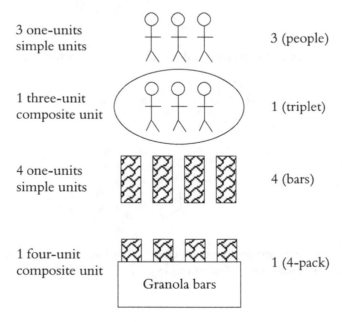

Unit structures continue to grow in complexity. For example, now compare the 3-unit of people to the 4-unit of granola bars. This produces another unit, a ratio:

③ If we think of the triplet of people as a unit of units and the 4-pack of granola
④ bars as a unit of units, then the ratio is a unit of units of units.

Psychologically speaking, 4 (bars) and 1 (4-pack) of granola bars are different and operating on them produces different results. For example, there are several ways of taking $\frac{1}{4}$ of our granola bars. If we take $\frac{1}{4}$ of a unit consisting of 4 single granola bars, we might get

In the first case, $\frac{1}{4}$ of 4 bars = 1 bar, and in the second case, we get $\frac{1}{4}$ of 4 bars = $4\left(\frac{1}{4}\text{-bars}\right)$. On the other hand, suppose we begin with 1(4-pack) of granola bars. We could unpack the box and then perform one of the operations just shown, or we could keep the box intact.

As we shall see later, these differences in the way a child operates on a composite unit are significant. They provide the teacher great insight into the child's thinking and his/her development of critical fraction ideas.

## NEW OPERATIONS AND QUANTITIES

When children worked with whole numbers, they operated on them principally by adding and subtracting. They began to develop some meaning for the operations of multiplication and division, but only in carefully chosen contexts using carefully chosen numbers and labels. Before the introduction of fractions, children develop only a very limited understanding of multiplication and division. This is because true understanding of the operations of multiplication and division can only come about when a student is able to construct composite units or units composed of multiple entities, and fraction notation is needed to help represent the complex quantities that result from multiplication and division.

When working with whole numbers, quantities had simple labels that came about by counting or measuring: 5 candies or 7 feet. The operations of multiplication and division often produce new quantities that are relationships between two other quantities. Furthermore, the label attached to the new quantity (the relationship) is not the label of either of the original quantities that entered into the relationship.

24 candies divided among 4 party bags is $\frac{24 \text{ candies}}{6 \text{ bags}}$ or $\frac{6 \text{ candies}}{1 \text{ bag}}$. We have a new quantity that is not measured by one of the original measures, *candies* or *bags*.

Also, whole number quantities could be physically represented. Students could draw a picture of candies or they could use beans or blocks or chips to represent things being counted. However, a quantity expressing a relationship such as 2.5 children per family or 12 miles per hour (mph) cannot be easily represented or conceptualized.

To further complicate the labeling issue, sometimes a quantity that is really a relationship between two quantities is given a single name. For example, consider the relationship between a certain distance traveled and the time it took to travel that distance. That relationship is so familiar that we chunk the two quantities into a single entity and refer to is as *speed*. When we refer to speed or to other *chunked* quantities in the classroom, it is important to discuss the quantities of which they are composed. Many students, well into their middle school years, don't know that speed is a comparison.

## INTERFERENCE OF WHOLE NUMBER IDEAS

In whole number operations, many students came to rely on the model of repeated addition to help them think about multiplication, and the model of sharing some set of objects among some number of children to help them think about the process of division. In the world of rational numbers, both of these models are defective. Consider these examples:

A car traveled an average speed of $52 \frac{\text{mi}}{\text{hr}}$ on a trip that took 3.4 hours. How far did it travel?

$$52 \frac{\text{mi}}{\text{hr}} \times 3.4 \text{ hr} = 176.8 \text{ mi.}$$

A car traveled an average speed of $51 \frac{\text{mi}}{\text{hr}}$ and consumed $1.5 \frac{\text{gal}}{\text{hr}}$ of gasoline on a certain trip. What was the car's fuel efficiency on that trip?

$$51 \frac{\text{mi}}{\text{hr}} \div 1.5 \frac{\text{gal}}{\text{hr}} = 34 \frac{\text{mi}}{\text{gal}}$$

You can see that in these examples, the repeated addition and sharing models are no help in answering the questions asked. It is necessary to build up new ways to think about these situations because the ways of thinking that were useful when working with whole numbers simply do not work anymore. A student must learn to think about the quantities and how they are related to each other in order to determine appropriate operations.

Children experience cognitive obstacles as they encounter fractions because they try to make connections with the whole numbers and operations with which they are familiar. Some of the ideas children develop while working with whole numbers actually interfere with their later ability to understand fractions and their operations. For example, most children think that multiplication makes larger and division makes smaller. They experience considerable confusion when they encounter fraction multiplications such as the following:

- $\frac{2}{3} \cdot \frac{1}{4}$ (start with $\frac{2}{3}$, multiply, and end with a product that is smaller.)

- $\frac{5}{8} \div \frac{1}{4}$ (start with $\frac{5}{8}$, divide, and end up with a quotient that is larger.)

The children whose work is shown at the beginning of this chapter probably remembered that in whole number division, the dividend (the number being divided) was always larger than the divisor. Each used a different method to deal with numbers that were too small to fit their concept of division, but then they both ran into the problem of deciding how to label the quantity their division produced. Mary Elizabeth's work shows what a bright little girl she is, but all students—even the brightest—experience a huge conceptual leap when they begin to work with fractions.

The problems are many. Even those we have mentioned here do not exhaust the list. For example, in whole number operations, multiplication is commutative, that is, 3 × 4 will give the same result as 4 × 3. However, as quantities become more complex, many people begin to question ideas as basic as commutativity. For example, it is difficult to see that 3 (5-units) and 5 (3-units) are equivalent if you think about 3 bags, each of which contain 5 candies and 5 bags each containing 3 candies. If you like candy, would you be satisfied choosing any one of these bags? Also, driving for 3 hours at 45 miles per hour is a very different trip from driving for 45 hours at 3 miles per hour. Therefore, some of the structural properties that were more transparent when working with whole numbers are still true on a more abstract level, but when placed in real contexts, it may be difficult to recognize them.

In addition to the problems already mentioned, other sources of difficulty for children arise in these facts:

- Even though a fraction is written using 2 numerals, it stands for one number.
- Even though $7 > 3, \frac{1}{3} > \frac{1}{7}$.

- There are new rules for adding and subtracting fractions: $\frac{1}{3} + \frac{2}{5} \neq \frac{3}{8}$.

- Sometimes though, $\frac{1}{3} + \frac{2}{5} = \frac{3}{8}$. Ratios written in fraction form do not follow the same rules as addition of fractions.

- Whole number rules for multiplication still work: $\frac{2}{3} \times \frac{4}{5} = \frac{8}{15}$.

## PROBLEMS WITH TERMINOLOGY

Sometimes we get careless with the way we use words and this can cause additional difficulties in communicating about an already complicated topic. Often the word *fraction* is used when rational number is intended, and vice versa. The word fraction is used in a variety of ways inside the classroom as well as outside the classroom. The many uses of the word are bound to cause confusion.

In particular, the word *fraction* has several meanings, not all of which are mathematical. For example, a fraction might be a piece of undeveloped land, while in church, it would refer to the breaking of the Eucharistic bread. In the statement "All but a fraction of the townspeople voted in the presidential election," the word *fraction* means *a small part*. When you hear that "the stock rose fractionally," it means *less than one dollar*. In math class, it is disconcerting to students that they need to learn a technical definition of the part—whole fraction when they already know from their everyday experience of the word that it means *any little bit*. When a fraction such as $\frac{4}{3}$ refers to more than one whole unit, the interpretation *a little bit* does not apply very well. The colloquial usage of the word is complicated enough, but multiple uses of the word in mathematics education is also problematic. Some people use the word *fraction* to refer specifically to a part—whole comparison. It may also refer to any number written in the symbolic form $\frac{a}{b}$. Many people further confuse the issue by using the words *fraction* and *rational number* interchangeably. We need to get this terminology straightened out so that we can communicate. We will begin by locating fractions in the development of number sets.

## DEVELOPMENT OF SETS OF NUMBERS

When a baby first begins to count, she says 1, 2, 3, 4, etc. Therefore, the following set of numbers is called the set of counting numbers (*C*): { 1, 2, 3, 4, ...}. The counting numbers (1, 2, 3, 4, 5, ...) are used to answer the question "How many?" in situations where it is implicit that we mean "How many whole things?"

When the baby gets a little older, he understands that it is possible to have "nothing." Until then, each number stood for a count of some concrete objects. Zero, however, is a count of the elements in the empty set. In other words, zero is the cardinal number that tells the size of a set that is empty. (Note that the empty set is represented as { } or Ø, but NOT {Ø}.) The whole numbers (0, 1, 2, 3, 4, ...) are also used to count how many whole objects are in a set of objects, with the added feature that they can answer that question even when the set is empty.

Zero is a special number. It separates the positives and the negatives, but it is not positive and it is not negative. But it *is* even. To prove this to yourself, recall the fact that evens and odds alternate, and begin counting down from an even number, say 6. When you get to 2, and skip the next number because it is odd, you must conclude that zero is even.

$$⑥ \quad 5 \quad ④ \quad 3 \quad ② \quad 1 \quad ⓪ \quad -1 \quad -2 \quad -3 \quad -4$$

Understanding why we have so many different sets of numbers consists of realizing what properties were gained by expanding a previous set.

The set of whole numbers (*W*) includes zero and *C*:

$$W = \{0, 1, 2, 3, 4, 5, \ldots\}$$

*W* has a special property: you now have a number (0) that you can add to any element of the set and that element will remain unchanged:

$$e + 0 = e$$

The set of fractions (*F*) includes the whole numbers that can be written in the form $\frac{a}{b}$ with the restriction that $b \neq 0$.

The special property that is added when you consider the set of fractions is the multiplicative inverse. This means that for every element of F, there is an element of F that you can multiply it by to get 1:

$$e \cdot \frac{1}{e} = \frac{e}{e} = 1$$

The set of integers (*Z*):

$$Z = \{\ldots, -3, -2, -1, 0, 1, 2, 3, \ldots\}$$

affords the use of additive inverses: $e + (-e) = 0$.

Finally, by joining fractions and their additive inverses, we get the set of rational numbers (*Q*). As in the set of fractions, all rational numbers may be written in the form $\frac{a}{b}$ with the restriction that *b* cannot be zero. The difference is that *Q* includes negative fractions. The rational numbers are used for answering the question "How much?" They are measures. In general, they measure how much there is of one quantity in relation to some other quantity. The set *Q* affords us all of the addition properties and the multiplication properties of fractions and integers combined.

Why is it important to know something about properties? Knowing some of the special properties of these sets can give you an edge when it comes to reasoning and mental calculations. Consider the following examples.

- The so-called "cancelling" and "reducing" or "lowering" fractions relies on the property of multiplicative inverses:

- $\dfrac{4}{6} = \dfrac{2 \cdot 2}{2 \cdot 3} = \dfrac{2}{3}$ because $2 \cdot \dfrac{1}{2} = 1$

- We can combine the additive and multiplicative properties of F to mentally carry out computations:

$$3\frac{1}{2} \cdot 2\frac{1}{4} = 6\frac{3}{4} + 1\frac{1}{8} = 7\frac{7}{8}$$

- You can use properties to eliminate needless computation. Without computing, you can see the answer.

$$\left(5 \cdot \frac{1}{5}\right)\left(-\frac{3}{5}\right) + \left(-\frac{5}{3} + \frac{5}{3}\right)\left(\frac{3}{7}\right) = -\frac{3}{5}$$

## KINDS OF FRACTIONS

Over time, fractions have undergone their own development. The earliest fractions were all reciprocals of integers: $\dfrac{1}{2}, \dfrac{1}{3}, \dfrac{1}{4}, \dfrac{1}{5}$, etc. Today we refer to these as unit fractions.

Much later, "vulgar" fractions or common fractions came into use. These are the fractions we use today $\left(\dfrac{1}{2}, \dfrac{3}{4}, \dfrac{5}{6}, \text{etc.}\right)$, in which the numerator designates a number of equal parts and the denominator tells how many of those parts make up a whole.

Sometime later, certain special fractions were recognized. When the denominators of fraction were powers of 10 (10, 100, 1000, ...) these were called *decimal fractions*. Eventually, commas or periods were used to separate these decimal parts from whole numbers, and so numbers are written 12,57 or 12.57, and today are known simply as decimals. Some countries still use a comma instead of a decimal point.

- 1.345 means

$$1 \text{ WHOLE} + 3\left(\frac{1}{10} \text{ of a whole}\right) + 4\left(\frac{1}{100} \text{ of a whole}\right) + 5\left(\frac{1}{1000} \text{ of a whole}\right).$$

Another special class of fractions is that in which the denominator is always 100. For example, $\dfrac{75}{100}, \dfrac{30}{100}$. Eventually the notation for 75 out of a 100 or 75 per 100 was changed to 75%. We derive the word *percent* stemming from the Latin word *centum* meaning *hundred*.

Although elementary textbooks have traditionally addressed decimals and percents as separate (and later) topics in the math curriculum, decimals and percents are really just special kinds of fractions with their own notation. There are several good reasons for arguing that right from the start of fraction instruction, children should be encouraged to express themselves in any or all of these forms. Children see decimals and percents more in everyday life more than they see fractions. As we know, learning in contexts is a complex and lengthy process, so "saving" children from decimals and percents until much later is a poor excuse that only cuts short their experiences. Most compelling is the fact that research has shown that by third grade, some children have already developed preferences for expressing quantities as decimals or percents. (In this book you will see some of their work.)

## WHAT ARE FRACTIONS?

Today, the word "fraction" is used in two different ways. First, it is a numeral. Secondly, in a more abstract sense, it is a number.

First, *fractions* are bipartite symbols, a certain form for writing numbers: $\frac{a}{b}$. This sense of the word fraction refers to a form for writing numbers, a notational system, a symbol, a numeral, two integers written with a bar between them.

Second, *fractions* are non-negative rational numbers. Traditionally, because students begin to study fractions long before they are introduced to the integers, $a$ and $b$ are restricted to the set of whole numbers. This is only a subset of the rational numbers.

The top number of a fraction is called the numerator and the bottom number is called the denominator. The order of the numbers is important. Thus fractions are ordered pairs of numbers, so $\frac{3}{4}$ is not the same as the fraction $\frac{4}{3}$. Zero may appear in the numerator, but not in the denominator.

All of these are fractions in the sense that they are written in the form $\frac{a}{b}$:

$$\frac{-3}{4}, \frac{\pi}{2}, \frac{\sqrt{4}}{2}, \frac{-12.2}{14.4}, \frac{\frac{1}{2}}{\frac{1}{4}}$$

However, they are not all fractions in the second sense of the word. Therefore, I will say *fraction form* when I mean the notation, and *fraction* when I mean non-negative rational numbers.

## RATIONAL NUMBERS

Although many people mistakenly use the terms *fractions* and *rational numbers* synonymously, they are very different number sets. Other important distinctions related to the rational numbers are made in the following examples.

- All rational numbers may be written in fraction form.

$\frac{3}{4}, \frac{\sqrt{4}}{3} \left( \text{usually written as } \frac{2}{3} \right), \frac{2.1}{4.1} \left( \text{usually written as } \frac{21}{41} \right)$, and $\frac{\frac{1}{2}}{\frac{1}{4}}$ $\left( \text{usually written as } \frac{2}{1} \right)$ are all fractions and rational numbers.

- Not all numbers written in fraction form are rational.

  $\frac{\pi}{2}$ is not a rational number although it is written in fraction form.

- Each fraction does not correspond to a different rational number.

  There is not a different rational number for each of the three fractions $\frac{2}{3}, \frac{6}{9}$, and $\frac{10}{15}$.

  Just as one and the same woman might be addressed as Mrs. Jones, Mom, Mother, Maggie, Dear, Aunty Meg, and Margaret, these fractions are different numerals designating the same rational number. A single rational number underlies all of the equivalent forms of a fraction.

- Rational numbers may be written as fractions, but they may be written in other forms as well.

  Terminating decimals are rational numbers. Non-terminating, repeating decimals are rational numbers. Percents are rational numbers. Non-terminating, non-repeating decimals are not rational numbers. Ratios and rates are rational numbers.

## FRACTIONS AS NUMBERS

When we speak of a fraction as a number, we are really referring to the underlying rational number. Understanding a fraction as a number entails realizing, for example, that $\frac{1}{4}$ refers to the same relative amount in each of the following pictures. There is but one rational number underlying all of these relative amounts. Whether we call it $\frac{1}{4}, \frac{4}{16}, \frac{3}{12}$, or $\frac{2}{8}$ is not as important as the fact that a single relationship is conveyed. When we consider fractions as single numbers, rather than focusing on the two parts used to write the fraction symbol, the focus is on the relative amount conveyed by those symbols.

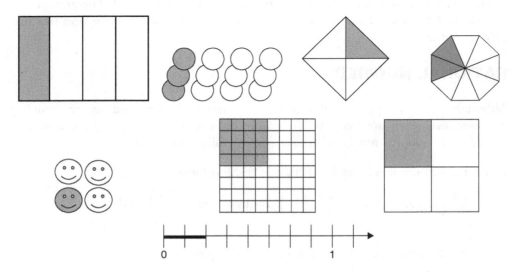

Regardless of the size of the pieces, their color, their shape, their arrangement, or any other physical characteristic, the same relative amount and the same rational number is indicated in each picture. $\Big($ Psychologically, for the purpose of instruction, when fractions are connected with pictorial representations, which fraction name you connect with which picture *is* an important issue. For example, you would not call the first picture $\frac{2}{8}$ or $\frac{4}{16}$.$\Big)$

## FRACTIONS, RATIOS AND RATES

A ratio is an ordered pair that conveys the relative sizes of two quantities. Under this definition, a part—whole fraction is a ratio; however, every ratio is not a part—whole comparison. A ratio may compare measures of two parts of the same set (a part—part comparison) or the measures of any two different quantities (e.g. cups of juice concentrate to cups of water). Often, ratios are expressed as "per" quantities. For example, miles per hour and candies per bag are both ratios or comparisons of unlike quantities.

The ratio—rate distinction is a bit more complex. When we are discussing a very particular situation, we use a ratio. However, if that ratio is one that is extendible to a broader range of situations, it is a rate.

- I am paid $8 an hour for working at the hamburger stand. $\frac{\$8}{1\ hour}$ is a rate because it applies whether I work 1 hour, 3 hours, or 40 hours.
- If I drive for 3 hours at 40 mph to my destination and then drive the same distance back at 50 mph, my average speed for the trip is $\frac{240\ miles}{5.4\ hours} = 44.4$ mph. 44.4 mph is a ratio that applies in this particular situation and would not be a rate.

Later in this book, we will explore ratios and rates and their distinctions from part—whole comparisons in more detail. However, right from the start we have to acknowledge that it is impossible to discuss real contexts without moving freely between part—whole comparisons and ratios (part—part comparisons). In everyday usage, we move back and forth between the two without making any distinction. The last two examples are cases in point: rate of pay and average speed. Technically, these are ratios (rates), but are typically written using fraction notation. Unfortunately, this is another conventional practice that complicates instruction. When it becomes necessary to make a distinction between the two types of comparisons, we will write part—whole comparisons using fraction symbols and ratios using colon notation (a : b).

- In Mr. Conroy's class, there are 12 girls and 13 boys.
  What part of the class is female? $\frac{12}{25}$
  What part of the class is male? $\frac{13}{25}$

What is the ratio of girls to boys? $12:13$
What is the ratio of boys to girls? $13:12$

- In Mrs. Hart's class the ratio of girls to boys is $3:2$.

  Can you make a part—whole comparison? Does this mean that she has only 5 students? No. There could actually be 30 girls and 20 boys, or 18 girls and 12 boys. Since we don't know how many children are in the class, we cannot write a part—whole comparison.

- John is making orange juice by mixing 2 cans of juice concentrate with 3 cans of water. Marcia is making orange juice using 4 cans of concentrate with 5 cans of water. There are many ways to convey information about this situation.

  In each recipe, what is the ratio of orange juice to water? John's ratio is $2:3$; Marcia's ratio is $4:5$.
  What part of each recipe is water? John's recipe is $\frac{3}{5}$ water and Marcia's is $\frac{5}{9}$ water.
  What does the ratio $1:2$ represent? The measure of John's juice concentrate to Marcia's is $2:4$ or $1:2$.
  What part of each recipe is concentrate? John's is $\frac{2}{5}$ concentrate and Marcia's is $\frac{4}{9}$.
  What is the ratio of the measure of John's water to Marcia's? $3:5$

## MANY SOURCES OF MEANING

As one moves from whole numbers into fractions, the variety and complexity of the situations that give meaning to the symbols increases dramatically. There are many different meanings that end up looking alike when they are written in fraction symbols. When we are using algorithms to add, subtract, multiply, or divide fractions, they are devoid of physical meaning and context. However, if we are teaching so that operations arise naturally from a very deep understanding and fraction sense, we need to be aware of a broad range of phenomena that are the sources of meaning underlying those fraction symbols.

Understand rational numbers involves the coordination of many different but interconnected ideas and interpretations. Unfortunately, fraction instruction has traditionally focused on only one interpretation of rational numbers, that of part—whole comparisons, after which the algorithms for symbolic operation are introduced. This means that student understanding of a very complex structure (the rational number system) is teetering on a small, shaky foundation. Instruction has not provided sufficient access to other ways of interpreting $\frac{a}{b}$: as a measure, as an operator, as a quotient, and as a ratio or a rate. We will address all of these interpretations later.

Having a mature understanding of rational numbers entails much more than being able to manipulate symbols. It means being able to make connections to many different situations modeled by those symbols. Part—whole comparisons are not mathematically or psychologically independent of other meanings, but to ignore those other ideas in instruction leaves a child with a deficient understanding of the part—whole fractions themselves, and an impoverished foundation for the rational number system, the real numbers, the complex numbers, and all of the higher mathematical and scientific ideas that rely on these number systems.

I reject the use of the word *fraction* as referring exclusively to one of the interpretations of the rational numbers, namely, part—whole comparisons. Because the part—whole comparison was usually the only meaning ever used in instruction, it is understandable that *fraction* and *part—whole fraction* became synonymous. However, we now realize that restricting instruction to the part—whole interpretation has left students with an impoverished notion of the rational numbers and increasingly, teachers are becoming aware of the alternate interpretations and referring to them as *operator, measure, ratio,* and *quotient.* Part—whole comparisons are on equal ground with the other interpretations and no longer merit the distinction of being synonymous with *fractions.*

# MULTIPLE INTERPRETATIONS OF THE FRACTION $\frac{3}{4}$

Fracturing or breaking, the activity by which fractions are created, provides a rich source of real-world connections and meanings that provide insight into the rational number system. To get an idea of the complexity and the rich set of ideas involved when a person truly understands the meaning of a fraction symbol, look at some interpretations for just one fraction, say $\frac{3}{4}$. These interpretations do not exhaust all of the possibilities, but they give a fair sample of the nuances in meaning when we consider the rational number $\frac{3}{4}$ in everyday contexts.

- John told his mother that he would be home in 45 minutes. $\frac{3}{4}$ means $1\left(\frac{3}{4}\text{-hour}\right)$

- Melissa had 3 large circular cookies, all the same size—one chocolate chip, one molasses, and one coconut. She cut each cookie into 4 equal parts and ate one piece of each cookie.

  She ate $\frac{3}{4}$ of the cookies but her share was $3\left(\frac{1}{4}\text{-cookies}\right)$.

- Cupcakes come 3 to a package. Suppose that you quartered the package without opening it and then ate one portion.

  You ate $\frac{1}{4}$ of the cupcakes but your share was

  $\frac{1}{4}$ (3-pack).

- For every 3 boys in Mr. Albert's history class, there are 4 girls.

  $\frac{3}{4}$ means 3 : 4 or 3 boys for every 4 girls.

  |  |  |  |  |
  |---|---|---|---|
  | BBB | BBB | BBB | BBB |
  | GGGG | GGGG | GGGG | GGGG |

- There are 12 men and $\frac{3}{4}$ as many women as men at the meeting. $\frac{3}{4}$ is a rule that prescribes how to act upon the number of men to obtain the number of women.

- Mary asked Jack how much money he had. Jack reached into his pocket and pulled out seven dimes and one nickel.

  Jack had $\frac{3}{4}$ of a dollar, which is \$0.75.

- Martin's Men Store had a big sale> −75% off.

  The store took $\frac{3}{4}$ off the marked price, which was 75% (or 75 cents off every 100 cents).

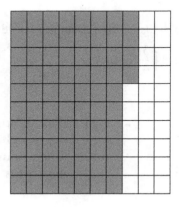

- Every time Jenny puts 4 quarters into the machine at the bus station, three tokens came out.

$\frac{3}{4}$ means a 3-for-4 exchange.

- Tad had 12 blue socks and 4 white socks in his drawer. He wondered what were his chances of reaching in and pulling out a sock to match the blue one he already had on his left foot.

Twelve out of the 16 socks in the drawer are blue. $\frac{3}{4}$ is the probability that the sock he chooses will be blue.

These are just a few of meanings that might be associated with the symbol $\frac{3}{4}$; there are many more. However, they illustrate the fact that beneath a single fraction symbol lies a world of meaning, multiple interpretations, representations, and associated ways of thinking and operating. As we are helping children to build alternate meanings for fractions, we will see that these personalities of the rational numbers are part of a complex web of knowledge that encompasses a whole world of multiplicative concepts.

## ACTIVITIES

1.  Write two problems that are appropriately solved by multiplication but which cannot be easily modeled by repeated addition.

2.  Write a division problem whose quotient has a label different from the labels on the divisor and the dividend.

3.  Write a problem appropriately solved by division which demonstrates that division does not always make smaller.

4.  Write a multiplication problem whose solution demonstrates that multiplication does not always make larger.

5.  What is the same about all of these?

6.  Using a pizza as the unit, draw the following fractional parts:

    a.  $1\left(\dfrac{3}{8}\text{-pizza}\right)$

    b.  $3\left(\dfrac{1}{8}\text{-pizzas}\right)$

    c.  $1\dfrac{1}{2}\left(\dfrac{1}{4}\text{-pizzas}\right)$

7.  Is zero a digit? A numeral? A number? Explain.

8.  Write in set notation:

    a.  Positive wholes
    b.  Non-negative integers
    c.  Non-positive integers
    d.  Even wholes

9.  Show that each of these is a rational number:

    a.  $-6$    b.  $0$    c.  $2\dfrac{1}{3}$    d.  $0.68$    e.  $54$

10. Write each of the following sums as a decimal.

    a.  $3 + \dfrac{1}{1000}$

    b.  $2 + \dfrac{3}{10} + \dfrac{4}{1000}$

c.  $\dfrac{5}{100} + \dfrac{8}{10000}$

d.  $1 + \dfrac{1}{10} + \dfrac{2}{10000}$

11. Why are fractions called equivalent rather than equal?

12. Which abbreviation should we teach children to write: mph or $\dfrac{mi}{hr}$ or mi : hr? Is there a good reason for choosing one above the other?

13. Explain what is meant by the statement that these two pictures show the same relative amount.

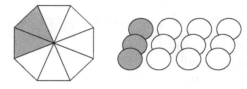

14. Name as many chunked quantities as you can.

15. Answer "Yes" or "No." If your answer is "No," give an example to explain why.

    a. Is every fraction a rational number?
    b. Is every rational number a fraction?
    c. Is every whole number a fraction?
    d. Is every whole number a rational number?
    e. Is every integer a rational number?
    f. Is every counting number a whole number?
    g. Is 0 an integer?
    h. Is 0 a rational number?
    i. Is every mixed number a fraction?
    j. Is every mixed number an integer?
    k. Is every mixed number a rational number?
    l. Is every negative integer a rational number?
    m. Is every whole number a rational number?
    n. Is every whole number a non-negative integer?

16. Which of the following are equal to $-4$?

    a.  $\dfrac{-8}{-2}$
    b.  $\dfrac{8}{-2}$
    c.  $\dfrac{-4}{1}$
    d.  $\dfrac{4}{-1}$
    e.  $\dfrac{-8}{2}$
    f.  $-\dfrac{8}{-2}$
    g.  $-\dfrac{-8}{-2}$

17.  Consider the following numbers:

$$-4.2 \quad 15 \quad -6 \quad -\frac{1}{8} \quad 0 \quad 5\frac{2}{3} \quad \frac{-4}{3} \quad -3\frac{2}{3} \quad \sqrt{8} \quad 564 \quad -32$$

   a.  Which are whole numbers?
   b.  Which are rational numbers?
   c.  Which are integers?
   d.  Which are natural numbers?
   e.  Which are integers?
   f.  Which are counting numbers?
   g.  Which are rational numbers?

18.  Express each of the following as an average speed (miles per hour):

   a.  15 minutes to go 4 miles
   b.  3.75 minutes per mile
   c.  230 miles in 4 hours
   d.  14 miles in 10 minutes
   e.  10 feet per second

19.  Write each number in expanded notation. For example, 30.205 means 3 (10) +
   $2\left(\frac{1}{10} \text{ of a whole}\right) + 5\left(\frac{1}{1000} \text{ of a whole}\right).$

   a.  204.05
   b.  3.0006
   c.  0.3051
   d.  1045.0602

20.  Consider the decimal fractions: (a) 0.0000001 and (b) 0.01. What problems do
   these present to children who are asked to compare their relative sizes?

21.  In a certain classroom, the ratio of girls to boys is 2:3. There are 12 girls in the
   class. Answer these questions about the class or write U for unknown.

   a.  How many students are in the class?
   b.  What fraction of the class is girls?
   c.  What is the ratio of boys to girls?
   d.  What fraction of the class is boys?

CHAPTER 3

# Relative Thinking and Measurement

## STUDENT STRATEGIES: GRADE 6

Discuss the student responses to the following problem. Which responses are correct? How are they different? Order the responses according to sophistication of reasoning.

Before, tree A was 8′ tall and tree B was 10′ tall. Now, tree A is 14′ tall and tree B is 16′ tall. Which tree grew more?

A        B

Before

A        B

Now

Robert

Both trees grew the same amount 6 ft.
B is always gone to be 2 ft. taller
then A.

Dan

A grew 75% of it height. but B grew a little less — 60% of it height.

P.J.

B climbed higher but not _higher_. I mean it higher but it didn't climb more feet because it was already higher. It didn't grow more. Its just higher. It seem like A grew more even though it didn't grow higher then B.

Pete

B grew more because it grew to 16.' That's more then A grew.

## TWO PERSPECTIVES ON CHANGE

The following situation highlights one of the most important types of thinking required for proportional reasoning: the ability to analyze change in both absolute and relative terms.

• Jo has two snakes, Slither and Slim. Right now, Slither is 4′ long and Slim is 5′ long. Jo knows that two years from now, both snakes will be fully grown. At her full length, Slither will be 7′ long, while Slim's length when he is fully grown will be 8′. Over the next two years, will both snakes grow the same amount?

Now...

Slither 4'

Slim 5'

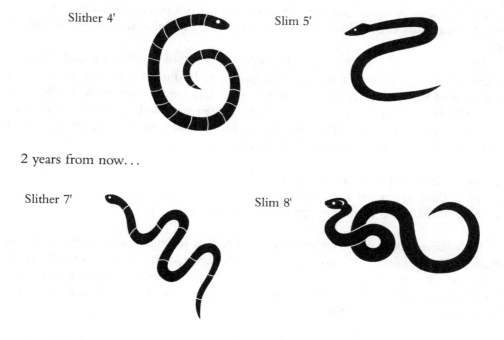

2 years from now...

Slither 7'

Slim 8'

Certainly, one answer is that snakes will grow the same amount because both will add 3 feet of length. So, if we consider only absolute growth—that is, actual growth independent of and unrelated to anything else—the snakes will grow the same amount. This perspective on change considers how much length will be *added*.

Another perspective, however, relates the expected growth of each snake to its present length. For example, Slither will grow 3 feet or $\frac{3}{4}$ of her present length. Slim will grow 3 feet, or $\frac{3}{5}$ of his present length. Which snake will grow more in the next two years? If we consider growth relative to present length, Slither will grow more than Slim because $\frac{3}{4} > \frac{3}{5}$. Therefore, from a comparative or relative perspective, the snakes will not grow the same amount!

Suppose that, in this comparative sense, Slim will grow the same amount as Slither. What should be his full-grown length? He should grow $\frac{3}{4}$ of his present length, or $3\frac{3}{4}$ feet. Therefore, Slim's length when fully grown would be $8\frac{3}{4}$ feet. Notice that you multiplied—not added—to find Slim's new length. For this reason, relative thinking is also called multiplicative thinking. Absolute thinking is additive thinking.

Our problem about Slither and Slim highlights the first and most basic perspective that students need to adopt before they can understand fractions. It is essential that they are able to understand change in two different perspectives: actual growth and relative growth, or absolute change and relative change. Note that the message here is *not* that one perspective is wrong and the other is correct. Both perspectives are useful. The word "more" has two different meanings, and we want children to entertain both of them.

Relative thinking entails more abstraction than absolute thinking and, through relative thinking, we create more complex quantities. In this computer age, students are accustomed to a barrage of sense data; understanding comes from perceptually based data. However, in mathematics, understanding often consists in grasping abstractions imposed upon sense data. This abstraction is not a *per*ception as much as it is a *con*ception. For example, try this mind experiment.

- Think about 5 people in an 8-person elevator.
- Now think about the same 5 people in a baseball stadium.
- Now think about the same 5 people in a 2-seat sports car.

Each statement should have given you a different feeling about crowdedness. You thought about the same 5 people each time; however, each statement caused you to compare your conception of how much space those people occupy to some other area. Your mental comparison resulted in a new quantity, density, and a method of measuring it, by comparing two quantities.

## RELATIVE THINKING AND UNDERSTANDING FRACTIONS

Relative thinking is critical in initial fraction instruction. In fraction instruction, relative thinking is entailed in the understanding of several important notions. These include the following:

- The relationship between the size of pieces and the number of pieces.
- The need to compare fractions relative to the same unit.
- The meaning of a fractional number. Three parts of five equal subdivisions of something conveys the notion of *how much* in the same way that the above example conveyed the notion of *crowdedness*.
- The size of a fractional number.
- The relationship between equivalent fractions. The fraction numeral $\frac{3}{5}$, for example, names the same relative amount as when the unit is quartered $\left(\frac{12}{20}\right)$ or halved $\left(\frac{6}{10}\right)$.

# ENCOURAGING MULTIPLICATIVE THINKING

The children's responses to the opening question about the trees demonstrates how difficult it is for children to move away from the additive thinking with which they are so familiar and to begin to think relatively. PJ's response also suggests the great difficulty children have in describing a relative perspective even when they recognize it as an alternative to thinking in absolute terms. Robert's response does not indicate that he is thinking relatively about this situation—which does not mean that he *never* does. Dan used percent of growth to show that he is comparing the amount of growth to the starting heights of the trees. Pete is using another kind of absolute thinking. He is considering only the final height of the trees and not taking into account that that the starting height of B was already greater than that of A.

Discussing problems such as the snake problem or the tree problem in a group setting is often helpful in encouraging a relative perspective. While third graders are most likely to be absolute thinkers, one or two in the class may begin to suspect that the difference in starting points might make a difference, and some useful discussion can follow. But it is difficult to predict the context in which children first begin to think relatively. Even when they do, it may be only in a limited number of situations. It may take time until a child begins to think relatively across a variety of situations, so it is important to present children the absolute-relative choice in many different contexts.

Distinguishing the situations that require multiplicative thinking from those that do not is one of the most difficult tasks for children. One difficulty is that our language does not supply us with new words with which to ask multiplicative questions. The same words that we use to discuss whole number relationships, take on different meanings in different situations. For example, when we ask "Which is *larger*?" in the context of comparing two lengths, additive or absolute thinking is appropriate. However, if we ask "Which is *larger*?" in the context of an area problem or an enlargement problem, multiplicative thinking is required. In other words, part of the challenge is to attach new meanings to old words and to associate contexts with appropriate operations—additive or multiplicative.

Become conscious of the way in which you ask questions and use every opportunity to ask both types of questions: one that asks children to think additively and one that asks them to think about one quantity in relation to another. Here are some examples:

Know what, Marcus? I have 6 cookies in my backpack.

Yeah, Clint, but I have 9!

- Questions that require absolute or additive thinking:

  Who has more cookies, Clint or Marcus?
  How many fewer cookies does Clint have?
  How many more cookies does Marcus have?
  How many cookies do the boys have altogether?

- Questions that require relative or multiplicative thinking:

  How many times would you have to stack up Clint's cookies to get a pile as high as Marcus's?
  What part of a dozen cookies does Clint have?
  Each boy has three chocolate chip cookies. What percent of each boy's cookies are chocolate chip?
  If Marcus ate one cookie each day, how many weeks would his cookies last?
  Cookies come 6 to a package. What part of a package does each child have?
  Marcus and Clint put all of their cookies together and shared them at lunchtime with their 3 friends. What part of the cookies will each child eat?

Early fraction activities often include questions about pizza. Students tend to answer "how many slices" were eaten rather than "how much" of the pizza was eaten, meaning "what portion of the pizza was eaten." To determine the number of slices is merely a counting problem and it does not help children to move beyond thinking with whole numbers. The question "How much pizza" implies "What part of the original amount of pizza?" and requires relative thinking.

- A pizza is cut into 8 equal slices. 3 people have two slices each.

  How many slices did they eat? 6 slices.

  How much (of the) pizza did they eat? $\frac{3}{4}$ of the pizza.

- Mr. Thomas had 3 vacation days last week.

  How many days did he work? 4 days.

  What part of a week did he work? $\frac{4}{7}$ of a week.

These are not simply word games. Just as relative thinking requires a cognitive change in perspective, a corresponding nuance occurs in the words we use to talk about multiplicative ideas. Relative thinking activities provide the opportunity for students to expand the range of applicability of certain words, which they have formerly only associated with additive concepts, for example, the word "more." Although most children will be familiar with the word as a signal word for addition/subtraction, the word can have a proportional or relational meaning.

# TWO MEANINGS FOR "MORE"

It is a peculiarity of our language that we do not have different words to signal absolute and relative comparisons (or additive and multiplicative comparisons). We simply say "Which is more?" "More" actually has two meanings and we need to be aware of both of them. It is inappropriate to routinely apply either operation (addition or multiplication) or to assume that both are equally applicable.

When you are trying to assess whether your students are thinking absolutely or relatively, it is useful to ask questions in an ambiguous way to see what sort of answer students will give without any prompting. For example, in the question about the number of girls in each family (#1 in the activity section at the end of the chapter), you will notice that the question is ambiguous. Clearly, the additive response is correct and most children say that both families have the same number of girls. However, if a student suggests that there is another way to look at the situation and can explain his or her perspective, you can be sure that the student is thinking relatively. If none of the students uses relative thinking, you can suggest the relative perspective with the follow-up question, "Which family has a larger *portion* of girls?" It is often the case that in a class discussion of the problem, either by the suggestion of one of their classmates or with a leading question from the teacher, absolute thinkers can be persuaded to look at the situation in a new way.

Sometimes children use incorrect additive/subtractive strategies. These incorrect strategies appear most often when there are not "nice" numbers involved (halves and easy multiples) or unit fractions and the children do not have adequate procedures for comparing the given fractions or ratios. Historically, these incorrect strategies have been studied in the context of mixture problems such as the following:

Which of the following drinks, A or B, will have a stronger apple taste?

| 3 c. apple |
| 5 c. water |

| 5 c. apple |
| 7 c. water |

Solve this problem without using any procedures for comparing fractions, then analyze the strategies used by these five students in the fourth grade. In particular, try to determine if each child used an additive (absolute) strategy or a multiplicative (comparative) strategy.

Anne   B because it has 5 apples, not 3.

TONY   THEY WILL TASTE THE SAME BCAUSE EACH HAS 2 XTRA WATERS.

Ed   The same because B just has 2 more of apple and 2 more water.

Sam   A because it has less water than B.

April   If you take away 3 A and 4 W from each pitcher, B still has apple juice in it, so B.

What operation did each child use to answer the question? Are the children relative thinkers? The answers that these children gave are all incorrect. None of them used relative thinking. These responses are very commonly given by younger children in mixture situations. However, it is difficult to conclude that they are not relative thinkers because relative thinking is not an all-or-none affair. It may be that they "get it" in other types of problems, but cannot yet understand mixture problems. For example, children get the point in the boy/girl problem (#1 in the activities at the end of the chapter) long before they can deal with mixtures. For this reason, it is important to vary the contexts when trying to encourage relative thinking.

## THE IMPORTANCE OF MEASUREMENT

Measurement lies at the very heart of human activity; humans have always been preoccupied with measuring their universe, and the units and methods of measurement are essential to science. Measuring is a starting point for mathematics. When studying whole numbers, the act of measuring occurs in its simplest form—counting discrete objects. However, when students begin to study the positive rational numbers, the emphasis shifts to measuring continuous quantities.

When talking about children's understanding, I have found that it is important to distinguish between the *act of measuring* and *measurement*. In other words, even when children are able to carry out the act of measuring with reasonable accuracy (i.e., choosing a unit of measure and displacing it without overlap or empty intervals), there is no guarantee that the child has learned the principles of measurement. Once again, this is not word play; rather, it is a critical distinction that has implications for the child's readiness to learn rational number concepts. It can be argued that concepts of measurement play a large role in the overall understanding of rational numbers and in multiplicative reasoning. In fact, every rational number interpretation may be conceived as a measure:

- A fraction measures the multiplicative relationship a part has to the whole to which it belongs.
- A ratio measures relative magnitude.
- A rate such as speed is a quantification of motion.
- A quotient is a measure of how much 1 person receives when $m$ people share $n$ objects.
- An operator is a measure of some change in a quantity from a prior state.
- As a measure, a rational number directly quantifies a quality such as length or area.

Conversely, you can conceive of any measurement as a ratio. What are you really doing when you measure with a standard unit such as a yard or a pound? A measurement of 6 meters is actually a ratio telling how your length compares to 1 meter. We do not usually make the comparison explicit, but a measure of 6 meters really means $\frac{6 \text{ meters}}{1 \text{ meter}}$.

Fractions are totally *about* measurement and measurement is *about* fractions!

- A 10% discount is a measure of how much you can expect to save.
- 5 miles per hour $\left(\frac{5}{1}\right)$ is a measure of how far you will travel in one hour.
- $\frac{1}{4}$ is a measure of how much of a candy bar you got when you shared with 3 friends.

All of these connections suggest that understanding measurement is a complex endeavor. It does not happen in a short period of time, but only with years of experience. Furthermore, it suggests that teaching about measurement entails more than teaching how to measure. Clocks, money, and weights and measures provide an excellent introduction to fraction ideas and language and should be revisited frequently as objects of study, not merely as tools for measuring.

Understanding measurement entails deepening one's understanding of three major principles: the compensatory principle, the approximation principle, and the recursive partitioning principle.

# THE COMPENSATORY PRINCIPLE

This principle states that the smaller the unit of measure, the more of those units you need to measure something, and conversely, the larger the units of measure you are using, the fewer of them it will take to quantify the same amount. For example, if you measure the length of a room using a meter stick, you will need to lay it end to end fewer times than if you measured the same length using a ruler. If you measure a certain distance in centimeters, your result will be a much larger number than if you measure that same distance in kilometers.

- If you purchase eggs by the dozen, you might think 6 eggs constitute $\frac{1}{2}$ of a package. If you buy a carton of 18 eggs (i.e., your measure is larger), you might think of eggs as $\frac{1}{3}$ of a package.
- We generally think of 96 years as a long human lifespan, but to a paleontologist, who thinks in millions of years it is but a flash in time.
- *Reducing* a fraction, also known as putting a fraction *in lowest terms* means using larger-sized pieces so that the number of pieces is reduced to the least number possible. Measuring with $\frac{1}{10}$-pieces requires a larger number of pieces than when measuring the same area with $\frac{1}{5}$-pieces.

$$\frac{4}{10} = \frac{2}{5}$$

## THE APPROXIMATION PRINCIPLE

A measurement is always approximate; that is, we can carry out the measurement process to whatever degree of accuracy is required by the job at hand. The decision about how accurate you need to be is usually made in context. If you are measuring the length of a room because you wish to install wall-to-wall carpeting, you might need a more accurate measurement than if you are purchasing an area rug. If you are measuring medicine, you need a more accurate measurement than if you are measuring water to mix up some iced tea.

- You may remember learning that you may use the decimal 3.14 to approximate the constant $\pi$. You might use $\pi = 3.14$ when roughly calculating how much liquid you can pour into a can, but engineers designing instruments that use high frequency alternating current to treat medical disorders require more precision.
- When you tell someone that you are 25 years old, you are using an approximation. More accurately, your age might be 25 years 2 months 11 days 13 hours. But who gets that precise about age?

These examples suggest that understanding the approximation principle means more than knowing and stating that a measurement is an approximation. Children need sufficient experience in many different contexts to know when greater or less accuracy is needed. If it is true that a measurement can be made more and more accurate, how do you know when to stop refining your measurement?

## RECURSIVE PARTITIONING PRINCIPLE

You can make any measurement as accurate as you need by breaking your unit of measure into smaller and smaller equal-sized subunits. As soon as you break a unit into smaller pieces, fractions come into play. There is an infinite number of fractions between any pair of fractions, no matter how close they are, and it is this property, typically referred to as the *density* of the rational numbers, that allows the closer and closer approximation of a measurement. This idea is a powerful one that has implications for higher mathematics. For example, the idea of getting *as close as you like* lies at the heart of calculus.

- Imagine timing a swim meet. If you time a 100-meter backstroke race to the nearest hour, you would not be able to distinguish one swimmer's time from another's. If you refine your timing by using minutes, you may still not be able to tell the swimmer's apart. If the swimmers are all well trained, you may not be able to decide on a winner even if you measure in seconds. In high-stakes competitions among well-trained athletes (the Olympics, for example), it is necessary to measure in tenths and hundredths of seconds.
- Suppose you are working on a project and you need to determine the length of a strip of metal in inches. Trying to measure as precisely as possible you might think to yourself: "The length is between $1\frac{7}{16}$ and $1\frac{8}{16}$, so I'll call it $1\frac{15}{32}$."

In mathematics, *partitioning* is the act of dividing a set or a unit into nonoverlapping and nonempty parts. When using the word *partitioning* in reference to fractions and measurement, we further require that the subparts be of equal size. Partitioning is the means by which an approximate measurement may be further refined and made more accurate. For example, you can measure a quantity of liquid more accurately with a quart measure than with a gallon measure, with a tablespoon more accurately than with a cup measure, and so on. How far you carry out the partitioning affects the accuracy of your measurement.

If you have more to measure but you cannot measure out another whole copy of the unit you are using, you adopt a new subunit of measure. To do this, you break the unit into some equal number of subunits and then measure the remaining amount using one of the subunits as your new unit of measure. If you still have more to measure, but you can not take out any more copies of the subunit you are using, you return to your original unit, partition it into even smaller subunits and then proceed to measure with one of them.

- If my gas gauge needle falls in between the $\frac{1}{2}$ and the $\frac{1}{4}$ marks, whether it is written on the gauge or not, I can judge when I have $\frac{3}{8}$ of a tank of gas left.
- When we tell time, we partition an hour. A minute is the name of one of 60 equal subunits of an hour. A second is the name of one of 3600 equal subunits of an hour.
- When we buy gas, the cost per gallon is quoted by partitioning $1 into 100 parts (cents) and then partitioning a cent into ten equal parts. For example, gas costs $2.83 + $\frac{9}{10}$ cents per gallon.
- A quarter or $0.25 is one of 4 equal parts of a dollar.
- In the United States, when we weigh fruits or vegetables, we partition a pound into equal parts called ounces.

Understanding the recursive partitioning of a unit of measure entails more than just breaking down into smaller pieces. How are each of those subunits named? How do different-sized subunits relate to each other? How small do subunits have to be? Will a larger subunit work?

- When adding fractions $\left( \frac{5}{6} + \frac{3}{8}, \text{ for example} \right)$, I can think of breaking the unit down into $\frac{1}{48}$-pieces. That will work. But the notion of *lowest common denominator* relies on the recursive partitioning principle as well as a sense of what level of refinement is sufficient for the task at hand.

## MEASURING MORE ABSTRACT QUALITIES

At some point late in the late elementary or middle school curriculum, students encounter attributes such as slope, speed and density. These attributes are inordinately difficult for them because nowhere in the current mathematics curriculum have they encountered characteristics whose quantification requires more than simple counts and measures. Part of understanding measurement is also knowing when counting and taking direct measurements are inadequate. For example, most students have never thought about how they might measure the oranginess of a drink or the crowdedness of an elevator. These are characteristics that cannot be measured directly. That is, their measure is a new quantity that is formed by a relationship between two other quantities.

Students need time to analyze such characteristics as color intensity, sourness, roundness, the oranginess of a drink, and the crowdedness of an elevator, and to engage in argumentation and justification about how to measure them. Consider the following problem in which two pitchers contain orange juice mixtures of different strengths. Each is made by mixing cans of juice with cans of water. Here are some questions that students need to discuss about this situation.

Pitcher A

3 cans o.j.
2 cans H$_2$O

Pitcher B

3 cans o.j.
3 cans H$_2$O

- Will one of the drinks have a stronger orange taste?
- How could you measure the oranginess of *any* such mixture?
- Does it matter that one of the pitchers has more liquid in it than the other one does? Why or why not?
- Suppose you obtained three measures from 3 different pitchers whose cans of o.j. to water were 3:4, 3:5, and 3:2. How would you use these numbers to rank the mixtures from the weakest to the strongest orange taste?

There are various ways to measure the oranginess of the drinks. Some students may be able to tell by inspection that the juice in A will taste more orangey because the 3 cans of o.j. concentrate are watered down with less water than the 3 cans in pitcher B. This answer shows good reasoning because it takes into account both the amount of juice and the amount of water in each pitcher. However, the task of constructing a measure of oranginess has not yet been accomplished. The purpose of the second question is to request an answer that does not depend on the specific numbers given in this problem. The measure of oranginess is actually a ratio: $\dfrac{\text{cans of o.j.}}{\text{cans of H}_2\text{O}}$ or $\dfrac{\text{cans of H}_2\text{O}}{\text{cans of o.j.}}$. The third question addresses a matter that puzzles younger students: How does the amount of liquid—5 cans in A vs. 6 cans in B—affect our answer? The answer is that the total amount of the mixture you have has nothing to do with the strength of the mixture. For example, you could have made 5 batches using the recipe 3 cans of juice + 2 cans of water and poured it into a huge pitcher, but it is going to have the same strength as if you mixed only 1 batch.

But we are not finished when we have the ratio. Interpretation is needed. Given several such ratios, how can we use them to judge the oranginess of the respective mixtures?

Let's first look at the ratio $\frac{\text{cans of o.j.}}{\text{cans of H}_2\text{O}}$. If there is no water $(3:0)$ then the mixture has as strong an orange taste as it can get. As we add cans of water, $\frac{3}{1} = 3, \frac{3}{2} = 1.5, \frac{3}{3} = 1$, etc., we can see that the divided ratios grow smaller and the orange taste grows weaker. Thus, the smaller the divided ratio, the weaker the orange taste. (Using the ratio $\frac{\text{cans of H}_2\text{O}}{\text{cans of o.j.}}$, the divided ratios grow larger, meaning that watery taste increases, which means that the orange taste grows weaker.)

It is important to note that the conclusion has to be the same, but more than one comparison may be used to measure oranginess and it is critical that the appropriate interpretation is attached to the ratio used. Thought and understanding and interpretation cannot be replaced by mechanically setting up ratios.

## OTHER STRATEGIES

A *unit rate* tells how many units of one type of quantity correspond to one unit of another type of quantity. Some common unit rates are miles per hour (miles per 1 hour) and price per one item. A rate is distinguished from a ratio because it is extendible; that is, a rate is used when it is clear that multiple copies of a unit will be under consideration. The divided ratio strategy we discussed in the last problem resulted in a unit ratio.

Pitcher A

5 blueberry
4 water

Pitcher B

2 blueberry
3 water

Here, if we divide $\frac{5 \text{ blueberry}}{4 \text{ water}}$, we get $\frac{1.25}{1}$, a unit rate. It means that pitcher A contains $1\frac{1}{4}$ measures of blueberry for 1 measure of water. When we do the same for pitcher B, we get $\frac{2 \text{ blueberry}}{3 \text{ water}} = \frac{0.66}{1}$, a unit rate that means there is $\frac{2}{3}$ measure of blueberry for 1 measure of water. Clearly, these unit rates tell us that the blueberry is stronger in pitcher A.

Another useful strategy is the *double counting* or *double matching* strategy. From an early age (kindergarten or first grade), children can double count. Double counting involves mentally coordinating two sets of counting numbers. In the following example, as the number of quarters goes up by one, the number of nickels goes up by 5.

How many nickels will I trade you for 3 quarters?

5 for 1

10 for 2

15 for 3

A variation of this strategy can be used to solve mixture problems. We can simultaneously measure 2 B's (measures of blueberry) and 3 W's (measures of water) out of both pitchers, then analyze what remains.

Rewrite the contents of each pitcher as follows:

B B B B B        B B

W W W W        W W W

Now, measure the contents of pitcher B, namely 2 B and 3 W, out of both pitchers.

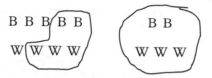

We have taken out of A the mixture that is the same as mixture B, but look at what remains. The other 3 B's in A would be matched by $4\frac{1}{2}$ W's if they were the same as the B mixture. But this is not the case. A has a lot less water diluting the blueberry than B does! A must have the stronger blueberry taste. Again, it's all in the interpretation.

Using yet another strategy, we might compare blueberry in A to blueberry in B and water in A to water in B. A contains $2\frac{1}{2}$ times as much blueberry as in recipe B. However A has less than $2\frac{1}{2}$ times the water that B has, so the blueberry in B is more diluted and A has the stronger taste.

- The Bland Company dyes textiles. They mix beakers of brown dye crystals with beakers of water in various quantities to create many different shades of brown, from dark brown to beige. The salesman offers you two choices. If you would like your fabric to be darker, which mixture should you choose?

Mixture A

Mixture B

This problem amounts to the following fraction comparison question: Which is larger, $\frac{5}{11}$ or $\frac{2}{5}$? Middle school children typically have a poor success rate with this fraction comparison. However, research has shown that when children's mathematics instruction includes the kinds of problems and discussions we have seen in this chapter, they are much more successful. Yes! In this problem context, they are more successful than they are with a bare-bones fraction comparison question. Look at the work done by a 6th grade student.

Jeremy

Mixture A

Mixture B

Take out of A the ingredients that make it the same color as B. Then A has a brown left. Chose A.

An interesting observation is that Jeremy prefers ratios to fractions. You can see that he measured 2B : 3W out of mixture A. Admittedly, the context is more conducive to ratio solutions, but it does illustrate our earlier observation that instruction can and does slip back and forth between part–whole comparisons and ratios without causing students any confusion. Jeremy's solution stands in stark contrast to the work of the fourth graders shown earlier in this chapter. None of them were using relative comparisons yet. Clearly, measurement ideas develop and deepen in the middle school years. This fact suggests that we continue to focus on measurement even while we proceed with fraction instruction. Rather than treating measuring and measurement as a specific unit of study, opportunities should be seized whenever possible during instruction to deepen students' understanding of measurement through problem-solving.

## ACTIVITIES

1. Which family has more girls?

The Jones Family

The King Family

2. Each of the cartons below contains some white eggs and some brown eggs. Which container has more brown eggs?

   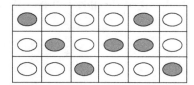

3. Bert solved this problem. Which container has more brown eggs? Is he correct?

Bert

I put them into 6 packs like this

then here I
have 2½ brown eggs
in each          (more)

here I have
2⅓ brown eggs
in each

4.  Assuming that both pizzas are identical, how much more pizza (the shaded portion) is in pan B? How many times could you serve the amount of pizza in pan A out of the pizza in pan B?

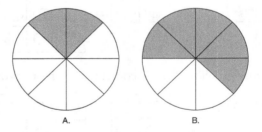

A.                    B.

5.  Dan and Tasha both started from home at 10 am to do some errands. Dan walked 2 miles to the post office, 3 miles from the post office to the dry cleaner, and then 1 mile from the dry cleaner to home. Tasha walked 2.5 miles to the drug store, 1.5 miles from the drug store to the bakery, and 3 miles from the bakery to home. Both arrived home at the same time, 12:30 pm. Assuming that their stops took a negligible amount of time. Who walked the farthest? Who walked the fastest? Which question requires relative thinking, the "farthest" question or the "fastest" question?

6.  One of your favorite stores is having a sale and you are trying to decide if it is worth your time to go. Is it more helpful to you to know that an item is $2.00 off or 20% off?

7.  The Moore Building has 2 elevators. The doors to both are open at the same time and you will choose the one that is less crowded. Elevator A is carrying 6 people and elevator B is carrying 9. How can you decide which one to enter?

8.  On a certain evening at a local restaurant, the 5 people sitting at table A and the 7 people sitting at table B ordered the drinks shown below. Later, the waitress was heard referring to one of the groups as "the root beer drinkers." To which table was she referring?

Table A:

Table B:

9.  Here is Leesa's (gr. 5) response to problem 8. Is she correct?

10. For each situation, ask a question that requires absolute (additive) thinking and then one that requires relative (multiplicative) thinking.

    a.  Crystal bought a 17-stick pack of gum. She and her 3 friends each chewed 2 sticks and saved the rest.
    b.  Four people bought a 6-pack of cola. Each of them drank 1 can and then they put the extras into the food pantry collection box.

c.  A pizza is cut into 8 equal slices. Three people each eat 2 slices and take the rest home.

d.  Mr. Thomas had 3 vacation days last month, but otherwise worked every day.

e.  Steve bought a dozen eggs. Three of them were brown and the rest were white.

11.  You are planning a party for 8 people and you decide to purchase 2 pounds of mixed nuts. If you have a party for 10 people, how many pounds of nuts should you purchase?

Analyze the following student work. Which children used productive strategies?

Dennis
Well, $8 - 6 = 2$
so  $10 - 6 = \frac{4}{=}$

Grant
I think  $\frac{8}{9}\ \frac{2}{3}$   It's a pattern.
$\overline{10\ \ 4}$

Caitlin
Prolly 2 more.  $8 + 2 = 10$ so
$2 + 2 = 4$

Mark
It is like this  [8 people 1 pound] [4 people 1 pound]
So I will buy 3 pounds and have some extra.

12.  In bowl A, I mixed 10 teaspoons of sugar with 8 teaspoons of vinegar. In bowl B, I mixed 8 teaspoons of sugar with 6 teaspoons of vinegar. Which bowl contains the most sour mixture?

13.  Here are the dimensions of three rectangles. Which one of them is most square?

$$114' \times 99' \qquad 455' \times 494' \qquad 284' \times 265'$$

14. Ty, a third grader, said that because 9 is bigger than 5, $\frac{1}{9}$ is bigger than $\frac{1}{5}$. Which measurement principle does he not understand, and what will you say to him?

15. Interpret Fred's comment. Which measurement principle does he fail to understand?

Oh, one more thing. Cut that pizza into four slices. I can't eat eight.

16. The India Ink Company mixes 3 parts of black dye with 1.5 parts of water. The Midnight Ink Company mixes 2 parts of black dye with 1 part of water. Which ink is blacker? Tell how you measure blackness of these inks.

17. Tom and 3 friends are going to share the cookies in Tom's bag. Jenny and her 4 friends are going to share the cookies Jenny has in her bag. The teacher tells you to join one of the groups.

Tom's bag          Jenny's bag

Which group is better for you?

What could *better* mean?

Find a way to measure what it means to be the *better* group.

18. A family with a physically challenged child needs to build ramps to their doors so that their home is wheelchair accessible. The base of one of the doorways is 5 feet off the ground and the base of the other doorway is 2 feet off the ground. Which ramp will be steeper?

19.  Who eats more in a day? Order these animals from smallest eater to biggest eater.

a.  weighs 187.5 kg
    eats 6.99 kg

b.  weighs 99 mg
    eats 100 mg

c.  weighs 563.6 kg
    eats 11.3 kg

d.  weighs 6096 kg
    eats 227 kg

e.  weighs 10 g
    eats 11 g

f.  weighs 4200 kg
    eats 185 kg

20.  Below you see the end of a strip whose left endpoint is placed at 0 on the ruler.

   a.  What is its length of the strip to the nearest inch?
   b.  To the nearest half inch?
   c.  To the nearest quarter inch?
   d.  To the nearest eighth of an inch?

21.  This figure has an area of 1 square inch. Draw a figure that has an area of $\frac{2}{3}$ in$^2$.

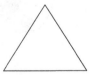

22.  The directions on my hummingbird mix say to mix sugar with the red liquid in the bottle. I am trying different mixtures to see which attracts more birds. Which of these has a more concentrated solution of sugar?

  sugar

red liquid

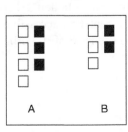

23. Order these juice mixes from least orangey to most orangey. Make sure that you can justify every decision.

| Mix A | Mix B | Mix C | Mix D |
|---|---|---|---|
| 2 c. concentrate | 1 c. concentrate | 3 c. concentrate | 4 c. concentrate |
| 3 c. water | 4 c. water | 5 cups water | 7 c. water |

24. Think about this situation and then analyze the following responses from fifth graders:

Here are two chocolate chip cookies. We would like a way to tell which is more chocolaty without tasting the cookies. How can we do this?

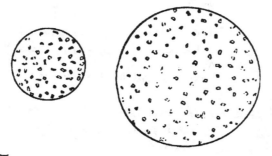

Tony

We could mark off how big 1 bite is like this ⟶ ◯ ◯

and then see how many choc chips are in 1 bite.

Mary

Count here Chips and then multiply by 8 to see which cookie has more chips.

Jim

Find out how many square inches are in each cookie and how many chips are in each cookie. The big one with more square inches in it should have more chocolate chips. If it doesn't then the little one will be more chocolaty.

25.    Solve this problem for yourself and then analyze the student solutions given below. Which mixture will have a stronger orange taste, A or B?

A
2 parts o.j.
3 parts lemon yellow

B
3 parts o.j.
5 parts lemon yellow

E.T.

$O-Y$    $Y$
$O-Y$

2:2 is like 1—1
1 extra Y
↑
This one will be more orange.

$O-Y$    $YY$
$O-Y$
$O-Y$

3:3 is like 1:1
but here 2 more Y

MS    I took out the parts that were the same in both mixtures. B still had 1 orange left so it is more orange flavored.

R

I took 2:3 out of 3:5

This will be very lemon because it is 1:2

26.    Is enlarging an additive or a multiplicative process? Do this mini-experiment to find out. You will need some graph paper with $x$- and $y$-axes marked.

Plot, label, and connect the vertices of a square or of a rectangle. Add 2 to each of the coordinates of each vertex of the figure. On the same graph as your original figure, plot and connect the resulting points. Next, multiply the coordinates of each of your original vertices by 2. Again, plot and connect the resulting coordinates. What can you conclude?

# CHAPTER 4

# Quantities and Covariation

## STUDENT STRATEGIES: GRADE 6

Solve this problem and then decide which quantities introduced by the four sixth graders are relevant to the situation.

When this boy drives from one end of the field to the other, will both wheels cover the same distance?

T.

The back wheel has to go a little more distance because its behind the other one.

⌐it has to go this much more

Angie.

The bigger wheel goes farther because it takes more time to turn completely around.

Pete

The front wheel is so small that it has to turn a lot and so it will go more distance.

Steve. The bigger wheel goes farther because it turns faster.

## BUILDING ON CHILDREN'S INFORMAL KNOWLEDGE

In this chapter, we are going to talk about quantities, their relationship to other quantities, and the way linked quantities change together (co-vary). You may be surprised when you talk to students about quantities and change. This is another neglected topic in the elementary school curriculum, so students have a difficult time knowing where to put their focus and how to express themselves when talking about quantities and change.

This chapter has two messages. The first is that children have a great deal of experience and intuitive knowledge. Whenever possible, it is best to build upon that knowledge. It is not the case that students *cannot* reason about quantities and change; it is simply that no one has asked them to think about these things before. Second, many of the powerful ways of thinking that are included in this book have roots in simple visual and verbal activities. You will see that it is not the case that we have to introduce lots of new material in our elementary and middle schools. Once you are aware of the issues and some of the obstacles, you can begin to ask questions about quantities and change in the course of every mathematics class.

## QUANTITIES UNQUANTIFIED

A quantity is a measurable quality of an object—whether that quality is actually quantified or not. For example, you can compare the heights of two people in your family without having to measure them. When one is standing beside or near the other, you can tell which is taller. If you are in New York, you can safely say that Philadelphia is closer than Los Angeles without checking a mileage table to get the distance between the cities. Relating quantities that are not quantified is an important kind of reasoning. Let's look at some examples.

- Yesterday you shared some cookies with some friends. Today, you share fewer cookies with more friends. Will everyone get more, less, or the same amount as they received yesterday?

  Of course, you know that everyone will receive less today. Both the number of people and the number of cookies might be quantified by counting; however, even without quantifying the number of people sharing the cookies, or the number of cookies being shared, you can answer that question. My question asked you to think about two ratios (the ratio of the number of cookies to the number of people), yesterday's ratio and today's. Try it again.

- Today fewer people shared more cookies.

  Again, you can tell that everyone would get more than they got yesterday. Suppose that today more people shared more cookies. Oops! We can't tell about that situation. Can you think of another situation in which the answer cannot be determined?

This type of reasoning is easy for children because it builds on their prior knowledge and experience. In fact, there are 9 different situations, only two of which are indeterminate, in which you can ask children to think about the ratio of cookies to children without quantifying either quantity.

| Change in the quantity *cookies per person* | | | |
|---|---|---|---|
| | Change in the number of people | | |
| Change in number of cookies | + | – | 0 |
| + | ? | + | + |
| – | – | ? | – |
| 0 | – | + | 0 |

This turns out to be a very useful way of thinking!

- Which is greater, $\frac{3}{4}$ or $\frac{2}{7}$?

  Think in terms of cookies and people. Yesterday we had 3 cookies for 4 people. Today we have fewer cookies and more people. Of course each person will get less today: $\frac{2}{7} < \frac{3}{4}$.

The process of analyzing what changes as well as what doesn't change is extremely useful in mathematics as well as in everyday life. It enables powerful reasoning, as opposed to noticing only obvious, surface-level information.

Suppose you are in a supermarket and you observe that the three people in front of you are all buying soup, milk, and bread. You think to yourself, "These items must be on sale. I wonder how much each of them costs."

A buys 2 soup, 1 loaf of bread, 2 milk and pays $8.
B buys 2 soup, 1 loaf of bread, 1 milk and pays $6.50.
C buys 3 soup, 2 loaves of bread, 1 milk and pays $9.50.

Look at the orders of person A and person B. What changes? What doesn't change?

A has 1 more carton of milk than B has and pays $1.50 more. Otherwise, they both have the same order. Now you know that milk costs $1.50.

From B's order, you can tell that S S B costs $5.
From C's order, you can tell that S S S B B costs $8.

Again, ask what changes and what doesn't change. S B costs $3.
Now look at B's order. If S B costs $3, a can of soup costs $2.

Now you can look at any one of the orders and tell that if milk costs $1.50 and soup costs $2, bread costs $1.

Suppose you know that the buckets in set (a) hold the same amount of liquid as the buckets in set (b).

(a)                    (b)

On the surface, this appears to be a simple statement of fact. However, by asking yourself "What changes between the two sets and what doesn't change?" you can dig more deeply into the statement and get additional information.

We can see that both (a) and (b) have one large bucket and one small bucket. Ignore the parts of each set that are the same. Because we are told that both sets hold the same amount of liquid, it must be the case that one large bucket holds the same amount as 2 small buckets. If you had not stopped and considered what changed and what didn't change as you looked from one set to the other, you may have missed less obvious information that can give you an edge in problem-solving.

In general, children need much more experience with questions that do not require numerical answers, questions that ask them to mine a given statement for additional information, and questions that force them to think about quantities and how they relate to each other.

- $\frac{2}{9}$ of a class is girls. Are there more girls or more boys in the class?

- There are twice as many boys as girls in my school. Are there more girls or more boys?

## QUANTIFIABLE CHARACTERISTICS

Before dealing with rational numbers symbolically, it is important to get children to discuss the relationships among quantities in real-world situations. The study of relationships begins on a visual level and may be clarified and extended when children develop a vocabulary, talk about those relationships, and analyze them. Visually and verbally analyzing relationships also teaches children to go beyond obvious, surface-level observations and to think more about why things work the way they do. It is important that reasoning about relationships occur long before symbolic instruction so that children learn that there is more to do when they first confront a situation than to merely extract the numbers and operate blindly with them. Even before we ask children to think about the relationships between quantities, it is important to make sure that they have a sense of what a quantity is.

I have found that many children do not necessarily focus on quantities when they read a problem. To find out which aspects of a situation they notice, I asked some middle school students to think about this situation:

You begin in front of your house and you ride your bicycle down the street. What changes?

There were many different answers and among them were:

- The trees go by
- I move away from my house
- My bicycle pedals go up and down
- My wheels go around
- I go by my friend's house

The students needed more direction to help them focus on quantifiable characteristics. I asked them to think of changes that could be measured. Then they said:

- How far away I am from my house
- How high and how low my foot goes off the ground
- How fast I go
- How much sidewalk a wheel passes when it goes around once
- How long it takes me to get to my friend's house

Now we were getting someplace! We could talk about quantities like circumference, speed, distance, and time. Time and time again, it becomes clear that we cannot assume that students know what we are talking about. It is so important to check to see what they are thinking about!

While on the surface, it seems that a teacher would have no trouble discussing these situations with children, in reality, it turns out to be difficult. The reason is that children (and even many adults) have trouble distinguishing a quantity (a measurable characteristic) from a physical description.

- Water is running from a faucet into a bathtub. What is changing?
  Physical description: the bathtub is filling up
  An appropriate quantity: amount of water (volume)

- You have a picture of Jack standing next to the giant at the top of the beanstalk.
  Physical description: the giant is much bigger than Jack
  An appropriate quantity: height

The point is that merely asking children to provide descriptions of a picture will not promote quantitative reasoning. Even when they are not attempting to take any measurements, discussing quantities entails knowing what the measurable characteristics are. Noting the distinction between description and quantity identification is a necessary step in mathematizing a problem situation. Anyone can look at the picture and see that the giant is taller than Jack is. Measuring the heights of the two characters uses mathematics to prove that assertion.

Students' responses to the tractor problem at the beginning of the chapter clearly demonstrate the difficulty that they have in discerning appropriate quantities and mentally coordinating them to make sense of what is happening. Consider all of the quantities that they introduced into the discussion:

- distance between the wheels
- distance each wheel travels
- how fast the wheels turn
- time it takes each wheel to complete one turn
- the circumferences of the wheels
- how many times a wheel turns
- number of turns of the smaller wheel as compare to number of turns of the larger wheel

Before they could begin to answer the question, they needed to argue about and to justify claims made about which of these quantities are appropriate to the situation. This took several class periods, but it was important that the students analyze the situation in depth. (By the way, both wheels cover the same distance.)

## DISCUSSING PROPORTIONAL RELATIONSHIPS IN PICTURES

Our earliest understanding of proportion occurs on a visual level even before we learn to walk. We rely on visual data to give us information about such things as scale, degree of faithfulness of models, perspective, and so forth. During their early elementary years, we can help children to build on this intuitive knowledge by making it more explicit and open to analysis. We can use pictures to help students to develop the vocabulary for thinking about and talking about proportions. Classroom discussion also needs to address ideas such as *stretching, shrinking, enlarging, distorting*, being *in proportion*, being *out of proportion*, and being drawn *to scale*.

We use the word *proportion* in several different ways, and it is important that students understand all of its uses. For example, it someone asks, "What proportion of the class is women?" they are really asking what fraction or part of the class is women? If it is said that the number of cases of a disease has reached epidemic proportions what is meant is merely that it has grown to a great size.

There are several different types of comparisons we can use to help students build the language of proportions well before they meet the symbols $\frac{a}{b} = \frac{c}{d}$. The first compares the picture of an object to something external, usually the real object. When we say that an object is drawn *in proportion*, we mean that there is a relationship between a real object and the sketch of that object, such that for all of the corresponding dimensions of the object, the ratios between drawn size and real size are equal. If a real person is 5 feet tall and has arms 2.2 feet long and in a portrait, the person is painted 3 feet tall, then his arms should not be 2.2 feet long or the portrait will be out of proportion. Technically speaking, to be in proportion, the comparison between every measurement on the real person and every corresponding measurement on the portrait should be the same. Proportions play an important role in caricatures. What would you say about this sketch of a well-known writer? Is he drawn in proportion? Why might the artist have drawn certain features *out of proportion*? What statement might the artist be trying to make with the distortions?

A second important sense of the word refers to relations within a single object—an internal proportion. For example, suppose you are asked to judge the proportions of this rectangle:

That means to judge the way in which the dimensions of the rectangle relate to each other. Without taking any actual measurements, you would take the width of the rectangle and visually lay it out against the length, making the judgment that there are about 4 of the widths in the length. You could say that the rectangle is about four times as long as it is wide, or you would say that the ratio of its width to its length is 1 : 4.

Finally, we would like children to be able to talk about different objects and their sizes relative to each other. By the time children come to school, they have a well-developed sense of proportion. For example, children are not fooled by the juxtaposition of two sketches such as that of the rabbit and the bear shown below. They know that the sizes of the animals are not their real sizes, nor do the sketches portray their relative sizes. Children understand implicitly that each drawing in itself is a faithful model of the real animal it represents, but taken together, the pair of drawings are not representative of a scene in which the real animals are standing next to each other. Children's first explanation for this might be that "they were shrunk by different amounts" or simply that "they don't look right." Again, it is a matter of developing some vocabulary by which students can think about and communicate about proportions. Both animals are scaled down, but they are drawn *on different scales*.

- The picture of the bear is drawn on a smaller scale than that of a real bear.
- The picture of the rabbit is drawn on a smaller scale than that of a real rabbit.
- The bear and the rabbit are not in proportion relative to each other.

Computers make it very easy to introduce scale. A picture in which two items are drawn in the correct proportions relative to each other can be altered by shrinking each item by a different factor to produce different effects. Numerical read-outs for absolute height, relative height, and aspect ratio, can help children not only with the language of change, but also, to obtain a deep understanding of the terms through their own experimentation on resizing the pictures.

## VISUALIZING, VERBALIZING, AND SYMBOLIZING CHANGING RELATIONSHIPS

Part of the preparation for later proportional reasoning is helping children to develop the ability to look at a situation, to discern the important quantifiable characteristics, to note whether or not quantities are changing in that situation, and if they are, to note the directions of change with respect to each other.

It is useful to have students make verbal statements about changing relationships and to use arrows to note the direction of change of each quantity. I have found that children have a tendency not to think too carefully about the way quantities change in relation to each other. Children have a tendency to believe that two quantities either increase or decrease together. Requiring a verbal statement about the situation causes them to focus more carefully on quantities, while the arrow notation will later serve as a reminder to reason up or to reason down.

- For example, we might show a picture of a child watching a balloon rise into the sky.

  The picture is static, but from their past experiences, students can imagine the kind of change that occurs in this situation. The balloon moves farther away and higher into the sky and as it moves away from us, it appears smaller in size.

  What quantities are changing? Height of the balloon, apparent size of the balloon
  Verbal statement of the quantitative relationships: the higher the balloon floats into the sky, the smaller it looks.
  Arrow notation: height of the balloon ↑ apparent size ↓

- We have a picture of three children with candy bars. Two other children are standing close by. The picture is titled *Sharing Candy*.

  What quantities are changing? The number of children and the amount of candy per child.
  Verbal statement: the more children who share, the less candy there is for each child.
  Arrow notation: number of children ↑ amount of candy per child ↓

In time, students quickly adopt the habit of referring to up-up situations, up-down situations, down-up situations, and so on. Later, this language and notation can be extended into more powerful ideas and the categories can be refined, for example, all up-up situations are not the same.

The balloon and the candy bar situations involve *covariation*. This means that linked quantities are changing together. Of course, it is not always the case that changing quantities are related.

- Yesterday at baseball practice, John had 3 hits in 10 times at bat. What will be the case after 3 days of practice?

  It would not make much sense to call this an up-up situation, and students need to be reminded to use their experience and common sense to distinguish those quantities that share a relationship from those that do not.

## COVARIATION AND INVARIANCE

All of this discussion about quantities, their relationships, covariation—where is it headed? The visualization and verbalization activities and discussions prepare students for another more abstract notion: the invariance of quantities. The most elementary forms of mathematical and scientific reasoning, whether it be logical, arithmetic, geometric, or physical reasoning, are based on the very simple principle of invariance of quantities. Simply put, it says something like this:

The whole remains, whatever may be the arrangement of its parts, the change in its form, or its displacement in space or time.

As simple as this seems, the principle of invariance is a very difficult instructional task. Invariance is not a priori datum of the mind, nor is it simply a matter of empirical observation. It is an abstraction and students reach it in their own time. It is related to many rational number ideas: equivalence, the idea of showing *the same relative amount*, and the relationship between the four quantities in a proportion, just to name a few.

One of the best ways to explain invariance is in term of structural relationships. They are not immediately apparent in a situation, but rather, they exist below the surface. We need to *read them into* the situation. For example, consider the following scenario.

I have 36 chips, 12 white and 24 black. I make the following arrangement:

Now I rearrange the chips.

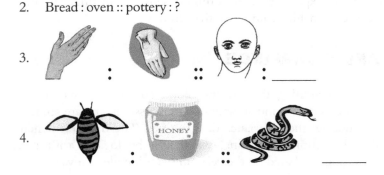

What changed? In both cases, the number of white chips and the number of black chips remained the same. Only the arrangement or grouping of the chips changed. In addition to the numbers of white and black chips, what remained invariant (unchanged)? (This is where we need to dig a little deeper and to consider underlying relationships.) In both arrangements, every group showed two black chips for every white chip. This constant relationship may be expressed as a ratio: 1 white:2 black.

Another way to encourage younger children to think about relational similarities is through the use of pictorial and verbal analogies. You may have encountered these on intelligence tests, college entrance examinations, or other standardized tests.

1.    Dog is to fur as bird is to? This is often written dog : fur :: bird : ?

2.    Bread : oven :: pottery : ?

3.    (hand) : (gloved hand) :: (face) : _____

4.    (bee) : (honey) :: (snake) : _____

5.

Analyzing analogies provides an alternate and more abstract means of studying relationships. In analogies, there is a relationship between the first pair of terms and the goal is to supply the missing term in the second pair so that it conveys a similar relationship. Historically, both psychologists and mathematicians have contended that there is a close connection between analogical reasoning and proportional reasoning, arguing that it is unlikely that a child will be able to understand all of the relations in a proportion if he or she cannot apprehend the relational similarity in analogies.

In discussing analogies with children it is important that they explain the relationship that led to their response. This is because it is often possible to complete an analogy merely by making associations and without thinking about relational similarity. For example, in the third problem stated above, a child might say "hair" because we typically associate hair with our heads. This response might have been made without considering the relationship between hand and glove. The relationship that explains the connection between hand and glove and between head and hand is that the first member of each pair is "protected and kept warm by" the second member.

## CUISENAIRE STRIPS

In addition to pictures, other concrete materials such as Cuisenaire strips or rods may be used to discuss relationships. Some people dismiss the idea of using manipulative materials in the mathematics classroom, based on the opinion that they are toys with questionable mathematical benefit. There are, however, two products that have a longer history than anything else in the trade catalogues because they are valuable thinking aids.

Cuisenaire rods and pattern blocks (I'll look at these later) are two superb tools for helping children to learn about fractions and the more advanced relationships in proportions. The commercially available Cuisenaire rods are brightly colored wood or plastic three-dimensional sets. As symbols for numbers, they are excellent proportional models. Cuisenaire rods are graduated in length from 1 cm (white) to 10 cm (orange). Their lengths have the same properties as numbers. The yellow rod (a 5-rod) is the same length as a red rod and a green rod laid end to end (3 + 2), and an 8-rod is twice as long as a 4-rod. Fractions require a comparison of two pieces, an ordered pair.

For fraction instruction, the fact that rods are three-dimensional is unimportant. It is the length of the rods that is critical. Thus it is easy and inexpensive to cut Cuisenaire-like pieces out of card stock so that all children can have access to these tools. For your convenience, patterns are included in *MORE*. As a caveat to these assertions, I might add that the teacher must always decide how long and how much to use any tool. Just because some clever person has figured out how to do everything but churn butter with a certain tool, doesn't mean that it useful or time-efficient to teach children to do so. A good guideline is this: if you, the teacher, have to read a thick manual to figure out how to use a tool, or take seminars or on-line courses to figure out how it works, then you will surely waste valuable classroom time teaching children about the tool, rather than about mathematics. Every teaching tool has its limitations and must be used judiciously.

The strongest recommendation for the use of Cuisenaire strips for teaching fractions is that they embody the idea that fractions show relationships between part and whole and that it is not the actual size of pieces that represent the part and/or the whole. A strip has no intrinsic value until we define a unit and compare it to that unit.

If black (7) is designated as the unit, then lime green (3) over black depicts $\frac{3}{7}$:

If yellow (5) is designated as the unit, lime green (3) over yellow represents $\frac{3}{5}$:

- Is the relationship of the magenta strip to the dark green strip the same as the relationship between the red and the magenta strips?

    Align the strips as shown here.

    magenta                         red
    dark green                      magenta

It is clear that magenta is more than half the length of dark green, while red is only half the length of magenta.

- Is the relationship between magenta and blue strips the same as the relationship between red and yellow strips?

    Align the strips or rods as shown here.

    red                             magenta
    yellow                          blue

Align the colored strips with white ones, which are one unit in length, in order to determine the relationships. Then you can see that magenta is twice the length of red, but blue is not twice the length of yellow. Now, you can also name the fractions or ratios that are being compared. We can tell that $\frac{2}{5} \neq \frac{4}{9}$ because equivalent fractions both show the same relationship.

Although these problems are presented in a concrete form, they involve higher order multiplicative thinking. The relationships in the problems closely resemble those in proportions. Notice that the explanation used in the first example examined the relationship within each pair of strips, and the second explanation examined the relationship between corresponding members of the pairs (first to first and second to second). In a proportion, both within ratios and both between ratios are the same, but not necessarily to each other.

## SCALE FACTORS

When talking about resizing objects, you are more likely to hear the term *scale factor*. A scale factor is a number that multiplies some quantity. Here, the word *scale* means changing size through a multiplicative operation, rather than in an additive way. In the first chapter, we discussed what it means for two quantities to be proportional to each other. It means that they have a constant ratio $\left(\frac{y}{x} = k\right)$ or, equivalently, one is a constant multiple of the other ($y = kx$). The constant of proportionality actually describes the way in which two quantities co-vary or change in an associated way. When you think about it, shrinking or enlarging an object entails changing quantities in a directly proportional way. Thus, a scale factor is not a new concept; it is a constant of proportionality in a directly proportional situation. It describes the change between two objects when one is a smaller or a larger version of the other. Most often, it refers to the relationship of a quantity to a previous state of that quantity.

You have a pile of sand. The storm blew in some more. When you are talking about the same quantity before it changed and now, you might say "There is twice as much as before." Possibly the wind blew some of the sand away, and you might say, "Now there is only half as much." Twice as much (a multiplier of 2) or half as much (a multiplier of 0.5) relate that quantity to a previous state. 2 and 0.5 are called *scale factors*.

Sometimes you see the term *scale ratio*. A scale factor is really just a ratio that has been divided. When the ratio is not divided, it is called a scale ratio. The ratio $2:1$, when written in fraction form is $\frac{2}{1}$ or 2 divided by 1. Therefore a scale factor of 2 corresponds to a ratio of $2:1$.

- A scale factor of 0.5 corresponds to a scale ratio of $1:2$.

## SIMILARITY

Here are two pictures of commonly recognized objects. What do you think they are?

Why do you have to concentrate on the images and perhaps even make guesses as to what you are seeing? The images are distorted. They have been resized in a way that does not preserve the proportions of the original objects.

When an object is shrunk or enlarged in such a way that all of its dimensions preserve the proportions within the original object, then we say that the objects are *similar*. Similar objects have to have the same shape; that is, one is just a smaller or a larger version of the other. One of the objects can be shrunk or enlarged until it is an exact copy of the other, that is, the original and the resized copy are *congruent* (same shape, same size). Unfortunately, the mathematical use of the term *similar* does not agree with the colloquial use of the term.

These sailboats are similar.

These dragons are similar.

These rabbits are not similar.

Human beings seem to have a built-in capability to recognize objects whether they are large or small in size, whether they are the real thing, or whether they are photographs or models with only some of the characteristics of real things. For example, even very small children recognize that the above sketches are models of a bunny. They will call each one a *bunny*, implicitly understanding that the picture does not have all of the characteristics of a real bunny—life, movement, furriness, size, and so on—and even though each is portrayed to a different degree of abstraction.

In our everyday use of the word *similar* we mean *showing some resemblance*, but mathematically speaking, similarity is a more precise notion. Unfortunately, we tend to underestimate the conceptual difficult of the mathematical idea of similarity because we think we know the meaning from its colloquial use and because the standard textbook definition is deceptively simple: objects are similar when they are the same shape. When we talk to children, we find out that, in fact, they develop their own notions about what it means to have the same shape, and their primitive notions of similarity may actually interfere with instruction if we are not careful to explore their ideas more carefully. Consider, for example, the following observation of an 8-year-old regarding the set of rabbits shown earlier. "These pictures are similar because they are all have the same shape—the bunny shape."

Mathematical similarity entails much more than merely looking at the two objects. It requires a search for quantities and relationships. Earlier in this chapter, we talked about analogies. When both parts of an analogy entail the same relationship, we say that the parts are similar. But remember, the relationship was hidden beneath the surface. The discovery of a constant ratio when two variables were changing together was also more than a perception; the ratio was not explicit in the given information. Thus, similarity is an elusive concept. The student needs to be looking below the surface for quantitative relationships that are not explicit. We discuss now some of the multiplicative relationships entailed in understanding similarity. Are the following two rectangles similar?

Let's consider the relationships *within* each rectangle.

In the first rectangle, comparing width to height, we get $9:6 = 3:2 = 1.5:1$
In the second rectangle, comparing width to height, we get $4.5:3 = 1.5:1$
Dividing both ratios, we get $W:H = 1.5$ Now we know that the rectangles are similar.

Alternatively, we could have reached this conclusion by considering relationships *between* the two rectangles:

Comparing the widths or the rectangles, we get $9:4.5 = 2:1$
Comparing the heights of the rectangles, we get $6:3 = 2:1$
The rectangles are similar because $W_1:W_2 = H_1:H_2 = 2$

What do these numbers mean? $9:6$ and $4.5:3$ are ratios comparing width to height within each rectangle, thus they are called *within* ratios or *internal* ratios. They are also called *aspect* ratios (more on this later in the chapter). Both ratios, when divided, equal 1.5, signifying that the rectangles are proportional. 1.5 is the constant of proportionality in the equation relating the width and the height of each rectangle: $W = 1.5 H$.

Each of the ratios $9:4.5$ and $6:3$ compares corresponding measurements from the two rectangles, thus they are called *between* ratios. When divided, both ratios equal 2; thus, the rectangles are proportional. 2 is the scale factor. It is important to note that a scale factor operates on all of the dimensions of a figure simultaneously. If the width, but not the height, had been shrunk or enlarged, we would have a distorted figure that is not similar to the original figure. 2 is also the constant of proportionality in the equations relating the widths and the heights of the two rectangles: $W_1 = 2W_2$ and $H_1 = 2 H_2$. Alternatively, we could have used the ratios $4.5:9$ and $3:6$. In this case, the scale factor would be $\frac{1}{2}$.

Regardless of the way in which equivalent ratios are constructed, the constant of proportionality is a special relationship lurking in the background, as in an analogy. Notice that it did not appear overtly in the given information. Furthermore, it is always important to interpret the ratios, scale factors, and constants of proportionality that you are using.

Thinking about fractional multipliers can help to interpret scale factors. If you multiply by 1 (the multiplicative identity), the quantity you multiplied remains unchanged. If you multiply a quantity by a fraction that is smaller than 1, your result is a smaller quantity. If you multiply by a factor that is larger than 1, the starting quantity gets larger.

- Apply a scale factor of 0.8 to rectangle A.

B will be similar to A and, because the scale factor is less than 1, B will be a smaller version of A. B's height is $3(0.8) = 2.4'$ and B's width is $4(0.8) = 3.2'$.

2.4' | B
3.2'

- A builder installs rectangular lap swimming pools. All of his pools are similar in shape. He shows you a model that measures 8' by 20'. Your space requires a pool that is only 6' wide. How long will it be?

You know that the pools are similar, so the pool you purchase (P) will be a scaled down version of the model (M). First, use the widths to find the scale ratio:
$$8:6 = 4:3 \text{ or } 6:8 = 3:4$$
You can do this either way. But you have to think about what these scale ratios mean.

M width: P width = 4 : 3 and Mw = $\frac{4}{3}$ Pw. (The model is wider than your pool.)

P width: M width = 3 : 4 and Pw = $\frac{3}{4}$ Mw. (Your pool is narrower than the model.)

I will apply the scale factor $\frac{3}{4}$ to the length of the model pool to get your pool's length.

$\frac{3}{4} \cdot 20 = 15$. The length of your pool will be 15′.

Let's see how children handle the concept of similarity. Children in grades 4, 5, and 6 tried to solve this problem:

Rami was looking at swimming pools. All of the pools had the same shape. They were larger versions of the pool at the store that measured 6′ by 8′. If he decides to buy a pool that is 10′ wide, how long will it be?

Grade 4 Ron

It must be 12′ long because 10 = 6 + 4.
So ? = 8 + 4. In case you don't beleve it, 8 − 6 = 2 and 12 − 10 = 2
so it must be right.

Grade 5

$\frac{6}{8} = \frac{3}{4}$

$\frac{3}{4} \cdot 10 = \frac{30}{4} = 7\frac{1}{2}$′

Grade 6

Ed $6 \times 1\frac{2}{3} = 6 + 4 = 10$

$8 \times 1\frac{2}{3} = 8 + \frac{16}{3} =$

$8 + 5\frac{1}{3} = 13\frac{1}{3}$′

When children were working with whole numbers, addition was a way to make something larger. The most difficult idea for children to grasp about the notion of similarity is that the same thing or enlarging does not involve addition, but rather, multiplication. Adding the same thing to both height and width of the rectangle will make the rectangle larger, but the amount you add is a different fraction of each side, thus stretching the shape more in one direction than the other. This is what happened in Ron's solution to the opening problem. Adding 4 to 6 increases the height of the rectangle by $\frac{2}{3}$ but adding 4 feet to 8 feet increases 8 by $\frac{1}{2}$. From Ron's response, we can imagine how deeply engrained his additive thinking is. Not only does he think that he can enlarge the rectangle by adding the same amount to its dimensions, but he even finds a second additive argument to convince himself that he is correct! Ed, the sixth grader, realized that 6 had been multiplied by $1\frac{2}{3}$ and so he correctly multiplied the other side of the rectangle by the same factor. Jan, the fifth grader compared the width to the length of the first rectangle and obtained $\frac{3}{4}$. However, she did not know how to use $\frac{3}{4}$ to find the missing length.

## INDIRECT MEASUREMENT

We have already talked about the importance of measurement, especially the role of ratios and proportions in measuring quantities that cannot be measured directly, such as slope, speed, oranginess of a drink, etc. Ratios were actually measures of some types of quantities. Ratios (specifically, the ratios that apply in similar triangles) may be used to obtain measurements of physical objects when you cannot reach to measure. For example, it would be difficult for you to measure the height of a flag pole, or of a tree, or of a tall building. You simply cannot climb up with a measuring tape and obtain information that you may wish to have, so you need an indirect way of obtaining it. Similar triangles can help you figure out the approximate height of the object. Let's say that this little groundhog is standing near a tree and he wants to know how tall the tree is.

The little groundhog is 18 inches tall, and he measures his shadow (because it is on the ground) from his heel to the end of his shadow, and sees that it is 3 feet long. He can also measure the tree's shadow; he measures from the base of the tree to the end of its shadow and gets 27 feet.

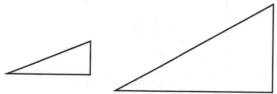

We have a situation that can be modeled by similar triangles. What is the scale ratio? To get the scale ratio, I will ask myself "How does the shadow of the tree relate to the shadow of the groundhog?" Scale ratio $= \dfrac{27}{3} = \dfrac{9}{1}$. So I get a scale factor of 9, meaning that the length of the tree's shadow is 9 times the length of the groundhog's shadow, so the height of the tree must be 9 times the groundhog's height.

$$H = 9(1.5) = 13.5'$$

## TESTING FOR SIMILARITY

Every rectangle that is similar to rectangle A has to have an internal ratio comparing width to height of $8:6 = 4:3$. Whether a rectangle is larger or smaller than A, if it is similar to A, its ratio of width to height will be $4:3$. Obviously, the scale factor will be different each time we construct a larger or a smaller rectangle, but the ratio $W:H = 4:3$ will remain the same.

People who work in video industries use this ratio frequently and so they have given it a name. *Aspect ratio* is the comparison of the width of an image compared to its height. For those in video industries, the term is insider-speak for the internal comparisons we have already discussed.

We can think of all of the rectangles that are a scaled-down or scaled-up version of A as members of the same family as A. In mathematics, this family is called an *equivalence class*. The ratio that describes all of them is the aspect ratio $4:3$. The equivalence class of $4:3$ includes $3.2:2.4$, $5:3.75$, $13.33:10$, $8:6$ and many other ratios. The graph of that equivalence class is shown here. Notice that the graph is a straight line and the slope between any two points is $\dfrac{4}{3}$. (Remember that $4:3$ or $\dfrac{4}{3}$ is 1.33 when divided.)

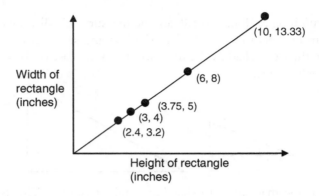

- Which of the other rectangles are similar to A?

    A.  $4' \times 6'$        B.  $6' \times 10'$        C.  $8' \times 12'$        D.  $2' \times 3'$

We know several different ways to check. We could write the aspect ratio of each rectangle. We could check between rectangles to see if each dimension of A was multiplied by the same scale factor to obtain the new rectangle. We could write the scale ratio between A and each of the others. But I am going to use a graph to determine the similar rectangles. Stack up the rectangles according to size, smallest to largest, and then put them on a graph so that their longer sides ($W$) are against the $y$-axis, and their shorter sides ($H$), are against the $x$-axis.

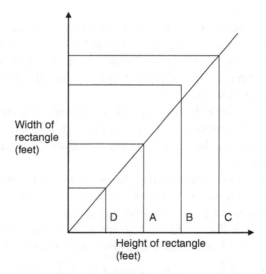

Draw a line through the origin, (0,0) and the upper right-hand corner of one of the tallest rectangle. The line represents the aspect ratio $W:H$. We can see that the width-to-height ratio for three of the four rectangles is the same. The ratios $3:2$, $6:4$, and

12 : 8 are all in the same equivalence class. The 10 : 6 ratio is in a different equivalence class. So A, C, and D are similar.

On your computer, it is very easy to create similar objects. Insert a piece of clip art into Microsoft Word. Try to resize (shrink or enlarge) the picture. The menu gives you the option of checking the following box:

☐ preserve (or maintain or lock) aspect ratio

If the box is checked, you can resize the clip art, such as the following heart, and every smaller or larger heart you create will be similar to the original. If the box is not checked, the aspect ratio will not be preserved and your heart can become distorted by resizing.

## MOCKUPS AND PUDGY PEOPLE

Aspect ratios, scale factors and similarity are important in many jobs that make use of scale drawings. It would not be cost-effective for manufacturers, architects, and other designers, for example, to build and test life-sized prototypes. You can visit Universal Studios and see how the film industry uses scale models when it is impractical to use build full-size objects. Imagine the size of King Kong if he were built to be taller than actual buildings! Children would not be able to carry Lightning McQueen, Mater, and Sally in their pockets if Disney-Pixar and Mattel did not make cars on a scale of 1 : 55.

One of the most common—but misunderstood—uses of stretching and shrinking is in the video industry. The two most common aspect ratios in home video are 4 : 3 (or 1.33 : 1, or *standard*) and 16 : 9 (or 1.78 : 1, or *wide-screen*).

A 4 : 3 screen works well with an older program, and an HDTV program works well on a 16 : 9 screen, but when you watch a program whose formatting does not match the shape of the TV screen you have, everything doesn't look quite right. People look pudgy or there are black spaces on your screen where the picture doesn't fill. Distortions and failure of the image to fill the screen happen because a 4 : 3 rectangle is not similar to a 16 : 9 rectangle. Every time you mismatch the video format with the shape of the screen for which it was intended, you have problems. Your choices are to (a) preserve the ratio or to (b) distort the picture.

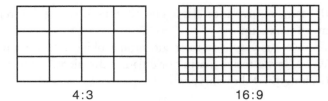

4:3                           16:9

Let's see how this works.

Suppose we take a video formatted for a 4:3 TV set and watch it on a 16:9 TV set. We need to make the 4 in the 4:3 image 4 times larger. Using a scale factor of 4, a 4:3 rectangle becomes a 16:12 rectangle (that is, 4(4:3) = 16:12). If we put 16:12 video on a 16:9 screen, a larger height gets mushed into a smaller height and that's when people look chubby or bloated.

An alternative solution is to make the 3 in the 4:3 image 3 times larger. Using a scale factor of 3, a 4:3 rectangle becomes a 12:9 rectangle (that is, 3(4:3) = 12:9). When we put a 12:9 image on a 16:9 screen, we cannot fill up the width, so we get black spaces on each side of the picture, but at least the picture still looks normal because we have preserved the aspect ratio and we have an image that is similar to the original.

4:3              16:9 with black bands          16:9 with squat objects
             aspect ratio preserved          aspect ratio not preserved

Now suppose we want to fit a wide-format image to a standard 4:3 screen. We can use a scale factor of $0.25 = \frac{1}{4}$. Then a 16:9 image changes to 4:2.5 (that is $\frac{1}{4}(16:9) = (4:2.5)$). The image will be similar to the original, but black bars will fill in across the top and across the bottom of the picture to take up the unused height of the screen. An alternative is to use a scale factor of $\frac{1}{3}$. Then $\frac{1}{3}(16:9) = (5.33:3)$. In this case, the image will be too wide for the screen and the sides of the image will get cut off.

16:9              4:3 with bands              4:3 with edges cropped
             aspect ratio preserved          aspect ratio not preserved

It's all mathematics! I have found that TV screen mathematics proves to be an interesting topic—no, a *riveting* topic—for middle school children. They love explaining to their parents why some TV images look the way they do!

## ACTIVITIES

1. Describe this caricature. What is the difference between a caricature and a life-like drawing? Make some conjectures concerning the reason why the artist may have drawn certain features out of proportion.

2. To advertise our go-to-school night, a local pizzeria made a 3-foot pizza in the gymnasium and served it to parents, teachers, and students. The three people who served the pizza estimated that each group was served the portion indicated in the picture. What can you say about the way they distributed the pizza?

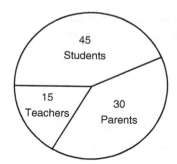

3. In each case, discuss possible responses and the relation on which they are based.

   a. picture : frame :: yard : ?
   c. food : body :: rain : ?
   e. sap : tree :: blood : ?
   g. pear : tree :: potato : ?
   i. conductor : train :: captain : ?

   b. giraffe : neck :: porcupine : ?
   d. car : gasoline :: sail : ?
   f. sandwich : boy :: carrot : ?
   h. tree : leaves :: book : ?
   j. wedding : bride :: funeral : ?

4.  Using Cuisenaire strips, decide whether or not the relationship in each pair is the same and state the reason for your conclusion. (Strips are available in *MORE*.)

    a.  yellow to white; orange to green
    b.  white to green; green to dark green
    c.  dark green to blue; green to magenta
    d.  brown to orange; magenta to yellow
    e.  green to blue; white to red

5.  Judge the proportions of width to length of these rectangles.

    a.        b.

    c.        d.

6.  Pretend you have a little dog who is as high as your knee when he is standing on all four feet. If you were a giant, 8 feet tall, how high would your dog be if he still came up to your knee?

7.  The given pair of Cuisenaire strips defines a relationship. Complete the second pair using the smallest number of strips possible so that it shows the same relationship.

    a.  white to yellow; magenta to ?
    b.  red to magenta; black to ?
    c.  yellow to red; orange to ?
    d.  (orange + red) to brown; green to ?
    e.  dark green to (orange + magenta); green to ?

8.  Dianne runs laps every day. Given each statement below (a–e), draw a conclusion about her running speed today. Think about which quantities are changing and which are invariant.

    a.  She ran the same number of laps in less time than she did yesterday.
    b.  She ran fewer laps in the same amount of time as she did yesterday.
    c.  She ran more laps in less time than she did yesterday.
    d.  She ran more laps in the same time as she ran yesterday.
    e.  She ran fewer laps in less time than she did yesterday.

9.  For each situation, list the changing quantities.

    a.  You are filling your car's gas tank.
    b.  You travel by car from Milwaukee to Chicago.

   c.  You make several credit card purchases.

   d.  You are scuba diving.

   e.  You are draining the water in your bathtub.

10.   In each scenario, tell which quantities change and which do not change.

   a.  I was standing next to a change machine and two people came up and used it. A man inserted a 50-cent piece and received 4 dimes and 2 nickels. Then a woman inserted a dollar bill and received 8 dimes and 4 nickels.

   b.  I put the first picture shown here into a copying machine. The second picture is what came out.

   c.  On my map of Wisconsin, the distance between Madison and the Milwaukee lakeshore was about 4 inches, or 80 miles. The distance between Green Bay and Madison was about 6.5 inches or 130 miles.

   d.  I measured the length of my room in inches and got 144 inches; I measured my room in feet and got 12 feet.

   e.

11.   a.  A stew recipe calls for $\frac{4}{3}$ as many cups of peas as cups of carrots. Are there more peas or more carrots?

  b.  Jim is $\frac{2}{3}$ as tall as Ted. Who is taller?

  c.  Half as many people have dogs as have cats. Do more people have dogs or do more have cats?

  d.  $\frac{1}{2}$ liter of juice costs \$3. Will $\frac{2}{3}$ as much cost more or less than \$3?

  e.  On go-to-school night, $\frac{3}{5}$ of the mothers who have children in the third grade class and $\frac{2}{3}$ of the fathers who have children in the class came to visit with the teacher. What can you say about this situation?

12.  Use arrow notation to show the direction of change (↑ or ↓) for two related quantities. Then fill in the blank. If this is impossible, tell why.

  a.  8 people clean a house in 2 hours; 2 people clean that house in _____ hours.
  b.  It costs \$30 to play 15 games; 3 games will cost ____.
  c.  It takes 4 hours to play 1 game of golf; 3 games will take ____ hours.
  d.  John is 10 years old and his mother is 3 times as old as John; Ben is 12 years old, and his mother is ____ years old.
  e.  6 people can rake a yard in 2 hours; 2 people can do it in ____ hours.
  f.  I pay 6% sales tax when I purchase 1 item; I will pay ____% tax when I purchase 5 items.
  g.  Three people eat their dinner in 30 minutes; it will take 9 people ____ minutes.
  h.  2 people deliver all the papers on a certain route in 30 minutes; 6 people do the route in ____ minutes.

13.  Use the "cookies and kids" method of comparing these fractions.

  a.  $\frac{4}{9}, \frac{4}{8}$    b.  $\frac{2}{7}, \frac{5}{7}$    c.  $\frac{4}{5}, \frac{5}{3}$    d.  $\frac{3}{7}, \frac{2}{5}$    e.  $\frac{3}{5}, \frac{3}{7}$

  f.  $\frac{2}{9}, \frac{1}{10}$    g.  $\frac{3}{7}, \frac{4}{9}$

14.  In Mr. Trent's science class, students sit 3 to a table. One day for mid-morning break, Mr. Trent put two candy bars on each table and told the students to share them. "But before you do," he said, "please push all 4 tables together." If you are a candy lover, would you like to get your share of the candy before or after the tables are pushed together?

15.  Two of the sales at Bob's Bakery are shown below. What does Bob charge for a whoopie pie and what does he charge for a cookie?

16.   Find the cost of a bear and the cost of a train. Think about what is changing and what is not changing.

$80

$76

17.   Find the cost of a helmet and the cost of a football.

$50

$50

18.   My computer indicates that a piece of clip art has an aspect ratio of 2.51 : 2.44. What does that tell you?

19.  Using this rectangle as a model, what is the largest similar rectangle that you could make on a piece of paper $8\frac{1}{2}'' \times 11''$ and what scale factor would give you that largest rectangle?

20.  A plastic dinosaur is a $\frac{1}{20}$-scale version of the one used in the movie Land of the Dinosaurs. How tall was the dinosaur in the movie?

21.  In Figure A, the squares are 1 unit by 1 unit. In figure B, the lengths in figure A have been enlarged by a scale factor of 2. What is the factor of enlargement of the area of figure A?

A

B

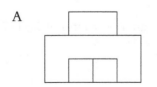

22. Using a metric ruler, make scale drawings of the objects whose actual dimensions are given here. Use a scale of 1 centimeter to 1 meter.

   a. a tennis court: 6 m by 11.5 m
   b. a sheet of paper: 0.25 m by 0.45 m
   c. a desktop: 1.75 m by 1.1 m

23. Draw a picture of this steamer that is twice its present size. It is drawn on $\frac{1}{4}$-inch graph paper. You can do this by using $\frac{1}{2}$-inch squares and drawing each line in a corresponding position on the larger grid.

24. Draw a smaller version of this butterfly using the same principle. Cover the butterfly with a grid of $\frac{1}{2}$-inch squares and copy corresponding parts onto $\frac{1}{4}$-inch graph paper.

25.  What was the scale factor in problem 24? Check the body length of the butterfly in the picture above and in the smaller version that you produced.

26.  Find the similar rectangles.

A.
$1\frac{1}{2}$
3

B.
1
$1\frac{1}{2}$

C.
$\frac{1}{2}$
1

D.
$\frac{1}{2}$
$1\frac{1}{2}$

E.
$\frac{1}{4}$
$\frac{1}{2}$

F.
1
3

G.
$\frac{3}{4}$
$1\frac{1}{2}$

H.
$1\frac{1}{4}$
$1\frac{7}{8}$

I.
2
3

J.
$\frac{1}{2}$
2

27.  Devise a test similar to the one we used for rectangles (nesting) to determine if any of these triangles are similar. How does your test work?

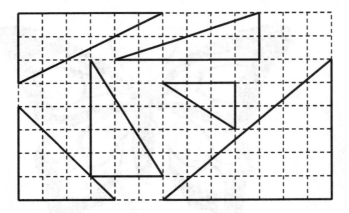

28.  An 8-inch square shrinks to become a 2-inch square.

   a.  What is the relationship between the sides of these squares?
   b.  What is the scale factor?

29.  Answers the following questions concerning figures A and B.

A                                                B

   a.  Describe the relationship of pyramid B to pyramid A.
   b.  What is the scale factor?
   c.  In the enlarging process, what happened to the right angles?
   d.  What happened to the length of the vertical segments?
   e.  What happened to the length of the horizontal segments?
   f.  What happened to the area of the figure?
   g.  What is the ratio of corresponding lengths?
   h.  What generalizations can you make about the effects of shrinking and/or enlarging?

30.  a.  Use the pizza parlor menu below to determine which cheese pizza is the best buy. All pizzas are round.

| Type | Diameter (inches) | Price |
|------|-------------------|-------|
| Small | 10 | $6.80 |
| Medium | 12 | $8.50 |
| Large | 14 | $12.60 |
| Giant | 20 | $28.00 |

   b.  Is the price proportional to the size of the pizza?

31.  Use the given scale factor to determine what each of the given measurements must have been before it was resized.

   a.  Scale ratio: $\dfrac{1}{14}$

2.5'

   b.  Scale factor: 25

0

80'

c.  Scale factor: 4.5

A = 25 ft²

32.  a.  Pretend that you could produce a video format to fit a TV with an aspect ratio of 6 : 5. How would it look on a TV whose aspect ratio is 12 : 8?
    b.  Suppose you could produce video in a 15 : 8 format. How would it look on a TV whose aspect ratio is 4 : 2?
    c.  Suppose you could produce video in a 16 : 12 format. How would it look on a TV with as aspect ratio of 8 : 6?

33.  There are recommendations concerning the optimal distance a person should sit from a TV. One such recommendation is that the ratio of the size of the TV screen to the distance between you and the screen should be 1 : 4.5. Answer the following questions based on this recommendation.

    a.  How far should you sit from a 32-inch TV?
    b.  How far should you sit from a 60-inch TV?
    c.  If your TV room allows for a maximum distance of 16 feet between you and the TV, what size TV should you use?

34.  The two trapezoids shown here are similar. Find the lengths of the segments A′B′, C′D′, and A′D′. Hint: Use the known corresponding sides to find out the scale ratio (or the scale factor) and remember that it acts upon *all* 4 sides of the figure.

35.  The following triangles are similar. Find the lengths of the segments A′C′ and B′C′.

36.  Based on the given information, find the missing measurement. Think! Do not set up proportions.

    a.  The scale of a map is 3 inches = 10 miles. Map measurement: 7.5 inches. Actual measurement: _____ miles.
    b.  The scale for a model is 1 inch = _____ feet. The model: 7 inches. The actual measurement: 14 feet.

  c. The scale of a map is 2 inches = 6 mi. Map: _____ inches. Actual distance: 24 miles.

  d. The scale for a model is 6 mm = 12 m. Model: 72 mm. The actual length: _____ meters.

  e. The scale of a map is 3 cm = 5 km. Map distance: _____ cm. Actual distance: 2.5 km.

37. Analyze this 6-year-old child's comment. She was asked if the second cat could be a smaller version of the first cat.

Emily: "Yeah. The first cat was shrunk into the second cat."

# CHAPTER 5

# Proportional Reasoning

## STUDENT STRATEGIES: GRADE 4

Analyze the student responses to this problem, thinking about these questions: (1) What is the unit? (2) How did each child think about the unit?

Jim ordered two pizzas. The shaded part is the amount he ate. How much of the pizza did he eat?

Kristin

$\frac{5}{4}$ because 5 little $\frac{1}{4}$ pieces
are shaded.

Jean

$\frac{5}{8}$ because there are 8 pieces
and 5 are colors.

TOM

1 And A bite.

Joe

It must be $\frac{5}{8}$ because $\frac{5}{4}$ is impossible. You
can't have more than a whole pizza.

# THE UNIT

In order to discuss fraction problems, we must first have some unit. (Alternatively, the unit has been called *the whole*, and *the unit whole*.) To answer the question "How much?" we need to use a unit of measure to determine the amount of stuff in question. Units are closely related to early measurement ideas. If you measure the same amount of stuff with different-sized measuring cups, the number of measures you get for your answer will be smaller or larger, depending on the size of your measuring unit.

Every fraction depends on some unit. For example, if I tell you that you can have half of my cookies, but I never tell you how many cookies I have, you cannot possibly know how many you are going to get. Yet, if I ask adults to draw a picture for $\frac{1}{2}$, the most frequent response is

or

They should be looking at me with puzzled faces! Unfortunately, due to the fact that fraction instruction has not always placed appropriate emphasis on the unit, they have a stereotypical view of the unit as one pizza or one cookie or one of something else.

In fractions, the unit need not be a single object. In whole numbers, *one* means *one object*. In fractions, *one* (1) means the whole amount you have before any breaking (fracturing) occurs, the whole collection of objects, a group regarded as a single entity, all things that are to come into consideration. Every fraction is a relative amount; that is, it tells how much you have relative to the unit.

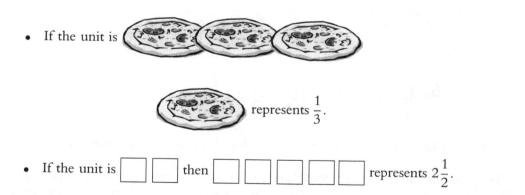

- If the unit is [pizzas] represents $\frac{1}{3}$.

- If the unit is ☐☐ then ☐☐☐☐ represents $2\frac{1}{2}$.

The significance of the unit and the fundamental changes that must occur in one's thinking at the beginning of fraction instruction cannot be overestimated. Children need to learn early in their fraction instruction that the unit may be something different in every new context and that the first question they should always ask themselves is "What is the unit?" Children who do not learn to look for that starting point, that reference point around which the entire meaning of the problem is built, usually make an inappropriate assumption (for example, the unit consists of a single whole entity, just as it did in whole number operations). Many students never develop any fraction sense or reasoning capacity—all because they never grasped the importance of the unit.

At the beginning of this chapter, the fourth graders' responses illustrate how difficult fraction ideas are for most children. In particular, they are struggling with the question "What is the unit?" Jean seems to understand that the amount eaten must be compared to the total amount available, but the others are reluctant to adopt the perspective that a unit may include more than 1 pizza. Tom's answer avoids fractions. Kristin and Joe realize that Jim ate 5 pieces, but they were not sure whether to compare the 5 to 4 pieces (meaning the unit is 1 pizza) or to 8 pieces (meaning that the unit is 2 pizzas). Joe is trying to make sense of the numbers, but he is still confused. A correct statement would have been that $\frac{5}{4}$ was impossible because "You can't eat more than you ordered."

Solve this problem for yourself and then analyze the responses given by the students and the teacher.

- Mr. McDonald took six of his basketball players out for pizza. They ordered 2 large pizzas, a cheese, and a pepperoni, and the seven of them each ate 1 slice of each pizza. If each pizza was machine cut into 12 equal slices, how much of the pizza was eaten?

John M.        They ate $\frac{14}{24}$ of the pizza.

Sally J.        $\frac{14}{12}$ of the pizza.

Andy S.        14 peaces

Their teacher wrote a reminder: Talk to John M. He is adding denominators.

The problem tells us that McDonald and his boys started with two large pizzas. The unit consists of the two pizzas or 24 slices. This means that if each person ate a slice of each pizza, 14 slices of the 24 total slices were eaten. John is correct.

Sally failed to identify the unit. She thought that 1 pizza or 12 slices was the unit, so she concluded that $\frac{14}{12}$ or $1\frac{1}{6}$ of the pizza was eaten. This actually says that they ate more pizza than they had! $1\frac{1}{6}$ of the pizza ordered would be $2\frac{1}{3}$ pizzas. They bought only 2 pizzas!

Andy did not answer the question. The question asks how much of the pizza was eaten, meaning how much of the pizza purchased was eaten. His response answers the question "How many slices were eaten?" Andy merely counted slices. This is not a counting question. The words "how much" demand a response that compares what was eaten to what they ordered.

It appears that the teacher is not sure what the unit is either. If he thinks that John was adding denominators, then we can safely assume that the teacher thinks that the unit is 1 pizza or 12 slices. The teacher thinks that John incorrectly added $\frac{7}{12} + \frac{7}{12}$ and got $\frac{14}{24}$.

## UNITS DEFINED IMPLICITLY

Deciding on the unit in a fraction problem should not be a matter of personal interpretation. In initial fraction instruction, the meaning of fractions derives from the context in which they are used, and each context, either implicitly or explicitly, should define the unit. The problems we give children to solve should either specify the unit or give enough information that the unit may be determined with a little reasoning. Some of the most widely used kinds of fraction questions in traditional texts confuse students, give them the impression that the unit is not important, or give them the impression that the unit is a matter of personal choice. The following question is not a good fraction question because the unit is not specified.

- What fraction is represented?

Several answers could be given:

5 if each dot is a unit

$2\frac{1}{2}$ if each column is a unit

$\frac{5}{3}$ or $\frac{3}{5}$ if you use a ratio interpretation

$1\frac{1}{4}$ if each set of 4 is a unit

A unit may be given explicitly or implicitly. If it is defined explicitly, then you are told at the beginning of the story exactly what the unit is. If the unit is given implicitly, then you are not told immediately what it is, but you are given enough information to find out what it is.

- John and his friends ordered 2 pizzas, each of them cut into 8 equal pieces. They ate 13 slices. How much of the pizza was left?

  The unit is defined explicitly as 2 pizzas or 16 slices.

  $\frac{3}{16}$ of the pizza is left.

- Reena has 4 candies left. If those candies are $\frac{2}{3}$ of the number she had before she started eating them, what was her original number?

  ⬤⬤
  ⬤⬤ is $\frac{2}{3}$ and we need to find the unit.

  If ⬤⬤
  ⬤⬤ is $\frac{2}{3}$, then ⬤ ⬤ must be $\frac{1}{3}$.

  If ⬤ ⬤ is $\frac{1}{3}$, then ⬤⬤
  ⬤⬤
  ⬤⬤ must be $\frac{3}{3}$ or 1.

## USING UNITS OF VARIOUS TYPES

It is important that children learn to work with units of many different types. If all they see is round pizzas, they try to use round pizzas even when they need to divide a pizza into thirds. Why not use a rectangular pizza in that case? Children have to know that the representation they choose will not affect the answer. Another reason for varying the type of unit is that it is psychologically different to divide a set of hard candies into three equal-sized groups than it is to divide a rectangular pizza into three equal-sized pieces. Different types of units can provide challenges for different children. Sometimes, one of the factors that affects a child's thinking about a problem is related to whether the child can see all of the pieces under consideration. For example, a package of cupcakes is not the same as a package of gum. Therefore, it is important that children's experiences not be limited. Problem difficulty may be varied by using problems involving units of all the following types:

- one continuous item, such as one pie

- more than one continuous item

- one or more continuous objects that are perforated or prepartitioned, such as a candy bar

- discrete objects (separate things, distinct parts), such as a group of hard candies

- discrete objects that typically come arranged in a special way, such as chocolates or eggs in a box

- composite units, that is, units consisting of single packages that have multiple objects inside, such as a package of cupcakes or a pack of gum.

## REASONING UP AND DOWN

When units are defined implicitly we have an excellent opportunity to use a process that I refer to as *reasoning up and down*, because it often entails reasoning up from some fraction to the unit, then back down from the unit to another fraction. As the name implies, this is mental work, not pencil work. Students should be encouraged to reason out loud. Here are some examples.

-  $= \frac{4}{5}$ of the ladybugs on my tree. How many ladybugs are on the tree?

  Think:

  Say aloud: 8 bugs $= \frac{4}{5}$

  2 bugs $= \frac{1}{5}$

  10 bugs $= \frac{5}{5}$ or 1

-  is $\frac{3}{4}$ of something. How much is $1\frac{1}{2}$ of that amount?

  Think: ——

  Say: If 6 sections make $\frac{3}{4}$

  then 2 sections make $\frac{1}{4}$ and

  8 sections make $\frac{4}{4}$ or 1

  ⬤⬤ is 1, so ⬤⬤⬤ is $1\frac{1}{2}$

Notice that there is a strategy to this reasoning process. Go from your starting fraction...to a unit fraction...to the unit...then finally to the target fraction. This is proportional reasoning. It does not take long until students are very successful with it and it helps them to establish useful ways of thinking from the very beginning of fraction instruction. We will continue to use reasoning up and down throughout the remaining chapters. You should reason out loud until you feel very comfortable with this process. Even if you can tell the answer, remember that the *process* is the goal!

Pattern blocks, available through trade catalogues, provide a useful alternative area model to the traditional pizza model for studying units and they support reasoning up and down. They are colorful, wooden blocks that are expensive if a classroom set is purchased. Plastic ones are less expensive. However, as with Cuisenaire rods, fraction activities require only 2 dimensions (area models), so cutting the pieces out of card stock is an equally effective alternative. In this chapter, you will use the pattern pieces provided in *MORE*.

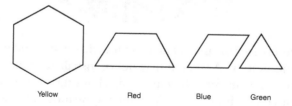

Yellow    Red    Blue    Green

- If red is the unit, what are the values of the other pieces?

  Red is $\frac{3}{3}$ and we can cover it with 3 green blocks. Green has a value of $\frac{1}{3}$. Two greens cover 1 blue, so blue is $\frac{2}{3}$. Because red is 1 and it takes 2 reds to cover a yellow, yellow must have a value of 2.

- If 2 yellows represent 1, what are the values of the other pieces?

  Because it takes 4 reds to cover the unit, red has a value of $\frac{1}{4}$. It takes 6 blues to cover the unit, so blue has the value $\frac{1}{6}$. Because it takes 2 greens to cover a blue, green must have a value of $\frac{1}{12}$.

## UNITS AND UNITIZING

Let's try a little mind experiment. Suppose I tell you we are going to solve a problem that uses a case of soda (24 cans). What sort of mental picture do you get?

Do you think about a huge cardboard carrying case full of cans or do you picture 24 individual cans of cola? Do you think about two twelve-packs? 4 six-packs? Any of these is a reasonable alternative. You could be thinking of that case as 24 cans, 2 (12-packs), 4 (6-packs), or 1 (24-pack).

Certainly, in the classroom, the mental picture that each student forms can be a source of miscommunication. A student may not be visualizing what the teacher thinks he/she is describing. Students may all be thinking about the same case of cola, 24 cans, but each individual could chose to think about the quantity in a way that was most familiar to them.

*Unitizing* refers to the process of constructing mental chunks in terms of which to think about a given quantity. It is a subjective process. It is natural; everybody does it. If we do not have a way to report to each other the way in which we are thinking about the quantity, lack of communication can occur. Imagine a classroom teacher, introducing a fraction problem about a case of cola to 20 or more children, each of whom is thinking about the cola packaged in the way that their parent typically buys it. I observed this very phenomenon one day in a fourth grade classroom. Chris, the teacher, gave this problem:

> Steve took a case of cola to Marcia's party, but it turned out that most of his friends drank water. He ended up taking three quarters of the cola home again. How much cola did he take home?

The children in Chris' class solved the cola problem and then in a class discussion, three answers were offered.

> Jim    I think  3.
> April   I say its  18.
> Joy     He took $1\frac{1}{2}$ home.

Suppose you were moderating the discussion that day. What would you say?

The problem explicitly specifies the unit: one case of cola. Depending on the size of chunk by which you think about the case, you can get different but equivalent answers. Jim, April, and Joy all failed to label their responses and should be reminded to do so. However, if we make the assumption that each of them knew that a case referred to some configuration of 24 cans, then it is possible that each of them was thinking correctly about the problem. Each could have used a different but equivalent form of the unit, 1 case. Jim could have been thinking that a case consisted of 4 six-packs, in which case 3 six-packs would be correct. April could have been thinking that a case consisted of 24 individual cans. In that case, 18 cans would be $\frac{3}{4}$ of a case. If Joy was thinking of a case as two 12-packs, then $1\frac{1}{2}$ (12-packs) would also be a correct response. Correctly labeled, their answers should have been 3 (6-packs), 18 cans, and $1\frac{1}{2}$ (12-packs).

## UNITIZING NOTATION

Unitizing is a natural process. In instruction, wouldn't it be better to recognize that fact and use unitizing to its fullest advantage? If we use a notation that allows students to tell us how they are "chunking" or thinking about a quantity, then we do not have to stifle a natural and useful process by insisting that everyone do things the same way. A notation that includes the number of chunks followed by the size of each group in parentheses is convenient:

$$\text{\# of chunks (size of chunk)}$$

- Let's think about 24 eggs.

  $$24 \text{ eggs} = 2 \text{ (dozen)} = 4 \text{ (6-packs)} = 1\frac{1}{3} \text{ (18-packs)} = 12 \text{ (pair)}$$

- Let's think about 32 crayons.

  $$32 \text{ crayons} = \frac{1}{2}\text{(64-box)} = 2\text{(16-boxes)} = 16\text{ (pair)} = 64\left(\frac{1}{2}\text{-crayons}\right)$$

Notice that in each case, the *quantity remained the same*; only the way I thought about it changed. I chunked it in different ways, but if you look carefully at each different statement of the quantity, you will see that it is always the same amount—24 eggs or 32 crayons. You could tell exactly how I was grouping the eggs because I told you explicitly, and you could tell whether I was making sense or not by checking to see that the quantity never changed, no matter how I expressed it.

## FLEXIBILITY IN UNITIZING

Ultimately, we want students to be able to think flexibly about any quantity they are given. There are advantages in being able to conceptualize a quantity in terms of many different-sized pieces. Depending on the context in which you are working, chunking a quantity in one way may be more advantageous than chunking it in another way. A person who is a flexible thinker and can choose or anticipate the best way to do something clearly has an advantage over someone who can do things in only one way. Some examples illustrate what this means.

- Suppose you go to the store and you see a sign that says kiwis are 3 for $0.67. You want to buy 9 kiwi fruits.

  If you think in terms of single kiwis, you will figure out that one kiwi costs 22.33333… cents. Now you need to multiply by 9 to get the cost of 9 kiwis. If you round before multiplying by 9, you magnify the error due to rounding by a factor of 9. In this case, it would definitely be easier to think about a group of 3 fruits. If we think of the 9 kiwis as 3 (3-packs), then the cost of 9 is just 3 times $0.67 or exactly $2.01.

• Think about a situation that requires sharing a case of cola (24 colas) among 4 people, or between 2 people.

If you need to share a case among 4 people, it is more convenient to think of a case as consisting of 4 six-packs. If you need to share a case between two people, would you deal out one can at a time? There is nothing wrong with using single cans, but it would certainly be faster to measure out each share and more convenient to carry home if you had 4 (6-packs) or 2 (12-packs). In mathematics, the ability to conceive of a commodity in terms of more than one-size chunk frequently adds convenience, simplicity, speed, and sophistication to one's mathematical reasoning.

Textbooks rarely encourage this flexibility; in fact, some of the procedures they ask children to practice work against the development of a flexible use of units. Let's try another mind experiment.

Imagine that you are faced with this decision in the supermarket and you do not have your calculator or even a pencil and paper. How would you do it? Think about this before reading any farther.

• The box of Bites costs $3.36 and the box of Bits costs $2.64. Which cereal is the better buy?

Some textbooks show students how to use the unit pricing method for *best buy* problems. Students are told to divide $3.36 by 16 to find the cost for one ounce of Bites. Then divide $2.64 by 12 to find the cost of one ounce of Bits.

Research has shown that you are likely to find several different solutions among adults. The so-called *unit method*, or comparing the cost of 1 ounce of each cereal, was rarely used in a sample of several hundred adults in real supermarkets. Most people find it difficult to divide mentally using a two-digit divisor, so they have developed other ways to compare prices without a calculator or pencil and paper.

The most common adult strategy was to think of 4-ounce chunks of each quantity probably because it is easier to divide using a single-digit divisor. That is, most adults think of 16 ounces as 4 (4-ounces) and 12 ounces as 3 (4-ounces). Thus, for the 16-ounce box, the cost of 4 ounces is $3.36 ÷ 4 = $0.84 and for the 12-ounce box, the cost of 4 ounces is $2.64 ÷ 3 = $0.88.

## CHILDREN'S THINKING

At the beginning of fourth grade, some children solved this "best buy" problem. Analyze their responses.

I want to get some juice to take on my bike trip. I like both apple and orange. The orange juice pack holds more and it costs $1.70. The apple juice pack costs $1.10. Which is the better deal?

DR

| 4 | 8 |
| 4 | |

| 4 | 12 |
| 4 | |
| 4 | |

EACH LITTLE DRINK
COST

$$2 \overline{\smash{)}110} \quad \begin{array}{r} 55 \\ -10 \\ \hline 10 \\ 10 \\ \hline 0 \end{array}$$

$$3 \overline{\smash{)}170} \quad \begin{array}{r} 56 \\ -15 \\ \hline 20 \\ 18 \\ \hline 2 \end{array}$$

APPLE IS A LITTLE LESS MONEY

Amy   You would pour the apple in the oj box. It would fit 1 whole + 1 half.

$$\boxed{1.10} \quad \boxed{55} = \boxed{\$1.65}$$

$$2 \overline{\smash{)}110} \quad \begin{array}{r} 55 \\ 10 \\ \hline 10 \end{array}$$   less than oj

Meg
each sip of apple costs

$$8 \overline{\smash{)}110} \quad \begin{array}{r} 13 \\ -8 \\ \hline 30 \\ -24 \\ \hline 6 \end{array}$$

each sip of orange costs

$$12 \overline{\smash{)}170} \quad \begin{array}{r} 14 \\ -12 \\ \hline 50 \\ -48 \\ \hline 2 \end{array}$$

If we are truly interested in helping children to develop their reasoning ability, rather than their facility in blindly following procedures, it is not useful to have them practice finding unit prices. To help children develop flexibility in situations like the best buy problem, encourage multiple solution strategies and discuss which strategies are easier, faster, or more reasonable. Under the conditions that you had no paper and pencil and no calculator, thinking in terms of 4 ounces makes the cereal problem easier to do in your head. In the case of the problem about buying kiwis, using a chunk of 3 fruits is nicer because it avoids the problem of a repeating decimal. A more compelling reason to encourage this flexible regrouping is that children naturally and easily use unitizing (although they don't call it that) long before they encounter the unit method (usually in middle school, in a chapter on ratios). The student work on the juice problem is a good example.

Meg used the unit pricing method; that is, she found the cost of one ounce of each cereal (ignoring decimals). We can safely assume that these students have not been taught *any* method for price comparison, so Meg's strategy was of her own choosing. D. R. and Amy also used intuitive and, ultimately, more sophisticated strategies. D.R. noticed that each drink could be represented as a multiple of 4 ounces. His "little drink" was clearly 4 ounces. He saw 2 chunks of 4 in the 8-ounce juice box, and 3 chunks of 4 in the 12-ounce juice box. Essentially, he used the adult method discussed above. Amy noticed that the orange juice pack held $1\frac{1}{2}$ as much as the apple juice box. This led her to calculate $1\frac{1}{2}$ times the price of the apple juice box. D.R.'s strategy and Amy's strategy are useful and correct intuitive strategies.

## CLASSROOM ACTIVITIES TO ENCOURAGE UNITIZING

Unitizing plays an important role in several of the processes needed to understand fractions, especially in sharing (partitioning) and in equivalence. Students who are better (more flexible) in their thinking are quicker to learn the concept of equivalence. They more quickly develop an understanding of fractions as quotients.

There are several ways to build on children's intuitive knowledge and to encourage flexibility in unitizing. First, as an oral reasoning activity in class, have students generate equivalent expressions for the same quantity. This *free production* activity encourages flexibility in their thinking. As children engage in these activities, several things are important:

1.  Students have a tendency to think only in terms of whole numbers. By thinking in terms of nontraditional chunks (not the same packaging that they find in stores), reformulate quantities so that chunks are fractional. Don't worry about the convention that says we should always express fractions in their lowest terms. It is more important to keep the focus on flexible thinking.

    - 1 case of cola = 24 cans = 2(12-packs) = 4(6-packs) = 12(pair) = 3(8-packs)
    - 1 case of cola = $48\left(\frac{1}{2}\text{-cans}\right) = 72\left(\frac{1}{3}\text{-cans}\right)$
    - 1 case = $1\frac{1}{2}(16\text{-packs}) = 2\frac{4}{10}(10\text{-packs}) = \frac{1}{2}(48\text{-pack})$
    - 18 eggs = $1\frac{1}{2}(\text{dozen}) = 3\left(\frac{1}{2}\text{-dozen}\right) = 6\left(\frac{1}{4}\text{-dozen}\right) = 4\frac{1}{2}(4\text{-packs})$

2.  Use some quantities (unlike cola) that do not come chunked in well-known ways.

    - 23 shoelaces = $11\frac{1}{2}(\text{pairs}) = 46\left(\frac{1}{2}\text{-laces}\right) = \frac{23}{24}(24\text{-packs}) = 5\frac{3}{4}(4\text{-packs})$
    - 1 chocolate bar = 12 blocks = 6 pair = 3(4-blocks) = 2(6-blocks)

# VISUAL ACTIVITIES

Unitizing, visualization, and fraction equivalence have a symbiotic relationship. As children do this reasoning out loud, they become more comfortable with fractions, they grow more comfortable with visualizing changes, their reasoning improves, and they generate equivalent fraction names without having to follow rules.

The following unitizing activity uses an area model, a partitioned rectangular area in which the subdivisions are not all the same size. The pieces of area include small, medium and large squares, and small, medium and large rectangles. This is a visual activity and children should be encouraged to reason aloud.

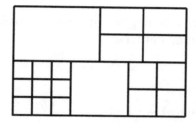

The following square and rectangular areas provide a means to talk about fractional parts of the area. First make sure that everyone can identify the following embedded figures: a large, a medium, and a small rectangle, as well as a large, a medium, and a small square.

- The large rectangle comprises the total area.
- A medium rectangle appears in the upper left hand corner.
- A small rectangle appears in the upper right corner.
- A large square appears in the middle third of the bottom half of the large rectangle.
- A medium square appears in the lower right corner.
- A small square appears in the lower left corner.

- Tell me how to see $\frac{1}{8}$.

  Sam: Look at the medium rectangle in upper right half of the large rectangle. One of the small rectangles there must be $\frac{1}{8}$ because there are 4 there and 4 more fit inside the medium rectangle, which means that there are 8 of them in the top half of the large rectangle. Oops! I forgot the bottom. There have to be 8 more down there, so one of them would actually be $\frac{1}{16}$. So stick two of the medium rectangles together then you will have 4 on the top and 4 on the bottom. So 2 small rectangles make $\frac{1}{8}$.

- Tell me how to see $\frac{1}{3}$.

    Jasmine: Look at the bottom half of the large rectangle. The large square is $\frac{1}{3}$ because 3 of them will fit in the bottom half. Oh, no! I just did the same thing Sam did. That large square has to be $\frac{1}{6}$ because you need 3 of them on the top half and 3 of them on the bottom half of the large rectangle. So look at the large square and all of the small squares together. That would be $\frac{1}{3}$ of the large rectangle.

Dot pictures are another unitizing activity. Again, visualization and reasoning are important, as well as reasoning out loud.

- Tell me how to see $\frac{1}{3}$.

    Rachael: 1(pair of columns) = $\frac{1}{3}$.

    Dan: 1 row = $\frac{1}{3}$.

- Tell me how to see $\frac{1}{9}$.

    Cory: 1(pair of dots) = $\frac{1}{9}$

- Tell me how to see $\frac{1}{36}$.

    Lisa: I have to think about the dots cut in half. Then $1\left(\frac{1}{2}\text{-dot}\right) = \frac{1}{36}$

## REASONING WITH RATIO TABLES

We have just used a reasoning up and down process to arrive at the unit in a fraction problem when it was given implicitly. That reasoning process is very natural for children. Research has repeatedly documented children's use of a *building up* strategy in solving proportions. With this strategy, they establish a ratio and then extend it to another ratio using addition:

2 erasers cost $0.29 How much do 6 cost?

$0.29 for 2
$0.29 for 2 more gives $0.58 for 4
$0.29 for 2 more gives $0.87 for 6.

The building up strategy is one that children use spontaneously and it is an intuitive strategy that works in many situations. However, there is a question as to whether some children see multiplicative relations when they persist in using additive strategies that give correct answers. Do they focus on the relationship between the two quantities? Do they realize that corresponding numbers of pizzas and numbers of people share the same relationship? Most often, interviews with students reveal that they do not. With the building up strategy, students often focus on each quantity separately. Successes with additive strategies do not necessarily encourage the exploration and adoption of more efficient strategies and should not be interpreted as proportional reasoning.

Let's look at "next steps" that will continue to build children's reasoning processes well after initial fraction instruction. Rather than teaching students an algorithm for solving proportions—a decision that dramatically decreases the chances that they will ever engage in reasoning—teachers have to trust that encouraging the reasoning up and down process will result in powerful and highly desirable ways of thinking. In time, children who start out reasoning up and down eventually deduce the algorithm. Although the end result is the same, the difference is that children who have engaged in the reasoning have also developed strategic planning, number sense, and confidence in using their heads to solve problems.

At first, children rely on halving and doubling, and they may use many steps to complete a problem. However, as students develop some strategies, the number of steps in their solutions decreases. As students gain more experience in the reasoning process, they are better able to anticipate how large a multiple they can use. In solving more difficult problems, they begin to strategize, planning in advance how they are going to move from givens to the target quantity. They become as adept with fractions and decimals as with whole numbers. Fewer steps signal their progress. More sophisticated, more strategic reasoning results in fewer and fewer steps until finally a student is solving proportions using the traditional algorithm.

It is wise to vary the kinds of questions, quantity structures, and numbers so that students are forced beyond their comfort zone, so that they must think about relationships and adopt increasingly efficient solutions. This may be done in several ways:

- Give problems whose quantities both decrease.
- Give problems whose quantities both increase.
- Give problems involving inversely proportional relationships.
- Give problems in which fractions are unavoidable so that students do not rely totally on whole number operations.
- Give problems whose solutions allow for combinations of multiplication/division and addition/subtraction operations.
- Give problems not solvable solely by halving or doubling.

Consider the work done by these children. They are purposely chosen from multiple grade levels so that you can see the increasing sophistication in their work. Sean was in grade 3, Amanda was in grade 4, and Gennie in grade 5.

If 3 pizzas serve 9 people, how many pizzas will I need to serve 108 people?

Notice that as the children got older, the number of steps in their solutions decreased, and they were able to take larger jumps—multiplying by 5, then by 10.

Their work illustrates the manner in which strategies become more efficient as students gain experience in reasoning up and down. Sean, the third grader, repeatedly doubled his numbers until he realized that he had passed the target number (108 people). He then went back and looked for pieces that could be combined to reach 108. Amanda, a fourth grader, used one less step, and seemed to be more keenly aware of her target number throughout the process. She first used a factor of 5, suggesting that she knew a larger jump was needed to go from 9 to 108, and performed two additions once she was in the area of her target number. Gen, the fifth grader, showed even fewer steps. She began with a factor of 10, suggesting that she had a better sense of the size of the enlargement needed. By sixth grade, students solve this simple problem in one step, saying that you would 12 times as many pizzas or 36, because you have 12 times as many people.

## PROBLEM TYPES

Problems involving proportional reasoning are of two basic types and it is important that students reason about both types. The first is a comparison problem. In a comparison problem, four quantities forming two ratios are given. The task is to find out whether the two ratios are equal or which is greater or smaller. Here is the work of some fourth graders.

- Which vehicle has a faster average speed, a truck that travels 126 miles in $1\frac{1}{2}$ hours or a car that travels 135 miles in $1\frac{3}{4}$ hours?

Eric

| miles | hours |
|-------|-------|
| 126 | $\frac{3}{2}$ |
| 42 | $\frac{1}{2}$ |
| 21 | $\frac{1}{4}$ |

| miles | hours |
|-------|-------|
| 135 | $1\frac{3}{4} = \frac{7}{4}$ |
| $19\frac{2}{7}$ | $\frac{1}{4}$ |

$\div 7$

The truck is faster because in 15 Min it does about 21 mi and the car does less than 20 mi.

- Last Saturday afternoon, the Smith family went to the Starr Theatre and all 6 of them got in for $10. The West family went to see a movie at the Odyssey and all 4 of them got in for $7. Which theatre has better Saturday matinee prices?

Colin

Smith

| # people | $ |
|----------|---|
| 6 | 10 |
| 3 | 5 |
| 2 | $\frac{10}{3} = $ 3.33 |

$\div 3$

best price

West

| # people | $ |
|----------|---|
| 4 | 7 |
| 2 | 3.50 |

The second kind of problem is one in which three quantities are given and the fourth quantity is missing; hence, these are called *missing value problems*. Again, we will observe the solutions of fourth grade students.

- If it takes 4 people 3 days to wash the windows at the Sun Office Building, how long would it take 8 people to do the job?

Joe

| #p | #d |
|----|----|
| 4 | 3 |
| 1 | 12 |
| 8 | $\frac{12}{8} = 1\frac{4}{8} = 1\frac{1}{2}$ d. |

- If Abe saves \$3.50 a week from his after school job at the grocery store, how much money can he save in 2 years (52 weeks = 1 year)?

Bill

\$364 in 104 weeks

| dollars | #weeks |
|---------|--------|
| 3.50 | 1 |
| 7 | 2 |
| 70 | 20 |
| 350 | 100 |
| 14 | 4 |
| 364 | 104 |

# RATIO TABLES

Eric, Colin, Joe and Bill organized their work using a vertical, two-column arrangement. Some people use a horizontal arrangement known as a *ratio table* or a *proportion table*. This is a matter of preference; both are convenient devices for keeping work organized. Here are some solutions that use proportion tables.

- A party planning guide says that 3 pizzas will serve about 7 people. How much pizza is needed for 350 people?

Two different and correct tables are given. Note that the same operation is performed on both quantities. Arrow notation records the operation.

$\times 100 \qquad \div 2$

| # pizzas | 3 | 300 | 150 |
|----------|---|-----|-----|
| # people | 7 | 700 | 350 |

$\times 5 \qquad \times 10$

| # people | 7 | 35 | 350 |
|----------|---|----|-----|
| # pizzas | 3 | 15 | 150 |

- Mark uses most of his time for school and sports and helping out in his dad's store. Mark had 38 hours of free time last week, and he spent 25 hours working at his dad's store. This week, he gave his dad the same portion of his free time but spent only $17\frac{1}{2}$ hours at the store. How much free time did Mark have this week?

| Free time in hours | 38 | 19 | $\frac{38}{5}$ | 26.6 |
|---|---|---|---|---|
| Hours of work | 25 | $12\frac{1}{2}$ | 5 | $17\frac{1}{2}$ |

Of course, there is always more than one correct way to build a ratio table. When students produce different tables, it is a good idea to have them present and discuss their strategies. If you are unsure about whether any operation has been performed correctly, remember that you can always check to ensure that all ratios in the table are equivalent. In the last problem, for example,

$$\frac{38}{25} = \frac{19}{12.5} = \frac{7.6}{5} = \frac{26.6}{17.5}$$

The appropriate use of the ratio table (or the two-column approach) is to systematically organize one's work as the operations of multiplication, division, addition, and subtraction are combined to produce equivalent ratios until some target quantity is achieved. However, this is not a trial-and-error process. A little advance planning is needed.

- 35 pounds of gravel cost $150, but I need only 18 pounds. How much will it cost me?

First, I will use what I know about numbers and operations to help me plan a way of moving from 35 pounds to 18 pounds.

$35 \div 5 = 7$
$7 + 7 = 14$, but I still need another 4 pounds
$7 \div 7 = 1$
$1 \times 4 = 4$
$7 + 7 + 4 = 18$

This gives the following scheme:

$35 \rightarrow 7 \rightarrow 1 \rightarrow 4$        $18 = 7 + 7 + 4$

Now I will carry it out.

| | ÷ 5 | ÷ 7 | × 4 | |
|---|---|---|---|---|
| Pounds | 35 | 7 | 1 | 4 | $7 + 7 + 4 = 18$ |
| Dollars | 150 | 30 | $\frac{30}{7}$ | $\frac{120}{7}$ | $60 + \frac{120}{7} = 77\frac{1}{7} = 77.14$ |

Some useful strategies that you will see emerging in your own work and that of your students include the following:

- Use multiplication and division by 2, 5, 10, and 100 as much as possible (because they are so easy to work with!).
- Keep exact answers (fractions) until the very last step. Converting to decimals produces a rounding error. As more operations are performed on that quantity, the amount of error increases.
- If you begin with a fraction, multiplying by the number in the denominator will give you a whole number.
- Sometimes you may go past the target quantity and then divide or subtract to get back to it.
- Use multiples and divisors wisely. If you have 5 and you want 2, one way to get there is to double 5 to get 10, then divide the result by 5.

This is not an exhaustive list. Instruction must play some role in encouraging students to build strategic tables. Strategy cannot be taught directly; ratio tables are individual constructions that record personal thought processes. Nevertheless, when the teacher models efficient processes or students discuss their strategies in class, others can see the benefit of shortcuts and jumps and they will incorporate some of those strategies into their own work.

## INCREASING THE DIFFICULTY

Try some problems involving 3 quantities. The key is to hold one of the quantities constant while you change the other two. Here is an example.

- If 8 men can chop 9 cords of wood in 5.5 hours, how long would it take 3 men (working at the same rate) to chop 3 cords?

| # men | Cords of wood | Time in hours | Notes |
|---|---|---|---|
| 8 | 9 | $5\frac{1}{2} = \frac{11}{2}$ | Given |
| 8 | 3 | $\frac{11}{6}$ | # men constant; other quantities ÷ by 3 |
| 24 | 3 | $\frac{11}{18}$ | Hold the wood; men × 3; time × $\frac{1}{3}$ |
| 3 | 3 | $\frac{88}{18} = 4.8$ | Hold the wood; men ÷ 8; time × 8 |

After students have been introduced to decimals, proportion tables involving decimals help to reinforce student understanding of decimal properties.

- If 15 cupcakes cost $3.36, find the cost of 38 cupcakes.

| Cupcakes | Cost | Notes |
|---|---|---|
| 15 | 3.36 | Given |
| 30 | 6.72 | × 2 |
| 5 | 1.12 | ÷6 |
| 3 | 0.672 | 30 ÷ 10 |
| 38 | 8.512 | 30 + 5 + 3 |

The cost of 38 cupcakes is $8.51.

- Cheese costs $4.25/pound. Nancy selects several chunks for a party and when they are weighed, she has 12.13 pounds of cheese. How much will it cost her?

|  | Pounds | Cost | Notes |
|---|---|---|---|
| a | 1 | 4.25 | Given |
| b | 10 | 42.50 | $a \times 10$ |
| c | 2 | 8.50 | $a \times 2$ |
| d | 0.1 | 0.425 | $a \div 10$ |
| e | 12.1 | 51.425 | $b + c + d$ |
| f | 0.05 | 0.2125 | $d \div 2$ |
| g | 0.01 | 0.0425 | $f \div 5$ |
| h | 0.03 | 0.1275 | $g \times 3$ |
| i | 12.13 | 51.5525 | $e + h$ |

The cheese will cost $51.55.

## ANALYZING RELATIONSHIPS

Seventh- and eighth-grade students preparing for algebra should be encouraged to analyze the structural relationships in a proportion more carefully. Make a column for each type of quantity and enter the three given quantities and the unknown in the appropriate columns. Within each column, one entry is a scale multiple of the other; find the scale factor that transforms the first entry into the second. Look between the columns and find the function or rule that relates the two quantity types. You will recognize this as a proportionality statement. In the following problem the constant of proportionality is 0.065. You will also notice that the amount you spend changes, but the rate of sales tax remains constant at $6\frac{1}{2}\%$ no matter how much you spend.

- I was charged $1.30 for sales tax when I spent $20. How much sales tax would I pay on a purchase of $50?

Sales tax is related to the amount of your purchase and it increases in a multiplicative way. If you spend $20, the amount of tax you pay is 4 times as much as you would pay if you spent $5. Similarly, the amount of tax you pay on a $50 purchase will be 2.5 times what you would pay on a $20 purchase. The factor that increases or decreases both quantities is called a *scale factor*.

In proportional relationships, we can always find a rule that relates one quantity type to the other. We can solve the sales tax problem because sales tax depends on the amount of purchase and we can express that relationship in a rule that holds no matter what specific dollar amount you spend. It is called a *function*. The rule tells you how to find one of the quantities when you know the other one. For a proportional relationship, the rule always looks the same:

$$\text{quantity B} = \text{constant} \cdot \text{quantity A}$$

- If it takes 4 men 3 hours to do a job, how long will it take 3 men to do it?

We know that it takes less time to get a job finished when there are more people working. Therefore, as the number of people increases, the work time decreases. It would take twice as many workers to cut the time half, and it would take three times as many workers to finish the job in $\frac{1}{3}$ of the time. This is known as an *inversely proportional relationship*. In inversely proportional relationships, one quantity varies with the other, but in the opposite direction. There are two scale factors and they are inverses. The product of the two quantities is a constant; in this case,

$$(\# \text{ men})(\# \text{ hours}) = 3,$$

so the function that relates the two quantities is $h = \dfrac{12}{m}$.

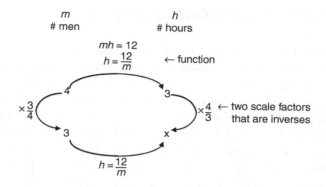

## PERCENT

Percentages are simply fractions (decimal fractions) whose denominator is always 100. So 30% means "30 per 100" or "30 out of 100" or $\frac{30}{100}$. The reasoning processes we have been discussing in this chapter are useful in thinking about percentages.

We use percents when we wish to indicate a certain proportion, rather than an absolute number. In other words, if I say 30% of my students were absent, I don't mean 30 students were absent. I mean that I took the fraction $\frac{\text{\# absent}}{\text{total \# students}}$ and scaled it up until the bottom number was 100. I am giving you an idea of the proportion of my students who were absent by using 100 because 100 is a familiar benchmark.

Percents are ubiquitous in everyday experience. Because they are used so frequently, especially in connection with metric measurement and money, children understand and use percentages at an early age: $\frac{1}{2}$ is like half a dollar or $0.50 and $\frac{50 \text{ cents}}{100 \text{ cents}}$ is 50% of a dollar; one quarter is $\frac{1}{4}$ of a dollar and $0.25 and 25 cents out of 100 cents is 25% of a dollar. In my long-term research classes, we never separated fractions, decimals and percents and treated them as individual instructional topics. Instead, we encouraged children to express quantities in as many ways as they could. Some children actually preferred to think in terms of percents (See Brian's work in the exercises at the end of this chapter.), while others showed a preference for decimals, so it was important not to cut off the powerful thinking that any of them used. All too often, we, the teachers, have in mind certain material that we want children to learn, but we cannot predict the connections that children will make or when they will make them. We have to be able to recognize and encourage all good thinking when it occurs.

## PERCENTS AS AN INSTRUCTIONAL TASK

In most textbooks, percents are a topic of instruction sometime after students have studied fractions. The failure to address percents until so late in the elementary curriculum and the attempt to treat the topic within the confines of a chapter means that students do not have sufficient time to learn to reason up and down with percent. This timing fails to build upon children's early experiences and intuitions, and later, the job of teaching percent is a harder task than it needs to be. In middle school and high school, we need worksheets for estimating percents, for using the 1% rule, the 10% rule, rules for finding the same percent, procedures for applying percents to the same base number, and pages with hundreds of carefully sequenced percent questions—all designed to teach by rules what could have been accomplished quite naturally by reasoning. The procedures these worksheets are targeting are natural to someone who has a good number sense, but it is questionable that number sense can be taught by rules.

When children are encouraged to reason up and down throughout fraction instruction, reasoning about percents is easy and natural. After children start using reasoning techniques, even shading percent grids is not terribly helpful because they can get the answers more quickly in their heads. There are two basic approaches that children use, both of which are based on scaling up and down.

a. The first strategy is to make sense of the given statement and reason from given to unknowns.
b. The second approach is to reason up or down after selecting some well-known benchmark.

Both approaches are illustrated below. If you cannot do this in your head, ratio tables are a convenient tool for recording your reasoning process.

## REASONING WITH PERCENTS

- $32 = \underline{\quad}\%$ of 40

  I will start with the given $\left( 32 \text{ out of } 40 = \dfrac{32}{40} \right)$ and scale up until I get 100 in the denominator.

  | 32 | 64 | 16 | 80 |
  |----|----|----|-----|
  | 40 | 80 | 20 | 100 |

  $\dfrac{32}{40}$ is equivalent to $\dfrac{80}{100}$ or 80%

  Another way: begin with a % that you know (say 50%) and reason to 80%

  I know that 20 is 50% of 40

So 4 is 10% of 40
12 is 30% of 40
32 is 80 % of 40

- 35% of _____ = 21?

  I will start with the given $\left(35\% = \dfrac{35}{100}\right)$ and scale up/down toward 21 in the numerator.

  | 35 | 7 | 21 |
  |----|----|----|
  | 100 | 20 | 60 |

  Another way: begin with 21 = 35% and scale up/down until you reach the whole, 100%

  21 is 35%
  42 is 70%
  3 is 5%
  60 is 100% (because 70% + 35% − 5% = 100%)

- 30 is _____ % of 80?

  I will begin with $\dfrac{30}{80}$ and scale up/down toward $\dfrac{x}{100}$

  | 30 | 15 | $7\frac{1}{2}$ | $37\frac{1}{2}$ |
  |----|----|----|----|
  | 80 | 40 | 20 | 100 |

  $$\frac{30}{80} = 37\frac{1}{2}\%$$

  Another way: Begin with a % that you know (say 50%) and scale up/down toward 30

  40 is 50% of 80
  20 is 25% of 80
  10 is $12\frac{1}{2}$% of 80
  30 is $37\frac{1}{2}$% of 80

# ACTIVITIES

1.  Which of these can be a unit in a fraction problem?

    a.           b.           c.

d.      e.      f.

2.  Use reasoning up/down to solve each problem, even if you can get the answer some other way. The goal is the reasoning *process*, not just the answer!

a.   $= 1\frac{1}{3}$    $\frac{2}{3}$ is how many stars?

b.   $= \frac{3}{5}$    $\frac{1}{2}$ is how many balls?

c.   $= 1\frac{1}{3}$    $\frac{5}{9}$ is how many sticks?

d.   $= 2\frac{2}{3}$     $\boxed{\phantom{xxx}} = 2$

e.   $= \frac{5}{6}$     $\boxed{\phantom{xxx}} = 1\frac{1}{2}$

f.   $= 1\frac{1}{4}$     $\bigcirc = \frac{3}{8}$

3.  Analyze the student responses (grade 5) to this problem:

    BJ and Reece bought a deck of baseball cards. BJ took $\frac{3}{8}$ of the deck and Reece took $\frac{5}{8}$ of the deck. BJ took home 15 cards. How many cards were there in the deck?

P.    40 in the deck

Rob

$$\frac{3}{8} = 15 \text{ cards}$$

$$\frac{1}{8} = 5 \text{ cards}$$

$$\frac{2}{8} = 10 \text{ cards}$$

$$15 + 15 + 10 = 40$$

4.  Frank ate 12 pieces of pizza and Dave ate 15 pieces. "I ate $\frac{1}{4}$ more," said Dave. "No! I ate $\frac{1}{5}$ less," said Frank. Why the argument?

5.  The shaded portion of this picture represents $3\frac{2}{3}$. How much do 4 small rectangles represent?

6.  What is wrong with this poster? Using blocks of the same size and without cutting any of them into pieces, how could these fractions be represented correctly?

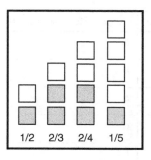

7.  Name the amount shaded in this picture:

    a.  when the unit is

    b.  when the unit is

c.  when the unit is

8.  In each case, draw a picture of the unit.

a.  represents $\frac{1}{3}$ of

b.  represents $1\frac{1}{2}$ of

c.  represents $\frac{1}{3}$ of

d.  represents $\frac{2}{9}$ of

9.  At a party, a cake is cut as follows:
    Kim takes $\frac{1}{6}$ of the cake; Bill takes $\frac{1}{5}$ of what remains; Connie takes $\frac{1}{4}$ of what remains; Andy takes $\frac{1}{3}$ of what remains; Kay and Jamal share the last piece. Tell what fraction of the cake each person received. Explain your thinking.

10.  Fill in this chart using Cuisenaire strips.

| Unit Strip | Fraction | Color Representing the Fraction (Relative to the Unit) |
|---|---|---|
| Brown | $\frac{1}{4}$ | a. |
| Magenta | $1\frac{3}{4}$ | b. |
| Lime Green | $2\frac{2}{3}$ | c. |
| Brown | $1\frac{1}{2}$ | d. |
| Blue | $\frac{1}{3}$ | e. |
| Red | $3\frac{1}{2}$ | f. |
| Dark Green | $1\frac{1}{3}$ | g. |
| Orange | $\frac{2}{5}$ | h. |
| White | 6 | i. |
| Black | $\frac{5}{7}$ | j. |

11.    Complete this table.

| Unit Strip | Add: | Color Representing the Sum (Relative to the Unit) |
|---|---|---|
| Orange | $\frac{2}{5}+\frac{1}{10}$ | a. |
| Brown | $\frac{5}{8}+\frac{1}{2}$ | b. |
| Dark Green | $\frac{1}{2}+\frac{1}{6}$ | c. |
| Orange + Red | $\frac{1}{3}+\frac{5}{12}$ | d. |
| Magenta | $\frac{1}{4}+\frac{1}{2}$ | e. |
| Brown | $\frac{3}{4}+\frac{1}{8}$ | f. |
| Blue | $\frac{2}{9}+\frac{1}{3}$ | g. |
| Brown | $\frac{3}{8}+\frac{1}{2}$ | h. |

12.    Use reasoning up/down to locate the following points on the number line. For example, to find $\frac{5}{8}$ using the number line in a,

2 spaces to $\frac{1}{4}$, 8 spaces to 1, 5 spaces to $\frac{5}{8}$.

a.  $\frac{7}{8}$

b.  $\frac{11}{24}$

c.  $\frac{7}{12}$

d.  $\frac{1}{3}$

e.  $\dfrac{5}{6}$

0                                    $\dfrac{3}{4}$

13.  Ruth's diet allowed her to eat $\dfrac{1}{4}$ pound of turkey or chicken breast, fresh fruit, and fresh vegetables. She ordered $\dfrac{1}{4}$ pound of turkey breast at the delicatessen. The sales person sliced 3 uniform slices, weighed them, and said, "This is $\dfrac{1}{3}$ of a pound." What part of the order could Ruth eat and stay on her diet?

14.  Use your pattern pieces in *MORE* to answer the following questions.

    a.  If the value of BLUE is 1, then the value of YELLOW is ?

    b.  If the value of RED is $\dfrac{1}{3}$, then the value of BLUE is ?

    c.  If the value of RED is $\dfrac{1}{4}$, then 1 = ?

    d.  If the value of GREEN is $\dfrac{1}{8}$, then $\dfrac{3}{4}$ = ?

    e.  If BLUE = 3, find the values of the other pieces.

15.  Tony ordered a small cheese pizza and a medium pepperoni. Each came sliced into 8 equal-sized pieces. He ate 2 slices of the cheese pizza and 3 of the pepperoni. How much pizza did he eat?

16.  Sixteen liters of water fill my fish tank to $\dfrac{2}{5}$ of its capacity. How many liters does it take to fill the tank?

17.  There are $7\dfrac{1}{3}$ pies left in the pie case. The manager has a fresh supply coming in and she wants to sell the rest of the pies in a hurry, so she offers a deal: buy one super slice $\left(\dfrac{1}{3} \text{ of a pie}\right)$ and get a second super slice free. How many of these specials can she sell?

18.  This rectangular area represents an acre of land. Draw the following quantities:

    a.  $3\left(\dfrac{1}{4}\text{-acres}\right)$

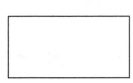

    b.  $1\left(\dfrac{3}{4}\text{-acre}\right)$

c.  $2\left(\dfrac{3}{4}\text{-acre}\right)$

d.  $2\left(\dfrac{1}{2}\text{-acres}\right)$

e.  2(pair of acres)

19.  You drank 34 colas last month. That is the same amount as:

a.  _____(6-packs)
b.  _____(24-packs)
c.  _____(18 packs)
d.  _____(8-packs)

e.  _____ $\left(\dfrac{1}{2}\text{-cans}\right)$

f.  _____ $\left(\dfrac{1}{4}\text{-cans}\right)$

g.  _____(pair of cans)

20.  Describe how you can see each quantity named.

a.  fourths    b.  eights    c.  thirty-seconds    d.  sixteenths    e.  sixty-fourths

21.  Use unitizing (thinking in different-sized chunks) to generate as many different names for the quantity as you can. Make sure that you write the quantity using the notation used in the chapter: # of chunks (size of chunk).

a.  15 stars
b.  16 colas
c.  26 eggs

22.  Describe how to see the fractional parts named.

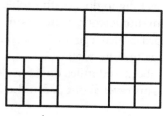

a.  $\dfrac{1}{4}$    b.  $\dfrac{1}{6}$    c.  $\dfrac{1}{18}$    d.  $\dfrac{1}{16}$    e.  $\dfrac{1}{12}$

23.    Name the fractional part that is indicated in each picture. Explain how you figured this out.

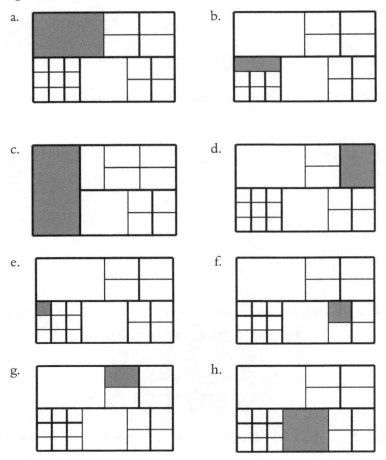

a.

b.

c.

d.

e.

f.

g.

h.

24.    Does each situation involve proportional relationships, inversely proportional relationships, or neither? How can you tell?

a.    Three pints of milk cost $1.59 and 4 cost $2.12.

b.    Two brothers drive to the basketball game in 15 minutes, and when John drives alone, he says it takes him 10 minutes.

c.    Six people clean a house in an hour and 3 people do it in 2 hours.

d.    One boy has 3 sisters, and 2 boys have 6 sisters.

e.    It takes me twice as long to do a math problem when I am watching TV as it does when I do my homework in my room.

f.    Tom can eat a hard-boiled egg in 20 seconds. In a recent contest, he ate 20 hard-boiled eggs in 5 minutes.

g.    Your car averages about 100 miles on 4.5 gallons of gas. On a full tank of gas (15 gallons) you can travel about 333 miles.

h. You spent $5.00 and paid $0.30 in sales tax and then paid $2.10 on a purchase totaling $35.

25. Solve each of these problems using a proportion table:

   a. If the school makes $1.15 on every raffle ticket sold, how much will it make when 128 tickets are sold?
   b. If a can of tennis balls costs $4.49, how many cans can be purchased for a tournament in which $70 has been allotted for balls?
   c. Matt runs a 10 km race in 45 minutes. At this rate, how long would it take him to run a 6.25 km race?

26. Solve each of the following problems, if possible, using a ratio table or a two-column approach. If a solution is not possible, state why.

   a. Mark can type 575 words in 15 minutes. At the same rate, how many words can he type in 1.25 hours?
   b. If 3 boxes of cereal are on sale for $6.88, and a day-care provider needs 17 boxes, how much will she pay?
   c. If Ellen has 537 points and 60 points may be redeemed for 1 baseball cap, how many caps can she get?
   d. If 1 inch on a map represents 195 miles, how far apart are two cities that are 2.125 inches apart on the map?
   e. For every $3 Mac saves, his dad will contribute $5 to his savings account. How much will Mac have to put into the account before he can buy a $120 bicycle?
   f. Five girls drank 3.5 quarts of lemonade on a warm day. If they were planning a party for 14 girls, how much lemonade should they prepare for the party?

27. Analyze each situation. Use a quantity diagram to show the multiplicative relationships. Are there any proportional relationships?

   a. A circle has a diameter of 3 feet. If you double the diameter, what happens to the area of the circle?
   b. The taxi I took from the airport started with a base charge of $1.50 and increased $0.20 for each tenth of a mile. How much did it cost me to go 2 miles? 10 miles? 50 miles?
   c. The width of a rectangle is half its length. If you triple the length of the rectangle, what will happen to the perimeter?

28. If 8 men can chop 9 cords of wood in 6.5 hours, how long will it take 4 men to chop 3 cords, assuming that all men work at the same rate?

29. In the Robo-Work Factory, robots assemble small sports cars. If 3 robots can assemble 19 cars in 40 hours, how many cars would you expect 14 robots to turn out in 8 hours?

30. For each situation, determine whether there is a proportional relationship or an inversely proportional relationship and write an equation relating the two quantity types.

    a. Your weight of 120 pounds is 54.54 kilograms, and your boyfriend, a blocker on the football team, weighs 320 pounds or 150 kg.

    b. When lightning strikes at 10 km away, you hear the crash about 30 seconds later; when it strikes at 20 km away, you hear the crash after 60 seconds.

    c. When you are 150 feet under water, the pressure in your ears is 64.5 psi (pounds per square inch) and at 10 feet under water, the pressure is 4.3 psi.

31. Solve by reasoning up and down.

    a. In 3 weeks, 4 horses eat 45 pounds of hay. How much will 1 horse eat in 4 weeks?

    b. Five robots produce 5 auto parts in 5 minutes. How many packages containing 2 parts each, can be produced if 10 robots work for 10 hours?

    c. If a hen and a half can lay an egg and a half in a day and a half, at the same rate, how many eggs can 2 dozen hens lay in 2 dozen days?

32. Teacher: to find $\frac{1}{2}$ of $\frac{1}{4}$ of the cake, we can divide the cake into 4 equal pieces.

Then, cut each quarter in half. Like this:

Then how can we name the piece we get when we take half of a quarter?

*Brian*: I think it is easier to just, like, say half of 25% is $12\frac{1}{2}$%.

*Teacher*: Well that is correct. But can you tell what the answer is in fraction form?

*Brian*: I don't really know. My brain thinks of percents.

*Teacher*: And what is $\frac{1}{2}$ of $\frac{1}{6}$?

*Brian*: 50% divided by 6 is like a little more than 8%. Something strange like $8\frac{2}{6}$%.

Analyze Brian's thinking. When you think you understand his method, solve these problems the way that Brian would do them.

    a. $\frac{1}{2}$ of $\frac{1}{5}$

    b. $\frac{1}{4}$ of $\frac{1}{4}$

c. $\dfrac{1}{8}$ of $\dfrac{1}{2}$

d. $\dfrac{3}{4}$ of $\dfrac{1}{5}$

33. Answer each question by reasoning.

   a. 25% of 80 = _____

   b. 15 = _____% of 50

   c. 45 is _____% of 60

   d. _____ is 20% of 70

   e. 65% of _____ = 58.5

   f. 28 is 40% of _____

   g. 15% of 80 = _____

   h. 36 is _____% of 90

   i. 27 is 45% of _____

34. Write the percent equivalent for each fraction. No computing! Do it by starting with a benchmark % (10%, 20%, 25%, 50%, or 100%) and its fraction equivalent and reasoning until you get to the target fraction.

   For example: $\dfrac{3}{25}$ = ?%. 1% = $\dfrac{1}{100}$, so 4% = $\dfrac{4}{100}$ = $\dfrac{1}{25}$ and $\dfrac{3}{25}$ must be 12%

   a. $\dfrac{3}{50}$

   b. $\dfrac{3}{2}$

   c. $\dfrac{25}{50}$

   d. $\dfrac{3}{5}$

   e. 3

   f. $\dfrac{1}{8}$ $\left(\text{hint: } \dfrac{1}{2} = \dfrac{1}{4} \text{ of } \dfrac{1}{2}\right)$

   g. $\dfrac{1}{6}$

   h. $\dfrac{5}{6}$

   i. $\dfrac{7}{12}$

35. Each of 2 hospitals in our city reported that on May 25, 50% of the babies born were males. Jack concluded that both hospitals had the same number of male newborns. Was he correct? Explain.

36.  Use reasoning alone to solve these problems. Record your reasoning in a ratio table if you need one.

   a.  There are 50 questions on a test and Jake gets 80% correct. How many did he get correct?

   b.  If the sales tax is 6%, what is the sales tax on a car for which you paid $15,000?

   c.  Suppose a special 1-year CD pays 4.5% on your money and you have $1800 invested. How much interest would it pay? (ignore compounding)

   d.  They say that the human body is 85% water. If this is true, how many pounds of water are there in a 200-pound man?

37.  Your total dinner bill at the Italian Restaurant is given below. Mentally compute the 15% tip that you should pay.

   a.  $16.80
   b.  $46.40
   c.  $125.60
   d.  $62.20

38.  Compute these percentages of $12.50 using a ratio table.

   a.  80%
   b.  47%
   c.  200%
   d.  120%
   e.  1.5%
   f.  60%
   g.  5.4%
   h.  350%

# CHAPTER 6

# Reasoning with Fractions

## STUDENT STRATEGIES: END OF YEAR, GRADE 5

Find 3 fractions that lie between $\frac{1}{8}$ and $\frac{1}{9}$.

Martin

## VISUALIZING OPERATIONS

Visual activities are useful for building meaning for fraction operations. Consider, for example, the following candy bar. By looking at the candy bar, you will be able to answer the list of questions that follow.

Half of the candy bar is how many pieces?

2 pieces is what part of the candy bar?

I have $\frac{1}{2}$ of the candy bar and you have $\frac{1}{3}$ of the candy bar. How much do we have altogether?

What part of the candy bar is missing?

I have $\frac{1}{2}$ of the candy bar and you have $\frac{1}{3}$ of the candy bar. Who has more? How much more?

How much of the candy bar is $\frac{1}{2}$ of $\frac{1}{3}$?

How many times will $\frac{1}{3}$ fit into $\frac{1}{2}$?

Of course, you will realize that these questions have taken you through all four fraction operations. The activity demonstrates that all four fraction operations may be perceived and performed without the use of any algorithms.

By changing the number of sections in the candy bar, you can increase the level of difficulty—still without teaching algorithms—and help students to approach fraction operations in a meaningful way. For example, ask yourself the same questions about this candy bar.

There are other reasoning games that also help to make fraction operations meaningful to students. The students I worked with for four years never grew tired of playing *Can You See*. Here is how it works. Just as it is in most of our visual activities, the objective is to describe to someone else exactly how to see certain quantities in a picture. This is a cake with plain icing on the top three sections, and jimmies on the bottom 4 sections.

- Can you see $\frac{3}{7}$?

  If the entire rectangular cake is the unit, then the plain pieces are $\frac{3}{7}$.

- Can you see $\frac{3}{4}$?

  If the part with the jimmies is the unit (the bottom 4 sections), then the plain part is $\frac{3}{4}$.

- Can you see $\frac{3}{4}$ of $\frac{4}{7}$?

If the whole cake is the unit, then $\frac{4}{7}$ of it is the bottom part with jimmies, and $\frac{3}{4}$ of $\frac{4}{7}$ is the part with plain icing which is $\frac{3}{7}$. So $\frac{3}{4}$ of $\frac{4}{7}$ is $\frac{3}{7}$.

- Can you see $1 \div \frac{3}{7}$? (Turn this into a measurement question: how many times can you measure $\frac{3}{7}$ out of 1?)

  If the whole cake is 1, then $\frac{3}{7}$ is the part with plain icing and I can measure it out of the whole cake $2\frac{1}{3}$ times. So $1 \div \frac{3}{7} = 2\frac{1}{3}$.

## EQUIVALENT FRACTIONS AND UNITIZING

Now, let's build upon the "can you see" activities. Looking at a given picture, tell how you can see a given fraction and then use unitizing (mentally chunking the area into different-size pieces) to name equivalent fractions.

- Shade $\frac{1}{12}$.

  First, I notice that there are 12 equal-size pieces, each consisting of half a row. To shade $\frac{1}{12}$, I color half of a row. (Half of a column would also work.)

Now suppose I think of this unit area as 36 little squares, then the shaded amount is $\frac{3}{36}$.

Next, think of the unit area in chunks that consist of $1\frac{1}{2}$ small squares each. There are 24 chunks each consisting of $1\frac{1}{2}$ small squares, so the shaded amount is $\frac{2}{24}$.

Next, I will think of the unit area in 4 chunks, each consisting of 9 small squares. Each chunk is $\frac{1}{4}$ of the unit area, so the shaded portion is $\frac{1}{3}$ of $\frac{1}{4}$.

"$\frac{1}{3}$ of $\frac{1}{4}$" is an acceptable response before children have learned fraction operations. It won't take them long to discover that $\frac{1}{3}$ of $\frac{1}{4} = \frac{1}{12}$, but there is no need to rush them. These visual and verbal activities pave the way for later algorithms.

Another possibility...

Think of the unit area as 18 chunks, each consisting of 2 little squares. Then the shaded portion is $\frac{1\frac{1}{2}}{18}$. It is also $\frac{1}{18} + \frac{1}{36}$.

## COMPARING FRACTIONS

Children need lots of informal experiences with fractions before proceeding to formal fraction operations because they need to build up some fraction sense. This means that students should develop an intuition that helps them make appropriate connections, determine size, order, and equivalence, and judge whether answers are or are not reasonable. Such fluid and flexible thinking is just as important for teachers who need to distinguish appropriate student strategies from those based on faulty reasoning.

It is not too difficult to think about the relative sizes of two fractions when their denominators are the same. For example, which is larger, $\frac{3}{5}$ or $\frac{2}{5}$? This is similar to a whole number situation because it is asking, "If all the pieces are the same size, do you have more if you have 2 of them or 3 of them?"

Similarly, if both numerators are the same, then the size of the pieces becomes the only critical issue. For example, which is larger, $\frac{3}{7}$ or $\frac{3}{5}$? In this case, we think, "If a pie has been cut into 7 equal pieces, then the pieces are smaller than those from an identical pie that has been cut into 5 equal pieces."

It can be more difficult to compare fractions if the numerators and the denominators are different, because then you are comparing different numbers of different-sized pieces. For example, "Would you rather have 3 pieces from a pie that has been cut into 5 equal-sized pieces $\left(\frac{3}{5}\right)$ or 4 pieces from a pie that has been cut into 9 equal-sized pieces $\left(\frac{4}{9}\right)$?" You need to decide which option gives you more: fewer pieces when the pieces are larger or more pieces when the pieces are smaller.

One way to think about the size of two fractions is to picture a number line with some familiar landmarks on it. If you can decide that one of the fractions you are comparing lies to the left of $\frac{1}{2}$, for example, and that the other lies to the right of $\frac{1}{2}$, then it is easy to tell which is larger.

- Compare $\frac{3}{4}$ and $\frac{1}{5}$.

$\frac{3}{4} > \frac{1}{2}$ and $\frac{1}{5} < \frac{1}{2}$.

So $\frac{3}{4} > \frac{1}{5}$.

It is often useful to enhance this strategy by using fractional parts of the denominator.

- The fraction $\frac{2}{3}$ is larger than $\frac{1}{2}$ because $\frac{1\frac{1}{2}}{3} = \frac{1}{2}$.

- $\frac{5}{11}$ is less than $\frac{1}{4}$ because $\frac{5\frac{1}{2}}{11} = \frac{1}{2}$.

- $\frac{5}{11}$ is greater than $\frac{1}{4}$ because $\frac{2\frac{3}{4}}{11} = \frac{1}{4}$.

- Which is larger, $\frac{3}{5}$ or $\frac{4}{9}$?

We have a pie cut into 5 equal slices. Half the pie would consist of $2\frac{1}{2}$ slices, so 3 slices is more than half the pie and $\frac{3}{5}$ lies somewhere to the right of $\frac{1}{2}$. Now think of a pie cut into 9 equal slices. Half the pie would consist of $4\frac{1}{2}$ slices. But we have only 4 slices, so $\frac{4}{9}$ lies somewhere to the left of $\frac{1}{2}$. Therefore, $\frac{4}{9} < \frac{3}{5}$.

When the fractions you are comparing lie on opposite sides of your reference point, this method works, but when you find that both fractions lie on the same side of your reference point, you need another method of comparison. At this point, it is common to ask "how far away from" the chosen reference point the fractions are. You may hear children say that $\frac{3}{5}$ is only 2 parts away from the unit and $\frac{4}{9}$ is 5 parts away, so $\frac{3}{5}$ must represent the larger amount. Beware of this faulty reasoning. Right answer! Wrong reason! The parts that are being compared here are of different sizes, just as they were in the fractions $\frac{4}{9}$ and $\frac{3}{5}$. It is sometimes true that a small number of large pieces can be greater than a larger number of small pieces. For example, $\frac{2}{4}$ is smaller than $\frac{6}{11}$ although $\frac{2}{4}$ is only 2 parts from the whole and $\frac{6}{11}$ is 5 parts away from the whole. The size of the parts matters!

- Which is larger, $\frac{2}{3}$ or $\frac{3}{5}$?

    $\frac{2}{3} > \frac{1}{2}$ and $\frac{3}{5} > \frac{1}{2}$

    How much larger than $\frac{1}{2}$ is $\frac{2}{3}$? $1\frac{1}{2}$ is half of 3, so 2 out of 3 is larger than $\frac{1}{2}$ by $\frac{\frac{1}{2}}{3}\left(\frac{1}{2} \text{ of } \frac{1}{3}\right)$.

    How much larger is $\frac{3}{5}$? $2\frac{1}{2}$ is half of 5, so 3 out of 5 is larger than $\frac{1}{2}$ by $\frac{\frac{1}{2}}{5}$.

    Now which is larger, $\frac{\frac{1}{2}}{3}$ or $\frac{\frac{1}{2}}{5}$? Because the pie cut into thirds has larger pieces than the pie cut into fifths, a half of a piece from the pie cut into thirds is larger than half of a piece from the pie cut into fifths.

    So, $\frac{2}{3} > \frac{3}{5}$.

- Compare $\frac{5}{11}$ and $\frac{1}{4}$.

    Both fractions are less than $\frac{1}{2}$ because $\frac{5\frac{1}{2}}{11} = \frac{1}{2}$ and $\frac{2\frac{3}{4}}{11} = \frac{1}{4}$.

    But $\frac{5}{11} > \frac{2\frac{3}{4}}{11}$, so, $\frac{5}{11} > \frac{1}{4}$

The ordering strategies we have discussed so far may be summarized as follows:

1.  Same-Size Parts (SSP). When comparing same-size parts, the fraction with the greater numerator has the greater value.

    $$\frac{5}{8} < \frac{7}{8}$$

2.  Same Number of Parts (SNP). When comparing fractions in which the numerators are alike (that is, you have the same number of parts in each), but the denominators are different (that is, the pieces are of different sizes) the larger number in the denominator indicates the smaller fraction.

    $$\frac{3}{5} > \frac{3}{7}$$

3.  Compare to a Benchmark (CB). When comparing fractions with different numerators and denominators, compare them to some benchmark: $\frac{1}{2}, \frac{1}{4}$, or 1.

    $$\frac{4}{5} > \frac{2}{7} \text{ because } \frac{4}{5} > \frac{1}{2} \text{ and } \frac{2}{7} > \frac{1}{2}$$

$\dfrac{9}{10} > \dfrac{8}{9}$ because $\dfrac{9}{10}$ is only $\dfrac{1}{10}$ away from 1, while $\dfrac{8}{9}$ is $\dfrac{1}{9}$ away from 1.

Sometimes younger children need visual models to help support their thinking as they compare fractions. The following area model is useful.

- Compare $\dfrac{3}{8}$ and $\dfrac{4}{9}$.

  Represent $\dfrac{3}{8}$ by slicing and shading a rectangle horizontally and $\dfrac{4}{9}$ by slicing and shading vertically.

  $\dfrac{3}{8} = \dfrac{27}{72}$ and $\dfrac{4}{9} = \dfrac{32}{72}$.

  $\dfrac{4}{9} > \dfrac{3}{8}$

Another method, which comes from the ancient Egyptians, uses unit fractions. These are fractions whose numerators are all 1, so they are easy to compare. It is easy to work with unit fractions because every unit fraction can always be written as the sum of other unit fractions. In fact, this can often be done in more than one way.

- $\dfrac{1}{5} = \dfrac{6}{30} = \dfrac{1}{6} + \dfrac{1}{30}$  $\qquad \dfrac{1}{5} = \dfrac{8}{40} = \dfrac{1}{8} + \dfrac{1}{20} + \dfrac{1}{40}$  $\qquad \dfrac{1}{5} = \dfrac{2}{10} = \dfrac{1}{10} + \dfrac{1}{10}$

- Compare $\dfrac{5}{6}$ and $\dfrac{3}{4}$.

  One technique is to think of the largest unit fraction that can be taken from $\dfrac{5}{6}$. $\dfrac{3}{6} = \dfrac{1}{2}$ and that leaves $\dfrac{2}{6}$ or $\dfrac{1}{3}$. So $\dfrac{5}{6} = \dfrac{1}{2} + \dfrac{1}{3}$. Similarly, $\dfrac{3}{4} = \dfrac{1}{2} + \dfrac{1}{4}$. Both fractions have $\dfrac{1}{2}$ as an addend, so we will compare them using the remaining addends. Because $\dfrac{1}{3} > \dfrac{1}{4}$ we get $\dfrac{5}{6} > \dfrac{3}{4}$.

- Compare $\dfrac{5}{9}$ and $\dfrac{7}{10}$.

  $$\dfrac{5}{9} = \dfrac{1}{3} + \dfrac{1}{9} + \dfrac{1}{9} \qquad \dfrac{7}{10} = \dfrac{1}{2} + \dfrac{1}{5}$$

  Substitute for $\dfrac{1}{2}$.  $\dfrac{1}{2} = \dfrac{3}{6} = \dfrac{1}{3} + \dfrac{1}{6}$

  $$\dfrac{5}{9} = \dfrac{1}{3} + \dfrac{1}{9} + \dfrac{1}{9} \qquad \dfrac{7}{10} = \dfrac{1}{3} + \dfrac{1}{6} + \dfrac{1}{5}$$

  Now we can see that both have $\dfrac{1}{3}$ as an addend, but $\dfrac{1}{6} > \dfrac{1}{9}$ and $\dfrac{1}{5} > \dfrac{1}{9}$. So, $\dfrac{7}{10} > \dfrac{5}{9}$.

- Compare $\frac{2}{9}$ and $\frac{3}{7}$.

$$\frac{2}{9} = \frac{1}{9} + \frac{1}{9} = \frac{1}{9} + \frac{1}{12} + \frac{1}{36} \qquad \frac{3}{7} = \frac{1}{7} + \frac{1}{7} + \frac{1}{7}$$

Here, each of the fractions comprising $\frac{3}{7}$ is greater than each of the fractions comprising $\frac{2}{9}$, so we conclude $\frac{3}{7} > \frac{2}{9}$.

Finally, don't forget the qualitative reasoning technique that we saw in a previous chapter. We compared cookies to children yesterday and today.

- Compare $\frac{4}{7}$ and $\frac{5}{6}$. Yesterday, 7 children shared 4 cookies. Today we have more cookies for fewer children, so $\frac{5}{6} > \frac{4}{7}$.

## FRACTIONS IN BETWEEN

Study the method this student used when he was asked to find 3 fractions between $\frac{1}{9}$ and $\frac{1}{8}$. His name was Martin and he produced this solution when he was at the end of fifth grade.

Martin's method for determining fractions that lie between two given fractions relied on the use of equivalent fractions. By rewriting a fraction using an equivalent expression, namely, a fraction within a fraction, he was able to name many fractions between the two he was given. Martin thought of $\frac{1}{9}$ as $\frac{\frac{8}{8}}{9}$ and he thought of $\frac{1}{8}$ as $\frac{1\frac{1}{8}}{9}$.

Then, keeping 9 in the denominator, any fraction that lies between 1 and $1\frac{1}{8}$ could be used in the numerator. Of course, it is easy to think of fractions that lie between 1 and $1\frac{1}{8}$. Any fraction less than $\frac{1}{8}$ when added to 1 will do it: $1\frac{1}{9}, 1\frac{1}{10}, 1\frac{1}{11}, 1\frac{1}{12}$, etc. You can get any number of these fractions that you want. Next, he wrote the mixed numbers as fractions. Finally, he divided by 9 by multiplying each denominator by 9.

- How would Martin find some fractions between $\frac{1}{4}$ and $\frac{1}{3}$?

  First he would write all of his fractions so that they had the same denominator. Let's say that he was going to use fourths. $\frac{1}{3} = \frac{?}{4}$ Because he knew that $\frac{1}{3}$ is $\frac{4}{3}$ divided by 4, he would write:

$$\frac{1}{4} \quad - \quad - \quad - \quad - \quad - \quad - \quad \frac{\frac{4}{3}}{4}$$

All of the fractions between $\frac{1}{4}$ and $\frac{1}{3}$ would then have denominators of 4 and numerators between 1 and $1\frac{1}{3}$. $\frac{1\frac{1}{4}}{4}, \frac{1\frac{1}{5}}{4}, \frac{1\frac{1}{6}}{4}, \frac{1\frac{1}{7}}{4}, \frac{1\frac{1}{8}}{4}, \ldots$ meet the requirements.

In addition to Martin's method, there are other ways to produce equivalent forms that can help you to reason about fractions. The next two examples suggest rewriting a fraction as the sum of other fractions.

- Find three fractions between $\frac{3}{5}$ and $\frac{4}{5}$.

  $\frac{4}{5} = \frac{3}{5} + \frac{1}{5}$, so if we add something less than $\frac{1}{5}$ to $\frac{3}{5}$, we will name a fraction less than

  $\frac{4}{5}$. Here are three examples: $\frac{3}{5} + \frac{1}{6} = \frac{23}{30}; \frac{3}{5} + \frac{1}{7} = \frac{26}{35}; \frac{3}{5} + \frac{1}{8} = \frac{29}{40}$.

- Find two fractions between $\frac{7}{8}$ and $\frac{9}{10}$. Study this technique used by another student at the end of sixth grade.

Alicia found the difference between the two fractions and then cut it into equal pieces to locate fractions at equal intervals between them. The difference between $\frac{9}{10}$ and $\frac{7}{8}$ is $\frac{1}{40}$ and if you split that into 3 equal pieces, each part would each be $\frac{1}{120}$.

$$\frac{7}{8} + \frac{1}{120} = \frac{106}{120} \qquad \frac{7}{8} + \frac{2}{120} = \frac{107}{120} \qquad \frac{7}{8} + \frac{3}{120} = \frac{108}{120} = \frac{9}{10}$$

Therefore, the fractions we want are $\frac{106}{120}$ and $\frac{107}{120}$.

I do not advocate teaching Martin's method or Alicia's method. That, after all, would be like teaching students another algorithm. Their work is highlighted here because it is a teacher's job to distinguish powerful methods from useless nonsense. Martin's and Alicia's work demonstrate the powerful thinking that can result when students are not rushed into algorithms and are given the time to reason with fractions. Their work also illustrates what we mean when we talk about a *rational number sense* and being able to comfortably and flexibly move around in the world of fractions.

## ACTIVITIES

1. Use reasoning to compare each pair of fractions. Use any of these reasoning methods: SNP, SSP, or CB, cookies and kids, shading areas, or unit fractions.

   a. $\frac{8}{14}, \frac{4}{9}$    b. $\frac{3}{17}, \frac{3}{19}$    c. $\frac{5}{13}, \frac{8}{13}$    d. $\frac{3}{2}, \frac{4}{3}$    e. $\frac{2}{3}, \frac{2}{5}$

   f. $\frac{5}{10}, \frac{7}{9}$    g. $\frac{7}{8}, \frac{3}{4}$    h. $\frac{1}{5}, \frac{1}{7}$    i. $\frac{5}{9}, \frac{3}{4}$    j. $\frac{2}{7}, \frac{3}{5}$

   k. $\frac{3}{8}, \frac{4}{9}$    l. $\frac{9}{19}, \frac{11}{21}$    m. $\frac{3}{7}, \frac{5}{8}$    n. $\frac{4}{9}, \frac{5}{11}$    o. $\frac{3}{8}, \frac{4}{9}$

   p. $\frac{6}{11}, \frac{7}{12}$    q. $\frac{3}{7}, \frac{2}{5}$    r. $\frac{2}{5}, \frac{5}{9}$    s. $\frac{8}{9}, \frac{10}{11}$    t. $\frac{13}{14}, \frac{11}{12}$

2. Use unit fractions to compare.

   a. $\frac{7}{8}, \frac{3}{5}$    b. $\frac{5}{6}, \frac{7}{8}$    c. $\frac{7}{8}, \frac{9}{10}$

3. Use Martin's method to find three fractions between the given fractions.

   a. $\frac{1}{6}, \frac{1}{5}$    b. $\frac{7}{14}, \frac{7}{13}$    c. $\frac{6}{8}, \frac{7}{8}$

4. Using each of the numbers 5, 6, 7, and 8 only once, construct a sum with the given properties:

   a. the smallest possible sum

   $$\frac{\square}{\square} + \frac{\square}{\square}$$

   b. the largest possible sum

   $$\frac{\square}{\square} + \frac{\square}{\square}$$

   c. the smallest positive difference

   $$\frac{\square}{\square} - \frac{\square}{\square}$$

   d. the largest possible positive difference

   $$\frac{\square}{\square} - \frac{\square}{\square}$$

   e. the smallest possible product

   $$\frac{\square}{\square} \times \frac{\square}{\square}$$

   f. the largest possible product

   $$\frac{\square}{\square} \times \frac{\square}{\square}$$

   g. the smallest possible quotient

   $$\frac{\square}{\square} \div \frac{\square}{\square}$$

   h. the largest possible quotient

   $$\frac{\square}{\square} \div \frac{\square}{\square}$$

5. What happens to the size of a positive fraction when the following changes are made:

   a. The numerator is increased by 1.
   b. The numerator is increased and the denominator is increased.
   c. The denominator is increased by 1.
   d. The numerator and the denominator are both multiplied by the same number.

6. Find three fractions equally spaced between $\frac{2}{5}$ and 1.

7. Mike says that the fraction $\frac{1}{a}$ can never be larger than 1. Is he correct? Explain.

# CHAPTER 7

# Fractions as Part–Whole Comparisons

## STUDENT STRATEGIES: GRADE 3

Third graders were divided into small groups to work at different math stations in their classroom. One group of seven was asked to draw a model and to explain the meaning of the fraction $\frac{5}{6}$.

Make as many observations as you can about the seven models that were produced.

# PART–WHOLE FRACTIONS: THE BIG IDEAS

- A *part–whole comparison* designates a number of equal parts of a unit out of the total number of equal parts into which the unit is divided. Here, *equal* means the same in number, or the same in length, or the same in area, etc., depending on the nature of the unit whole, that is, whether it is a count, a length, or an area.

- The symbol $\frac{a}{b}$ means a parts out of $b$ equal parts. However, one part does not mean the same as one piece. A part may consist of more than one piece. For example, the unit may be a set of 18 baseball cards. Then $\frac{1}{6}$ means one out of 6 equal parts, where a part consists of 3 cards.

- The amount in a part depends on how many equal-sized parts are formed. Increasing the number of parts decreases the amount in each part. The fewer the number of parts, the greater the amount in each part. Thus, $\frac{1}{3}$ of a cake (fewer parts) will represent more cake than $\frac{1}{6}$ (more parts) of the same cake.

- Many different fractional names designate the same amount. Two different fractions that represent the same amount are called *equivalent*. When we write $\frac{3}{6} = \frac{1}{2}$ we mean that these fractions represent the same relative amounts.

- When we speak of *unitizing*, we mean conceptualizing the unit in terms of different-size chunks. This could be a mental or a visual process. For example, remember the case of soda (the unit is 24 cans of soda) that could be mentally represented as 4(6-packs) or 2(12-packs). Unitizing is related to equivalent fractions: 2(6-packs) out of 4(6-packs) = 1(12-pack) out of 2(12-packs) because the same unit (24 cans) is merely chunked in different ways.

- In every fraction problem, it is important to identify the unit and to make sure that each fraction is interpreted in terms of that unit. You cannot compare fractions based on different units. When we are doing abstract calculations (adding or subtracting fractions, for example, that do not refer to any specific material object) we do not worry about units. However, in instruction, when giving children concrete objects to think about, we will do nothing but confuse the issue if we do not know what the unit is.

- In every problem, the unit must be stated explicitly, or given implicitly. When it is given implicitly, you can reason up and down until you know what the unit is.

- Use discrete and continuous units of various types, and use units that are composed of more than one object. The reason is that after many years of using a single round cake or a single round pizza as the unit, children don't know how to deal with a unit that consists of more than one object.

- Do not accept a counting number as an answer to a fraction problem. For example, when dealing with a pizza problem, *2 pieces* is not an acceptable answer. The question "What part of a pizza" or "How much pizza" requires a fraction answer.

## UNITIZING AND EQUIVALENCE

Consider the following rectangle. $\frac{3}{5}$ of the rectangle is shaded. This is because the area of the entire rectangle has been divided into 5 equal parts and we are comparing the area of 3 of those parts to the area of all 5 parts.

We could think of the same rectangle (the same unit area) as being composed of 20 small squares. The shaded portion would then be called $\frac{12}{20}$ of the rectangle.

If we think of the rectangle as being composed of the small rectangles formed of two of those small squares, then the shaded part would be called $\frac{6}{10}$ of the rectangle.

Here, unitizing (thinking in terms of different sized chunks) helps us to generate equivalent names for the same amount.

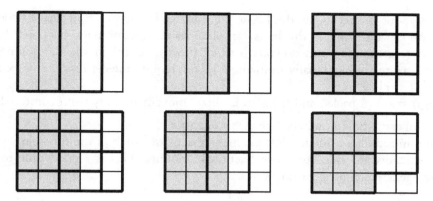

By having students designate in parentheses the size of chunk they are looking at when they use a particular fraction name, it becomes clear to others how they were thinking.

The seven equivalent names pictured above are as follows:

$$\frac{3}{5} \text{ (columns)} = \frac{1\frac{1}{2}}{2\frac{1}{2}} \text{ (pairs of columns)} = \frac{1}{1\frac{2}{3}} \text{ (3-packs of columns)} = \frac{12}{20} \text{ (squares)} =$$

$$\frac{6}{10} \text{ (pairs of squares)} = \frac{3}{5} \text{ (4-packs of squares)} = \frac{2}{3\frac{1}{3}} \text{ (6-packs of squares)}.$$

To express part of a whole, both the part and the whole should be expressed in the same size chunks.

- What part of a dollar are 3 US quarters?

$$\frac{3 \text{ quarters}}{1 \text{ dollar}} = \frac{3}{4} \text{ (quarters) (What a coincidence!)}$$

- 4 cans of soda is what part of a 6-pack?

$$\frac{4 \text{ cans}}{6\text{-pack}} = \frac{4}{6} \text{ (cans)} = \frac{2}{3} \text{ (pairs of cans)}$$

- 14 eggs is what part of a dozen?

$$\frac{14 \text{ eggs}}{1 \text{ dozen}} = \frac{14}{12} \text{ (eggs)} = \frac{7}{6} \text{ (pair of eggs)} = \frac{2\frac{1}{3}}{2}\left(\frac{1}{2}\text{-dozen}\right) = \frac{1\frac{1}{6}}{1} \text{ (dozen)}$$

An important fact about unitizing is that it entails the mental coordination of number of pieces and size of pieces, an important measurement principle and an important concept for developing a strong fraction sense. The larger the size of the chunks in which we thought about the unit, the smaller the number of pieces we needed to cover the rectangle. Conversely, the smaller the size of chunks in which we thought about the rectangle, the larger the number of pieces we needed to cover it. Furthermore, unitizing is the basis for understanding equivalent fractions. It asks children to reason up and down, a mental process useful in the development of proportional reasoning. Finally, unitizing does not require integer results (for example, $\frac{8}{12}$ (eggs) $= \frac{1\frac{1}{3}}{2}$ (6-packs) and helps to facilitate movement away from comfortable or nice numbers: whole numbers, halves, and quarters.

Many introductory fraction lessons include activities such as the following one, in which students are asked to shade fractional amounts. This is a good time to have students generate equivalent fractions.

- Shade $\frac{5}{6}$.

Now generate equivalent fractions:

$$\frac{5}{6} \text{ (columns)} = \frac{15}{18} \text{ (pair of squares)} = \frac{60}{72}\left(\frac{1}{2}\text{-squares}\right) = \frac{7\frac{1}{2}}{9} \text{ (4-packs)} = \frac{10}{12} \text{ (3-packs)} =$$
$$\frac{30}{36} \text{ (squares)}$$

## PROBLEMS IN CURRENT INSTRUCTION

Although fractions build on a child's preschool experiences with fair sharing, the formal ideas connected with visual representations, fraction language, and symbolism are intellectually demanding. In Chapter 2, we mentioned many of the cognitive hurdles that lie between whole numbers and fractions. Most initial fraction instruction begins with drawing and shading. Unfortunately, this method often contributes to the difficulty of learning fractions.

- Children sometimes do not divide the unit into equal-sized shares.
- Sometimes children make decisions about equivalence and order when the fractions they are using refer to objects that are not the same size (a small pizza divided into 8 pieces and a larger pizza divided into 8 pieces).
- Children make decisions about fraction equivalence or fraction comparisons on the basis of drawings that are incorrect.

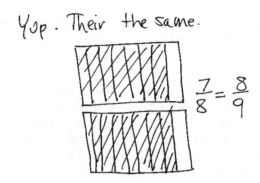

Yup . Their the same.

$$\frac{7}{8} = \frac{8}{9}$$

Most of the time when I see children struggling in part–whole instruction it is because instruction has been playing upon children's weaknesses, rather than building upon their strengths. Many of the so-called misconceptions and problems that have been identified are a result of the fact that adults expect artistic talent or hand-eye coordination that simply is not there in all third and fourth graders. There is considerable instructional time spent trying to fix these problems, which, in a year or so, would fix themselves. Most third and fourth graders do not have sufficient knowledge of the area of a triangle to know how to divide it equally into three parts. A common remedy for this problem is to have students partition sheet after sheet of odd-shaped figures. It is well known that students have trouble dividing a circular model into 3 or 6 equal parts, so in some classes, valuable class time is wasted practicing "Y-ing" circle after circle until they can get those thirds to look equal. In other classes, I have seen students measure and mark the sides of their rectangles with rulers so they could "get their eighths equal." This raises the question about which model or models for teaching fractions bring the greatest return.

## FRACTION MODELS

There are many commercial products for teaching fractions. However, traditional fraction instruction has typically failed to use these products effectively.

- Many fraction models are used beyond their usefulness.
- Important ideas and questions are not being asked.
- These products are ascribed magical power. Manipulatives and "hands-on" activities are sacred cows, presumed to have the power to impart valuable fraction knowledge. Such tools may be colorful and fun, but engaged hands do not necessarily mean engaged minds.
- Each model accommodates a limited number of fractional denominators.

No one model is a panacea; every model has some useful features, but wears out at some point, and it up to the teacher to use it wisely. If you have to spend valuable class time teaching students how to work with the model, it is wasted time that is not being used to teach fractions. It is important that instruction use various models so that children do not become habituated to the extent that they can think about fractions in only one way and fail to transfer that knowledge when they are faced with an alternate model.

Area models are fraction models in which 1 whole is an area. That is, the unit whole is a certain given area and that area is partitioned (divided up into equal-size pieces) to produce fractions. Fractions strips, fraction circles, rectangular cakes and pizzas, Cuisenaire strips and rods, and pattern pieces are all area models. Equally important (but most neglected) are discrete models. In a discrete model, individual objects or sets of such objects form the unit whole. Money and bi-color chips are examples of discrete models.

We have already discussed the value of Cuisenaire strips and pattern pieces. Both may contribute to the development of proportional reasoning when used appropriately. However, longitudinal research has shown that fraction achievement was greatest when students actively and thoughtfully engaged in partitioning a unit. We will read more about this in the chapter that discusses fractions as measures. Next, we will consider the use of fraction strips, an inexpensive and highly effective model for comparing fractions, and paving the way for fraction computation. A key feature of these strips is that students must partition them to answer important questions.

## FRACTION STRIPS

Fraction strips, such as those available in trade catalogs, are two-dimensional strips, all of the same length. One strip shows halves, the next, thirds, the next, fourths, etc. If a problem is about running distances, for example, the strips can be used as a unit length. All of the strips have the same area, so if the problem is about a rectangular cake, for example, the unit is a unit area. These are useful for helping the children to observe, that $\frac{2}{6} = \frac{1}{3}$ by placing the thirds and the sixths strips one above the other. Likewise, they can observe useful facts when comparing unit fractions. For example, although $2 < 10$, $\frac{1}{2} > \frac{1}{10}$. I have seen teachers cut all of the pieces apart. This turns out to be a disaster. First of all, the number of pieces is unmanageable and there are too many little pieces of paper flying around the classroom, but more importantly, cutting the pieces apart fails to convey the concept that every fraction is based upon the same unit.

In *MORE*, you will find a different version of fraction strips. The chief difference is that they are designed to involve students in the partitioning process. Besides being inexpensive and easy to reproduce for all children in the class, the strips are partially partitioned so that students have some landmarks as they partition continuous objects. Alternatively, if you provide students with a clear plastic sheet and a marker, they can trace the strips that are appropriate for a given problem and do their work on the plastic.

# COMPARING PART-WHOLE FRACTIONS

When it comes to comparing fractions, you can find worksheet after worksheet asking children which is longer $\frac{2}{3}$ or $\frac{3}{4}$? By coloring fraction strips, it is easy to see that $\frac{2}{3}$ of a candy bar is more than $\frac{1}{2}$ of that candy bar.

But this activity can be more productive by asking a more challenging question. We want to help children move beyond qualitative judgments, such as longer, shorter, more, less, etc., toward a quantitative response. The more important question is "How much larger?"

To answer *how much more*, we divide the candy bars so that each has the same number of pieces, or pieces of the same size. In this case, if we further divide each of the three sections in the first candy bar in half and we divide each half of the second candy bar into three equal pieces, then both will contain 6 equal pieces. The shaded amounts are then $\frac{4}{6}$ and $\frac{3}{6}$, respectively.

This enables us to compare the pieces. $\frac{2}{3}$ is $\frac{1}{6}$ larger than $\frac{1}{2}$.

Secondly, when children engage in the partitioning process to try to answer the questions "How much more?" they quickly learned about common denominators. This question requires a common denominator, so that right from the start of instruction, you are already preparing students for addition and subtraction that will come later.

- Which is more, $\frac{5}{6}$ of a cake or $\frac{2}{3}$ of that cake? (5 out of 6 equal pieces, or 2 out of 3 equal pieces). How much more?

  $\frac{2}{3}$ pieces $= \frac{4}{6} \left( \frac{1}{2}\text{-pieces} \right)$. This says that on the cake showing 2 out of 3 pieces, if I cut all of the pieces in half, then 2 out of 3 will look like 4 out of 6 equal pieces. Therefore, $\frac{5}{6} > \frac{2}{3}$. Furthermore, $\frac{5}{6}$ of a cake is $\frac{1}{6}$ more than $\frac{2}{3}$ of a cake.

- Maurice has $2\frac{3}{4}$ cakes. Sam has $2\frac{2}{3}$ cakes.

  Who has more? How much more?
  Write the fraction subtraction problem that tells how much more.
  How much do the boys have altogether?
  Write the fraction addition problem that tells how much they have together.

Since both boys have 2 cakes plus something more, we need only compare the "something more."

$$2 \text{ out of 3 pieces} = \frac{2}{3} \text{ (pieces)} = \frac{8}{12} \left(\frac{1}{4}\text{-pieces}\right).$$

$$3 \text{ out of 4 pieces} = \frac{3}{4} \text{ (pieces)} = \frac{9}{12} \left(\frac{1}{3}\text{-pieces}\right).$$

This says, partition each of the pieces in Maurice's third cake into 3 equal pieces and then his cake is 9 out of those 12 pieces. Partition each of the pieces in Sam's third cake into 4 equal pieces. Then his cake is 8 out of the resulting 12 pieces.

This means that now both cakes have the same number of pieces and the same size pieces.

Now we can see that Maurice has $\frac{1}{12}$ cake more than Sam has.

$$2\frac{3}{4}2\frac{2}{3} = \frac{1}{12}$$

Together, the boys have $2\frac{3}{4} + 2\frac{2}{3} = 2\frac{9}{12} + 2\frac{8}{12} = 4\frac{17}{12} = 4 + 1\frac{5}{12} = 5\frac{5}{12}.$

## DISCRETE UNITS

The fraction strips we have been using are continuous objects. Children also need to work with units that consist of sets of discrete objects, that is, objects that are detached from each other. These might be candies, coins, or bi-color chips.

The part–whole comparison depicted here is $\frac{2}{3}$.

- Is $\frac{6}{9}$ equivalent to $\frac{2}{3}$?

  By unitizing (mentally or visually re-grouping), it is easy to see that $\frac{6}{9}$ is like $\frac{2}{3}$.

  We know that $\frac{6}{9}$ is equivalent to $\frac{2}{3}$ because we can see that it is 2 columns out 3 columns.

- Is $\frac{6}{9}$ equivalent to $\frac{18}{27}$?

  Let's unitize again. Instead of individual dots, if we think of $\frac{1}{3}$-dots, then we get

  $$\frac{6 \text{ dots}}{9 \text{ dots}} = \frac{18\left(\frac{1}{3}\text{-dots}\right)}{27\left(\frac{1}{3}\text{-dots}\right)}$$

How do we compare fractions? You will remember that we used several methods; however, two of them were a) SSP (creating same-sized parts), and b) SNP (creating same number of parts). When working with sets of discrete objects, we can use either of these strategies.

SSP is a process that equalizes the denominators of the fractions we want to compare. It is finding a common denominator for those fractions.

- Compare $\frac{3}{4}$ and $\frac{5}{8}$.

  A 2-clone of $\frac{3}{4}$ is $\frac{6}{8}$.

Visually, you can verify that you have 3 columns out of 4 total columns. There is no need to clone $\frac{5}{8}$ because we can already see that $\frac{3}{4}$ is greater. We can also see the benefits of using different models in fraction instruction. With the chip model, we can easily answer the question: How much greater is $\frac{3}{4}$ than $\frac{5}{8}$? $\frac{3}{4}$ is clearly $\frac{1}{8}$ larger than $\frac{5}{8}$.

- Compare $\frac{7}{9}$ and $\frac{5}{6}$.

A 2-clone of $\frac{7}{9}$ and a 3-clone of $\frac{5}{6}$ produce sets of the same size, and fractions with the same denominators. We can make a simple visual comparison by rearranging the chips that represent $\frac{5}{6}\left(\frac{15}{18}\right)$. Then we can see that $\frac{5}{6} > \frac{7}{9}$ by $\frac{1}{18}$. $\frac{15}{18} > \frac{14}{18}$.

Another way to compare fractions is to clone them until their numerators are the same. This is the SSP strategy.

- Compare $\frac{3}{8}$ and $\frac{4}{9}$.

A 4-clone of $\frac{3}{8}$ gives $\frac{12}{32}$. A 3-clone of $\frac{4}{9}$ gives $\frac{12}{27}$. $\frac{4}{9}$ is greater because $27^{\text{ths}}$ are larger pieces than $32^{\text{nds}}$ are.

- I baked chocolate and vanilla cookies. What part of the following batch of cookies is chocolate?

4 (6-packs) out of 6 (6-packs) are chocolate. So $\frac{4}{6}$ of the cookies are chocolate.

Of course, I could name them in other ways. For example,

$$\frac{4}{6}(\text{6-packs}) = \frac{2}{3} \ (\text{dozen})$$

- Suppose I want to make smaller packages of cookies, but I always want 2 parts out of 3 parts to be chocolate. How can I do this:

  a. If I want to put 6 cookies in a package?
     I need 6 cookies divided into 3 equal parts; that is, 2 cookies in each part. Put 4 chocolate and 2 vanilla.
  b. If I want to put 18 cookies in a package?
     I need 18 cookies divided into 3 equal parts; that gives 6 cookies in each part. Put 12 chocolate and 6 vanilla.

The importance of allowing lots of time for children to work with many different fraction models cannot be overemphasized. At the beginning of the chapter, you saw the work of 7 children who were given the freedom to use whatever model they wanted to illustrate the fraction $\frac{5}{6}$. These children had been instructed using continuous and discrete models, with unit wholes that sometimes consisted of more than one object. Notice the models they chose for the task. Although they had only begun fraction instruction in third grade, they already had a broader range of experiences than children get from cutting fraction circles or single pizzas. Only one person chose to use a single round object! Note that more than one child chose to use sets of objects, and several of them used more than 6 objects in their set. Note that sharing had a very strong influence on the children's thinking. Students C, E, and G all created sharing scenarios, but still managed to illustrate the part–whole fraction: 5 out of 6 shares of hard candies were distributed (C), 5 out of 6 candy bars had someone to eat them (E), and 5 out of 6 people got cookies (G). It is a little early to tell and evidence is sparse in this example, but as the classroom teacher, I would be watching student G to see if he/she prefers ratios to part–whole comparisons.

## MULTIPLICATION

Area models, such as a rectangular area, are best for introducing fraction multiplication.

- $1\frac{1}{2} \times \frac{2}{3} = ?$

  I will use a unit area.  $1 =$

Color $1\frac{1}{2}$ copies of that unit area.

Next, divide the area into thirds using horizontal lines.

Finally, shade $\frac{2}{3}$ of the colored region.

How do we name the shaded area? Remember that we must refer back to the unit area to name our fractional answer. 6 colored and shaded sections represent what part of the unit are? They constitute 1 whole unit area. Therefore $1\frac{1}{2} \times \frac{2}{3} = 1$.

## PARTITIVE AND QUOTATIVE DIVISION

Not only do children need to experience many different meanings and models for fractions, but it is important that they recognize that there is more than one wording for a problem that signifies division. There are two types of division questions: partitive division questions and quotative (also known as measurement or subtractive) division questions.

In a partitive division problem, you are given the total number of groups, and you are trying to find the number of items in each group. For example, if John has a package of 30 cookies to share fairly with his 5 friends, the question is how many cookies will each boy receive (an absolute question) or what part of the whole set of cookies will each boy receive (a relative thinking question). In this case, each boy would get $\frac{5}{30}$ or $\frac{1}{6}$ of the package. Notice the connection here to fractions as quotients. The whole set of cookies (1 whole set) shared 6 ways means that each person gets $\frac{1}{6}$ of the cookies. Partitive division is division that is based on partitioning or fair sharing.

In a quotative division problem, you are given a number of objects and quoted a certain number per person and the question to be answered is how many people can be served. For example, John has 30 cookies and if he gives each person 3 cookies (a rate of 3 per person), how many people can he serve?

Notice the connection to rates. In this type of division you are quoted a rate: cookies are to be distributed at the rate of 3 per person. In reality, this question can be symbolized: $30 \div \frac{3}{1} = ?$ It happens that this is a simple rate called a *unit rate* that reduces this problem to a whole number division. A quotative division problem that involves a fractional divisor is:

Mr. Brown has a hank of rope that measures $9\frac{3}{8}$ yards long. Each boy in his scout troop needs a piece $\frac{5}{8}$ yards long. How many pieces of the required length can he cut?

Quotative division is also called measurement division and subtractive division because you are given a measurement that can be subtracted repeatedly to obtain your answer. You can count how many times you can measure $\frac{5}{8}$ yard out of $9\frac{3}{8}$ yards, or you can count how many times you can subtract $\frac{5}{8}$ yard from $9\frac{3}{8}$ yards.

- How many marbles would I have to give Jim if he won $\frac{2}{3}$ of my marbles?

In this case, I am working with discrete objects. My unit is 12 marbles and I can think of the 12 marbles as 3 (4-packs). 2 (4-packs) out of the 3 (4-packs) gives the required relationship $\frac{2}{3}$. I will need to give him 8 marbles.

## DIVISION

Children should be encouraged to reinterpret a fraction division problem in terms of the meaning of division.

- $2 \div \frac{1}{2} = ?$

- Think: How many times can I measure $\frac{1}{2}$ out of 2?

$$2 \div \frac{1}{2} = 4$$

- $4\frac{3}{8} \div \frac{5}{8} = ?$

$$\frac{8}{8} + \frac{8}{8} + \frac{8}{8} + \frac{8}{8} + \frac{3}{8} = \frac{35}{8}$$

How many times can I measure $\frac{5}{8}$ out of $\frac{35}{8}$? 7 times. So $4\frac{3}{8} \div \frac{5}{8} = 7$.

Division with remainders should be introduced a little bit later. The reason is that division is the first instance where we do not refer back to the unit whole to name a fractional answer. In a division problem, the divisor becomes the unit and the remainder must be named in terms of the divisor. This is a tough idea!

- $2\frac{2}{3} \div \frac{5}{6} = ?$

Recall the meaning of division. How many times can I measure $\frac{5}{6}$ out of $2\frac{2}{3}$?

Begin by representing $2\frac{2}{3}$.

Subdivide to represent sixths.

In the shaded region representing $2\frac{2}{3}$ $\left(\text{or } 2\frac{4}{6}\right)$, I can see 3 sets of $\frac{5}{6}$ with $\frac{1}{6}$ left over.

What part of the divisor $\left(\frac{5}{6}\right)$ is $\frac{1}{6}$? Remember, we were measuring out chunks of

size $\frac{5}{6}$. Look at what is left over and see what part of $\frac{5}{6}$ it is. The one piece that is

left over is $\frac{1}{5}$ of our divisor. So $\frac{1}{5}$ is the remainder. $2\frac{2}{3} \div \frac{5}{6} = 3\frac{1}{5}$.

- $3 \div \frac{2}{3} = ?$

Let ( ) = 1. Then ( )( )( ) = 3.

Subdivide into thirds.

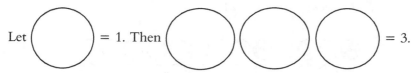

I can measure $\frac{2}{3}$ out of 3 a total of 4 times, but I have a piece of size $\frac{1}{3}$ left over.

Remember that we are measuring out chunks of $\frac{2}{3}$. What part of the divisor $\frac{2}{3}$ is left

over? The remaining piece is $\frac{1}{2}$ of $\frac{2}{3}$, so my answer is $4\frac{1}{2}$.

- I have three acres of land. How much land is $\frac{5}{9}$ of my land?

In this case, the unit is 3 acres. I can think of 3 acres as 9 $\left(\frac{1}{3}\text{-acres}\right)$. Then 5

$\left(\frac{1}{3}\text{-acres}\right)$ would give 5 parts out of 9 parts.

Make sure that children shade some fraction strips. Then it is easy to see that the

shaded portion, 5 $\left(\frac{1}{3}\text{-acres}\right)$, is equivalent to $1\frac{2}{3}$ acres.

$\frac{5}{9}$ of 3 acres = $\frac{5}{3}$ acres = $1\frac{2}{3}$ acres.

- If you want to shade $\frac{7}{6}$ of these dots, how many should you shade?

You could think of 18 dots as 9 (pairs), 3 (6-packs), 6 (3-packs), etc. I need 6 equal parts, so I will think of 18 as 6 (3-packs). 7 of those 3-packs or 21 dots would be $\frac{7}{6}$ of the dots but since I have only 6 (3-packs), I'll need another set of dots so that I can color the $7^{\text{th}}$ (3-pack). $\frac{7}{6}$ of 18 = 21.

- What is $1\frac{1}{4} \div \frac{2}{3}$? How many copies of $\frac{2}{3}$ can I measure out of $1\frac{1}{4}$?

$\frac{5}{4}$ (pieces) $= \frac{15}{12}\left(\frac{1}{3}\text{-pieces}\right)$ and $\frac{2}{3}$ (pieces) $= \frac{8}{12}\left(\frac{1}{4}\text{-pieces}\right)$. How many times can you measure 8 pieces out of 15 pieces? $\frac{15}{8} = 1\frac{7}{8}$.

## OTHER RATIONAL NUMBER INTERPRETATIONS

As we study the other rational number interpretations in the next four chapters, you will begin to notice that in teaching part–whole fractions, we stepped out of a strict part–whole interpretation and began to intersect with all of the other interpretations. We have already noted that so many problems cross over to the ratio interpretation. Problems about sharing and comparing take us into a quotient interpretation. Teaching multiplication through cross-hatched shading is really an operator interpretation. The measurement ideas and partitioning fraction strips as unit lengths take us into the measure interpretation. Fraction division also uses measurement ideas. It is important to recognize each of these personalities of the rational numbers so that you can provide your students a diverse experience and a richer interpretation for fractions.

## ACTIVITIES

1.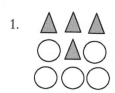

   a. The triangles are what part of the group of objects pictured above?
   b. What is the unit in question 1a?
   c. 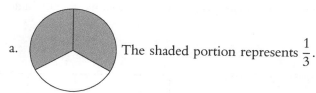 is what part of the set of triangles?
   d. How many items are in the unit in question 1c?
   e.  is what part of the set of circles?
   f. How many items are in the unit in question 1e?

2. In each case, draw the unit.

   a.  The shaded portion represents $\frac{1}{3}$.

   b. The shaded portion represents $1\frac{1}{2}$.

   c. The shaded portion represents $\frac{1}{3}$.

   d.  The shaded portion represents $\frac{2}{9}$.

e. The shaded portion represents $\frac{1}{10}$.

f. The shaded portion represents $\frac{2}{3}$.

g. The shaded portion represents $\frac{2}{3}$.

3. One rectangle = 1 whole area. Using only the subdivisions given, shade each fractional area named.

a. $\frac{3}{4}$

b. $\frac{5}{6}$

c. $\frac{2}{9}$

d. $\frac{5}{8}$

e.  $\dfrac{2}{3}$

f.  $\dfrac{7}{12}$

g.  $\dfrac{7}{18}$

h.  $\dfrac{3}{16}$

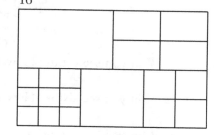

4.  Answer each of the following questions, clearly indicating the way in which you unitized.

   a.  3 days are what part of a work week?
   b.  24 shoelaces are what part of pair?
   c.  One pair of shoelaces is what part of two dozen shoelaces?
   d.  8 colas are what part of a 12-pack?
   e.  8 colas are what part of a 6-pack?
   f.  3 quarters are how many half dollars?
   g.  17 quarter-acres are what part of an acre?
   h.  17 quarter-acres are what part of a half-acre?

5.  Represent each of the following relationships in a drawing.

   a.  Five ninths of the committee members are women.

   b.  I have 4 acres of land and I have $\dfrac{5}{6}$ of it planted in corn.

   c.  I have 10 acres of land and $\dfrac{2}{5}$ of it is a lake.

   d.  I had 2 cakes, and $\dfrac{5}{6}$ of them were eaten.

6.   What part of the square does the circle cover?

7.   Which is larger and by how much, $\frac{4}{5}$ of an acre or $\frac{5}{6}$ of an acre?

8.   Answer the following questions using this picture.

   a.   Can you see thirds? How many flowers are in $\frac{2}{3}$ of the set?

   b.   Can you see sixths? How many flowers are in $\frac{5}{6}$ of the set?

   c.   Can you see ninths? How many flowers are in $\frac{7}{9}$ of the set?

   d.   Can you see twelfths? How many flowers are in $\frac{7}{12}$ of the set?

   e.   Can you see eighteenths? How many flowers are in $\frac{11}{18}$ of the set?

9.   Using this set of hearts, rank these fractions, smallest to largest: $\frac{5}{6}, \frac{2}{3}, \frac{5}{9}$.

10.  Color $\frac{7}{8}$ of these rectangles. How many will you color?

11.  First, determine what is important to understand about this question. Can you tell if these fourth grade children understand it?

     Name the part that is shaded in each picture.
     Do these fractions name the same amount? How do you know?

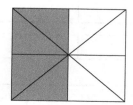

Mike

In the circle $\frac{2}{2}$ is shaded. In the box $\frac{4}{4}$ is shaded. They can't be the same amount because one is a box and one is a circle.

DEREK

$\frac{2}{4}$ IS COLORED IN THE CIRCEL AND $\frac{4}{8}$ IS COLORED IN THE RECTANGEL. THEY ARE THE SAME BECAUSE HALF THE PICTURE IS SHADE.

Adam

$\frac{1}{2}$ is shaded in both pitcures. It is the same fraction but not the same amount. You can tell like this

12. Figure out how to cut these cakes so that the cake in each pan will have pieces of the same size.

a.

b.

c.

d.

e.

f.

13. Compare these fractions using fraction strips (provided in *MORE*). Be sure to answer how much more is in the larger area.

   a. $\frac{2}{3}$ of an acre and $\frac{3}{5}$ of an acre

   b. $\frac{7}{9}$ of a mile and $\frac{5}{6}$ of a mile

   c. $\frac{3}{4}$ of a cheese cake and $\frac{7}{10}$ of that cake

   d. $\frac{5}{6}$ of a cake or $\frac{7}{8}$ of a cake

   e. $\frac{7}{9}$ of a pizza or $\frac{2}{3}$ of a pizza

   f. $\frac{5}{6}$ of a cake or $\frac{3}{4}$ of a cake

14. Maurice has

   Sam has

   How much do they have altogether?

15. What is $1\frac{2}{9} \div 1\frac{2}{3}$?

16. What is $2\frac{1}{3} \div 1\frac{1}{4}$?

17. Make multiplication models to show the following products:

   a. $1\frac{1}{3} \cdot \frac{3}{4}$    b. $\frac{5}{8} \cdot \frac{1}{2}$    c. $1\frac{5}{6} \cdot \frac{2}{3}$

18.    $1\frac{3}{4} \div \frac{2}{3} = ?$

19.    Use fraction strips to solve the following.

Who gets more, a person in group A, or a person in group B?

a.  In group A, 3 people share 2 cakes $\left(\text{represented as } \frac{2}{3}\right)$. In group B, 4 people share 3 cakes $\left(\text{represented as } \frac{3}{4}\right)$.

b.  In group A, 8 people share 5 cakes. In group B, 12 people share 9 cakes.

c.  In group A, 4 people share 1 pizza. In group B, 9 people share 2 pizzas.

d.  In group A, 3 people share 2 cakes. In group B, 8 people share 5 cakes.

e.  In group A, 6 people share 5 pizzas. In group B, 5 people share 4 pizzas.

20.    Model each division problem with fraction strips and answer how many boxes (and/or what fraction of a box) this candy maker was able to fill.

a.  On Monday, Mrs. Diehl made $\frac{7}{8}$ lb. of candy. How many $\frac{1}{4}$ lb. gift boxes did she fill?

b.  On Tuesday, she made $\frac{3}{4}$ lb. of candy. How many $\frac{1}{8}$ lb. gift boxes did she fill?

c.  On Wednesday, she made $1\frac{1}{4}$ pounds of candy. How many $\frac{3}{8}$ lb. gift boxes did she fill?

d.  On Thursday, Mrs. Diehl made $2\frac{1}{2}$ pounds of candy. How many $\frac{1}{4}$ lb. gift boxes did she fill?

e.  On Friday, she made $\frac{5}{3}$ lb. of candy. How many $\frac{1}{2}$ lb. gift boxes could she fill?

21.    Some fifth-grade students who were just beginning to add fractions worked with rectangular pizzas consisting of a unit, halves, fourths, sixths, eights, twelfths, and twenty-fourths, as shown here.

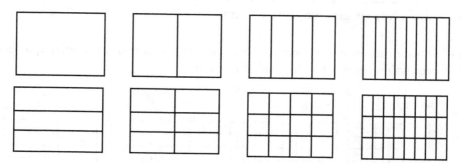

Their task was to use the pizza pieces to find this sum: $\frac{1}{3} + \frac{1}{6}$. Analyze their work. Was the student correct?

22.  Two sisters were told to share a piece of cake. The older girl cut the cake and gave her sister a piece. Then the younger girl protested, "Your half is bigger than my half." What does *half* mean to this little girl?

23.  John split a long licorice stick so that he and his two friends each got a fair share. Just after he cut it and before anyone had eaten any, another friend came along. They decided to give the fourth boy a fair share. How can they split the candy so that everyone gets the same amount?

24.  Shade the amount indicated above each unit area and use unitizing to generate equivalent names for the shaded amount.

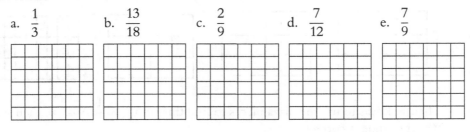

    a. $\dfrac{1}{3}$      b. $\dfrac{13}{18}$      c. $\dfrac{2}{9}$      d. $\dfrac{7}{12}$      e. $\dfrac{7}{9}$

f. $\frac{1}{3}+\frac{1}{4}$    g. $\frac{1}{9}+\frac{5}{18}$    h. $\frac{5}{6}+\frac{1}{18}$    i. $\frac{1}{4}+\frac{1}{6}$    j. $\frac{1}{2}+\frac{1}{12}$

25.  Grace, Lindsay, Troy, and Carson each thought about this problem in a different way. Analyze their solutions.

$$1\div\frac{2}{3}$$

*Grace*

$\frac{2}{3}$ is twice as big as $\frac{1}{3}$ and I know $\frac{1}{3}$ goes into 1 three time. So $\frac{2}{3}$ can go in only half as many times.

*Lindsay R*

$1 = 3\left(\frac{1}{3}'s\right) = 1\frac{1}{2}\left(\frac{2}{3}'s\right)$

*Troy*

   $1 = 6\left(\frac{1}{6} \text{ pieces}\right)$

   $\frac{2}{3} = 4\left(\frac{1}{6} \text{ pieces}\right)$

After I take out 4 from the 6, I have $2\left(\frac{1}{6} \text{ pieces}\right)$ left. This is   $\dfrac{2\left(\frac{1}{6} \text{ pieces}\right)}{4\left(\frac{1}{6} \text{ pieces}\right)}$

*Carson*

       $2\div\frac{2}{3} = 3$

So $1\div\frac{2}{3} = 1\frac{1}{2}$

# CHAPTER 8

# Fractions as Quotients

## STUDENT STRATEGIES: MULTIPLE GRADES

Solve this problem for yourself and then analyze the students' solutions given below.

If the girls share their pizzas equally, and the boys share their pizzas equally, who gets more pizza, a girl or a boy? How much more?

Tyrone, Grade 3

A girl gets more. Each one gets a bite on the extra piece.

Emilia, Grade 4

The girls get more. They get $\frac{1}{3}$ more than the boys. They each get $\frac{1}{8}$ more.

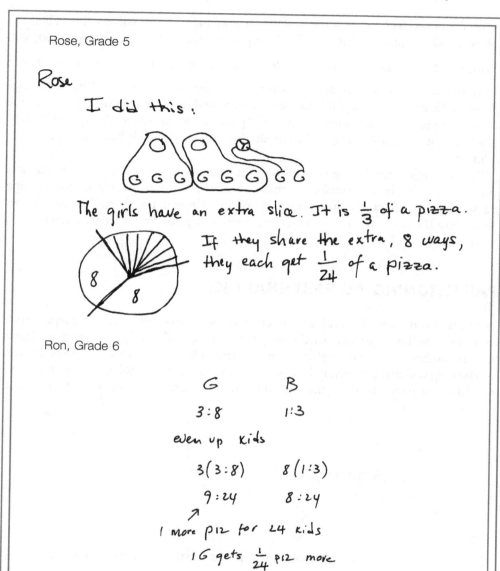

Rose, Grade 5

Rose

I did this:

The girls have an extra slice. It is $\frac{1}{3}$ of a pizza.
If they share the extra, 8 ways,
they each get $\frac{1}{24}$ of a pizza.

8

8

Ron, Grade 6

| G | B |
|---|---|
| 3:8 | 1:3 |

even up kids

3(3:8)     8(1:3)

9:24       8:24

I more piz for 24 kids

1 G gets $\frac{1}{24}$ piz more

## QUOTIENTS

A rational number may be viewed as a quotient, that is, as the result of a division. At an elementary level, $\frac{3}{4}$ may be interpreted as the amount of cake each person gets when 3 cakes are divided equally among 4 people. Later, in high school, one might look at the problem this way: I wish to divide three cakes among 4 people. How much cake will each person receive? Let $x =$ the amount of cake each person will receive. Then the solution will be obtained by solving the equation 4x=3. To solve the equation, you perform a division to get $x = \dfrac{3}{4}$. Still later, in more advanced mathematics, one might study the rational numbers as a quotient field. The study of rational numbers as a quotient field is well beyond the elementary and middle school child, but the foundations for building a solid understanding are laid in the early years. In fact, at their most basic level, quotients arise in fair sharing, an activity well known to preschool children.

Partitioning or fair sharing is a process that begins in preschool years, but is no less important during the elementary and middle school years. To some extent, partitioning plays a role in all of the interpretations of the rational numbers. In this chapter we explore the ways in which classroom activity can promote understand fractions as quotients.

## PARTITIONING AS FAIR SHARING

Partitioning—the act of breaking or fracturing a whole—is the action through which fractions come into existence. Partitioning is the process of dividing an object or objects into a number of disjoint and exhaustive parts. This means that the parts are not overlapping and that everything is included in one of the parts. When we use the word in relation to fractions, it is with the additional stipulation that those parts be of the same size.

is the unit area.

is a partition, but it is not suitable for representing the fraction $\dfrac{3}{4}$ because the pieces do not all have the same area.

The process of partitioning lies at the very heart of rational number understanding. Fractions and decimals are both formed by partitioning. (Note that decimals are based on a division of a unit into 10 equal parts, and each of those parts, into 10 equal parts, etc.). Locating a faction on the number line depends on the division of the unit into equivalent spaces. The roots of the understanding of equivalence—a mathematical notion that applies far more widely than in the fraction world—are laid when performing different partitions that result in the same relative amounts. We could go on. Partitioning is fundamental to the production of quantity, to mathematical concepts, and to reasoning and operations.

In fraction instruction, there are many good reasons to engage students in lots of partitioning activities and for a prolonged period of time. In addition to the fact that partitioning is a fundamental mechanism for building up fraction concepts and operations, it makes use of an activity that has long been part of children's everyday experience: fair sharing. There are very good at sharing cookies and candies, and in that process of sharing, they have experienced the need for fractions when everything did not work out nicely and they had to break food. Most children come to school with some experience in sharing because it has been expected of them since they were toddlers. Even if they do not have a good operational sense of fair sharing, they have primitive ideas and strong opinions about what is fair and what isn't! Thus, partitioning activities build on children's experience and help them to extend their knowledge into new territory.

Even though they have good intuitive strategies for sharing, they may need some reminders about the ground rules for partitioning:

- The unit must be divided into equal shares.
- If a unit consists of more than one item, the items must be the same size.
- *Equal* means equal in amount, but shares do not always have the same number of pieces.
- Equal shares do not have to have the same shape.
- When we have a choice about the shape we use, for example, in representing a cake, we anticipate the number of pieces we will need and choose the shape accordingly. Sometimes it is easier to use a rectangular cake than a round one.

## PARTITIONING ACTIVITIES

Some teachers may avoid partitioning activities in the first and second grades because children do not always have good hand—eye coordination at that age, and they have trouble drawing the correct number of parts and making them all the same size. However, these problems may be circumvented by giving students prepartitioned pictures so that drawing pictures is not an end in itself. The goal should be to keep their concentration on the reasoning process, on the number of shares, and the fairness of shares, rather than on the ability to draw them accurately. For second and third graders, it is a good idea to begin with units in which there are perforations or some form of scored cutting lines. For example, stamps come in perforated sheets (save them from your junk mail), and candy bars are scored for breaking.

Partitioning is best introduced visually. For example, without using your pencil, try to "see" each person's share in the following situation.

● Share 3 pizzas among 6 people.

In your mind, you should see one share as half a pizza.

It is a good idea to ask children to partition visually in order to encourage them to see bigger pieces. When young children in grades K-3 engage in partitioning activities, a common strategy is to divide every piece of the unit into the number of shares needed. This means that if a number of objects are to be shared by three people, they will routinely cut every piece into three parts.

If several objects are to be shared by six people, they will divide every one of the pieces into six parts.

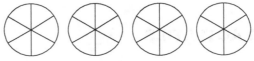

One of the goals of instruction that uses partitioning is to create shares as efficiently as possible. More efficient partitioning requires some form of mental comparison of the amount of stuff to be divided to the number of shares. It involves knowing that you have enough stuff that you will not run out if you give each person a little more or make each share larger. Anticipating or estimating or visualizing that relative size before you start cutting reduces the total number of cuts needed to accomplish the job. The object of partitioning is to be able to name how much is in each share. The more fragmented a share is, the more difficult it will be to name the total amount in that share. By having students look for one share while the pictures are on an overhead, rather than on a paper in front of them, they more easily see shares in larger pieces.

## CHILDREN'S PARTITIONING

It takes children a very long time and many, many partitioning activities to get to the point where they can answer the questions you were asked: How much pizza does each person get? What part of the total pizza is that? I am going to present some pictures of children's work that will help you to see why these questions are so difficult and why it takes so long until children can answer them. Children of many different ages were asked to solve this problem:

Tell how much pizza 1 person will get when 3 people share 4 identical cheese pizzas. Draw a picture to show what each person will receive.

Here are two student papers. Look at A and B and judge which one is more sophisticated. (Remember, the goal is to be able to answer the question: How much does each person receive?)

You can tell that student B's response is more sophisticated. That student actually named the amount $1\frac{1}{3}$ pizzas. Can you tell why student A could not answer the question? One person's share consists of many pieces and before the student could name how much pizza is in one share, that student would have to have a way to patch together all of the pieces.

Here are two more student papers, answering the same question: If 3 people share 4 identical pizzas, how much pizza will each person get?

These solutions are very close, but there is a difference. The difference comes in the way the last pizza was distributed. Each student marked the pizza with 6 equal pieces. Student B "dealt" out the pieces in the fourth pizza: person 1, person 2, person 3, person 1, person 2, person 3. Student A did not cut all of the pieces as marked. Instead, realizing that each person could get 2 pieces, this student made fewer cuts and gave each person a chunk equivalent to 2 slices.

Now look at one more set of student solutions. See if you can rank these four solutions in order from lowest to highest level of sophistication.

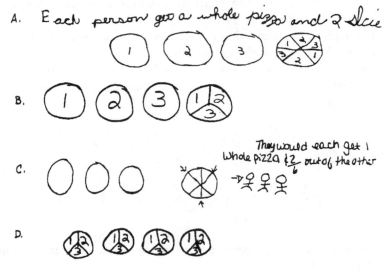

The students rank this way: D, A, C, B. Student D cut every pizza into 3 equal parts and dealt out the pieces like cards. Student A realized that each person could get a whole pizza, but when it came to sharing the last pizza, cut and dealt out 6 slices. Student C, although he or she marked 6 pieces on the fourth pizza, realized that each person could get two of those slices and didn't do as much cutting. This person was able to name the amount of pizza: $1\frac{2}{6}$. Student B showed the most direct solution, with no extra marking or cutting.

The student work was differentiated by the following characteristics: preservation of pieces that do not require cutting, economy in marking, and economy in cutting. These snapshots enabled you to "see" children's cognitive growth from primitive to more complex. Third graders typically use the "cut-em-all-up-and-deal-em-out" strategy. Because of their lack of experience with fractions, and their comfort with counting, a fair share still means *the same number of same size pieces*. The more fragmented a share was, the farther the student was from being able to tell how much pizza was in a share. Students who marked but did not cut, were beginning to chunk the pieces in a share: they were making discoveries about equivalence. Marking without cutting suggests a transitional phase in which a student can still see and count pieces, but is beginning to believe that the sameness of shares has something to do with amount, rather than number of pieces. Students with the best number sense anticipated the fact that there was enough for everyone to get a whole pizza and they knew that dividing the fourth pizza three ways meant that everyone would get $\frac{1}{3}$ of it.

The research from which this student work comes was snapshot research. That is, it looked at children's work at different grade levels. The children had not had specific instruction on partitioning. This type of student work is useful for helping us to understand what children do on their own accord, and hence, how instruction might have to play a role if we want something to happen differently. The research was clear about *how* and *how slowly* children would get to the point where they could answer *how much*. It was also clear that equivalence was the chief concept that facilitated more sophisticated strategies. When instruction supported children's partitioning activities with discussions of equivalence, children's solutions became more unified and they more quickly progressed to the point where they could answer *how much*.

## EQUIVALENCE

It is important that partitioning be much more than fun drawing and shading. As we have seen children's partitioning work can produce many different results and well-crafted comparisons and discussions of those results can push student thinking to new levels.

Some children were given the task of showing how 6 people might share 4 identical rectangular pizzas. Here are some of the pictures they produced. In each case, the shaded area represents 1 share.

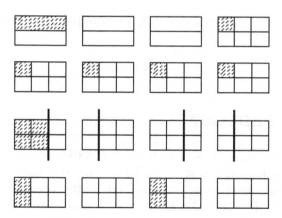

By visually rearranging the shaded parts in each picture, it was easy for children to understand that one person was going to get the same amount of pizza in each case. To facilitate discussion, each piece in a share was given a fractional name and, after agreeing that all of these shares were the same amount, students could agree that all of the symbolic statements were also equivalent.

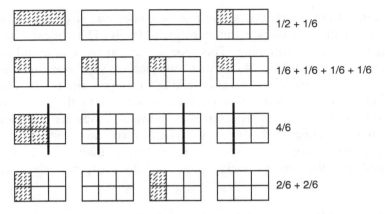

The following discoveries resulted from the activity:

$$\frac{1}{2}+\frac{1}{6}=\frac{4}{6}$$

$$\frac{1}{6}+\frac{1}{6}+\frac{1}{6}+\frac{1}{6}=\frac{4}{6}$$

$$\frac{2}{6}+\frac{2}{6}=\frac{4}{6}$$

The most important question could then be answered: How much pizza does each person get?

$$\frac{4}{6} \text{ of a pizza}$$

## SHOULD WE REDUCE?

Teachers never fail to ask me how important it is in the early stages of instruction to insist on putting fractions in lowest terms. Those who were taught that fractions must *always* be written in lowest form are surprised by my response. Do not insist on reducing too early in the game! There are reasons not to reduce—and you have just encountered one!

Two classes did this partitioning problem on the same day. Because children tend to do more marking than they have to, no one in either class produced a drawing that suggested that one person's share was called $\frac{2}{3}$. One teacher was content to let the students call a share $\frac{4}{6}$ and went on to the next partitioning task. The other teacher produced her own drawing and added it to the ones the students had produced.

After some more discussion, the class realized that $\frac{4}{6} = \frac{2}{3}$. However, her students missed the opportunity to notice the most important aspect of a partitioning activity. Fractions are quotients (answers to division problems). When we divide $a$ things among $b$ people, each person's share is $\frac{a}{b}$. When we divide 4 pizzas among 6 people, everyone gets $\frac{4}{6}$ of a pizza. By requiring an answer in lowest form, the second class had no "ah-ha" experience.

## UNDERSTANDING FRACTIONS AS QUOTIENTS

How long should students participate in partitioning activities? How do we know if a student understands quotients? Many adults believe that there is nothing to it! As students, they were told to remember that a fraction symbol means division, so when you want to enter $\frac{a}{b}$ into your calculator, you enter $a \div b$.

Understanding quotients consists in being able to answer the following questions without having to do any work at all. That is, students need to partition until they say "I don't have to draw any more. I already know the answers to these questions."

1.   How much is one share?
2.   What part of the whole amount is one share?

Let's demonstrate with the following problem:

•   Five people are going to share three identical pepperoni pizzas. How much will each person get? What part of the total pizza is one share?

When 3 pizzas are divided among 5 people, each person gets $\frac{3}{5}$ of a pizza. If 5 people share the pizza, each share is $\frac{1}{5}$ of the unit whole, the total pizza. The number of pizzas being shared is irrelevant to answering the second question. Whether the 5 people are sharing 3 pizzas, or 300 pizzas, each share is $\frac{1}{5}$ of the pizza. In this case, $\frac{1}{5}$ of the total pizza is $\frac{3}{5}$ of a pizza.

In this context, the fraction symbol $\frac{a}{b}$ has multiple meanings. First, it stands for a division ($a \div b$). It is also the rational number that is the result of that division $\left(\frac{a}{b}\right.$ of a

pizza$\left.\right)$, a quotient. It stands for *a pizzas per b people*, a ratio.

## MORE ADVANCED REASONING

Unfortunately, instruction has made very little use of partitioning. It is used implicitly in the beginning of fraction instruction when part—whole fractions are defined: the denominator tells the number of equal parts into which the whole is divided. Students usually make some pictures to represent part—whole comparisons, but then picture drawing is abandoned. This is unfortunate because, although children may quickly *see* that one amount is larger or smaller than another, it takes some time before they are able to quantify differences. "How much more?" is a very difficult question.

As you can see by the range of responses given by the children from multiple grades at the start of this chapter, it takes years to go from "a bite" to "$\frac{1}{24}$ of a pizza." Quantifying *how much more* or *how much less* requires some knowledge of basic fractions ideas and these develop between grades 3 and 6. Nevertheless, even the youngest child used an effective strategy. What is so remarkable about the children's responses is that they intuitively all used the same strategy. You can see that each of them reinterpreted the girls' situation in terms of the boys'.

All of the children took a ratio (#boy pizzas to #boys) and *measured it out of* or *divided it out of* the ratio (#girl pizzas to #girls). Using a kind of double matching process, they reconceptualized the girl's ratio (#girl pizzas : #girls) using the boys' ratio (#boy pizzas:#boys). Quotients and ratios are inextricably linked in this activity.

Let's pretend that the girls are going to get the same amount of pizza per person as the boys got. First group, OK. Second group, OK. The third group doesn't quite work. We end up with 1 pizza for 2 girls. We now know that overall, the girls' group has more pizza, relatively speaking, because in that third grouping, only 2 girls have to share a pizza.

How much extra pizza do the girls have? If those last two girls got the same amount that everyone else got, they would each get $\frac{1}{3}$ of a pizza. So that means there is an extra $\frac{1}{3}$ of a pizza on the girls' side. If they all shared that extra piece, they would all get $\frac{1}{8}$ of $\frac{1}{3}$ or $\frac{1}{24}$ of a pizza. So each girl gets $\frac{1}{24}$ of a pizza more than each boy gets.

The children's responses at the start of the chapter differed mainly in their ability to quantify *how much more*. For the third grader, it was "a bite." The fourth grader realized that the extra $\frac{1}{3}$ pizza would be shared by the 8 girls, but she did not partition the entire pizza and ended up with the wrong number of pieces. The fifth grader partitioned correctly and got $\frac{1}{24}$. The sixth grader did not partition at all; he was able to reason with ratios.

If you know how to subtract using common denominators, you can work out the difference between a girl's share and a boy's share: $\frac{3}{8} - \frac{1}{3} = \frac{1}{24}$. As Ron did, you could get that difference by using ratios. He found equivalent pizza-to-children ratios that have the same number of children in each:

$$(3:8) = (9:24) \text{ and } (1:3) = (8:24)$$

This says that when the number of boys and the number of girls is the same, namely 24, the girls have 1 more pizza. 1 pizza for 24 girls means that each gets $\frac{1}{24}$ of a pizza more than the boys get.

## SHARING DIFFERENT PIZZAS

Suppose, now, that you are ordering two different kinds of pizza. Customarily, people will eat some of each.

- 4 people shared 3 pepperoni pizzas and 1 veggie pizza. How much did each person get?

$$\frac{3}{4} \text{ pepperoni} + \frac{1}{4} \text{ veggie}$$

- 12 people shared pizza. If one person's plate had $\frac{1}{6}$ cheese pizza $+ \frac{1}{6}$ pepperoni pizza $+ \frac{1}{12}$ veggie pizza, how many pizzas of each type were ordered?

$\frac{1}{12}$ means 1 pizza was shared by 12 people; $\frac{1}{6}$ means that 1 pizza was shared by 6 people, so for 12 people, there must have been 2 pizzas. Therefore, the 12 people must have ordered 1 veggie pizza, 2 cheese pizzas, and 2 pepperoni pizzas.

• 12 people ordered some pizzas. One person had $\frac{2}{3}$ cheese pizza + $\frac{1}{4}$ mushroom pizza on his plate. What was the group's order?

$\frac{2}{3}$ means that 2 pizzas were shared by 3 people; so 8 pizzas must have been shared by 12 people. $\frac{1}{4}$ means that 1 pizza was shared by 4 people, so 3 pizzas must have been shared by 12 people. They ordered 8 cheese pizzas and 3 mushroom pizzas.

• 24 people went to a restaurant and ordered 18 cheese pizzas. The restaurant had 1 table for 12 people, 1 table for 6 people, 1 table for 4 people, and 1 table for 2. How should the waiter distribute the pizzas? How much pizza does each person get?

While this is a kind of division problem, it is complicated because, as we divide the pizzas among the tables, we have to preserve proportionality. Everyone needs a fair share regardless of where they are sitting. For this division process, we can use a tree diagram to help organize tables and pizzas. A rectangle denotes a table, the number of people sitting at the table is the number underneath the rectangle, and the number of pizzas served to that table is the number inside the rectangle.

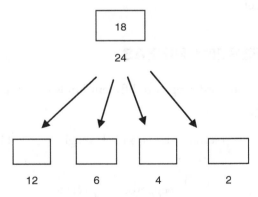

Here is an illustration of the way students reasoned down to get the required numbers of pizzas.

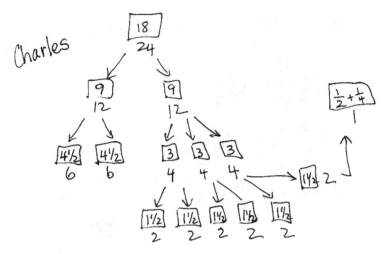

Notice that this thinking holds constant the ratio 18 pizzas to 24 people, but changes numbers of people and numbers of pizza. Thus, if we continued to serve pizza at the same rate, how much would we distribute to different numbers of people? Charlie worked his way down to an appropriate serving for 1 person.

• Would you get more if you were in group A, where 4 people are sharing 3 pizzas or in group B, where 7 people are sharing 5 pizzas?

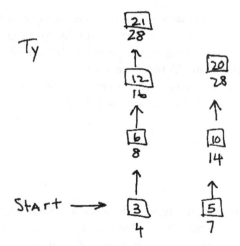

Ty started with each group and reasoned up. Finally, he reached a point at which both groups had 28 people, but their corresponding numbers of pizzas were different. A person in the group where 4 people shared 3 pizzas actually got more pizza.

• A family of 6 shared 3 cheese pizzas and 4 veggie pizzas. How much did each person get?

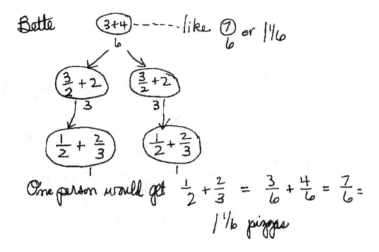

Bette kept the portions of the two different pizzas separate. She realized that it was not appropriate to add different kinds of pizza, so she suggested that *if* we could put all of the pieces together it would be *like* having 7 pizzas for 6 people or $1\frac{1}{6}$ pizzas for each person.

For teachers, there are a number of points to be taken from the children's work.

- Partitioning activities should be presented early in the curriculum and continued for several years.
- The process of quantifying *how much more* develops over a long period of time.
- Quotient and ratio thinking work very naturally together and children use both from an early age. There is no reason to delay the mention of ratios until middle school, as is currently done in most curricula.
- Although quotients are basically about division, the reasoning entailed in answering the question "How much more?" prepares students for addition and subtraction.

## ACTIVITIES

1. Some children drew pictures to show how much each person would get if 3 people shared 4 candy bars. Their partitions are shown. For each picture, write the fraction denoting each piece of a share and determine all of the equivalent parts that you would like the children to discover as they compare these partitions.

2.  If 5 people share 4 candy bars, how much will each person get?

3.  If 4 people share 2 (6-packs) of cola, how much will one share be? What part of the unit is one share?

4.  Three people shared 8 (6-packs) of cola. Students A, B, and C drew pictures to show one share of the cola. Rank the students' strategies according to their sophistication.

5.    Five people shared two pre-partitioned candy bars. Students A, B, C, and D showed how much each person would receive. Analyze the student's work.

6.    At table A, there are 3 children. At table B, there are 4 children. The information below shows how many cookies they share at each table. Decide whether each situation is fair. If not, who gets more, a child at table A or a child at table B? How much more? Do not draw pictures. Reason out loud.

|     | 3 children at table A share | 4 children at table B share |
|-----|-----------------------------|-----------------------------|
| a.  | 3 cookies                   | 5 cookies                   |
| b.  | 7 cookies                   | 8 cookies                   |
| c.  | 8 cookies                   | 10 cookies                  |
| d.  | 9 cookies                   | 12 cookies                  |
| e.  | 1 cookie                    | 1 cookie                    |
| f.  | 4 cookies                   | 5 cookies                   |
| g.  | 2 cookies                   | 5 cookies                   |

7.  Who gets more, a girl or a boy? How much more?

a.  5 cakes          8 cakes

b.  2 cakes          3 cakes

c.  5 cakes          4 cakes

d.  3 cakes          7 cakes

e.

f.

g.

h.

i.

8.  Provide an example showing that equal shares do not have to have the same number of pieces.

9.  Provide an example showing that fair shares do not have to have the same shape.

10. Analyze student responses to this problem. Rank their strategies according to sophistication, giving reasons to support your ranking.

Six children share these candy bars. How much candy does each person get?

Nicole

A get □ and $\frac{1}{3}$

$\frac{1}{6} + \frac{1}{3}$.

B gets the same.

C " " "

D " " "

Steve

Everybody gets $\frac{2}{3}$ of a candy bar.

Eric

Give to each

$\square\square\square$ + □ = $\frac{4}{6}$

of a candy bar.

11. Solve the next question in two ways. First, use the ratio of girl pizzas to # girls to reinterpret the boys' side. Then use the ratio of boy pizzas to # boys to interpret the girls' side. Who gets more, a boy or a girl?

GGG                    BBBBB

12. The symbol $\frac{3}{4}$ designates (a) an operation; (b) a number; and (c) a ratio. Use an example to explain this triple meaning.

13.   A family of 6 shared 3 cheese pizzas and 4 veggie pizzas. How much did each person get?

14.   A class of 20 people had a pizza party for which they ordered 12 pizzas. At the restaurant, some of them sat 4 to a table, and some of them sat 2 to a booth. How many pizzas should the waiter deliver to a table of 4? How many to a booth?

15.   Can someone who is served $\frac{1}{2}$ cheese pizza $+ \frac{1}{3}$ pepperoni pizza be sitting at a 2-for-5 table? Prove your answer.

16.   18 pizzas were ordered for 24 people. Was the distribution of 6 pizzas to 8 and 12 pizzas to 16 people fair?

17.   A group of 30 people ordered some pizzas. One of the people was served $\frac{2}{5}$ of a veggie pizza and $\frac{1}{5}$ of a cheese pizza. What must have been the group order?

18.   My friends and I ordered 3 cheese pizzas and 4 pepperoni pizzas for the 8 of us. Much did each of us get?

19.   Sixteen people ordered some pizzas. One person got $\frac{1}{4}$ of a cheese pizza and $\frac{1}{2}$ of a pepperoni pizza. What must have been the group order? If that person was sitting at a table for 2, how many pizzas and of what type were delivered to his table?

# CHAPTER 9

# Fractions as Operators

## STUDENT STRATEGIES: GRADE 6

Solve this problem yourself. Then tell what happened when each child went to the computer and carried out his or her plan. Tell what size picture (as a fraction of the original) each child produced. (In this case, and throughout the chapter, I will use the word *size* to mean linear dimensions, not area.)

You had a picture on your computer and you made it $\frac{3}{4}$ (or 75%) of its original size. You changed your mind and now you want it back to its original size again. What fraction of its present size should you tell the computer to make it in order to restore its original size?

After solving the problem, the children were given a picture $\frac{3}{4}$ of its original size on a drawing program that allowed them to scale pictures up and down, and they carried out their plans. (The program allowed for scaling any percent from 10% to 1000% of the original dimensions.)

Brigid

First I would make it 4 times bigger then it is now. I would get a picture 3 times its size. This is how I figured it out

Then I would divide by 3 to get its regular size.

Take $\frac{1}{3}$ of it.

1. 400%
2. 33%

Do these steps.

Elliot

To get it to 3/4 you had to do 75% of the original. So that means you took off 25% of its size. To get it back, you could enlarge it 25% by ~~one~~ setting the number at 125%.

Stella R.

If I put this strip of paper in, it will be [12 in.]

$\frac{3}{4}$ will be [9 in.] ( It will get skinny too.)

So I have to do 9 in. x ? = 12 in.

9 x 1 = 9       100 %

9 x $\frac{1}{3}$ = 3       33.333 %

So I will do [133.33 %]

## OPERATORS

In the operator interpretation of rational numbers, we think of rational numbers as functions. In this role, rational numbers act as mappings, taking some set or region, and mapping it onto another set or region. More simply put, the operator notion of rational numbers is about shrinking and enlarging, contracting and expanding, enlarging and reducing, or multiplying and dividing. Operators are transformers that

- lengthen or shorten line segments;
- increase or decrease the number of items in a set of discrete objects; or
- take a figure in the geometric plane, such as a triangle or a rectangle, and map it onto a larger or smaller figure of the same shape.

An operator is a set of instructions for carrying out a process. For example, $\frac{2}{3}$ *of* is an operator that instructs you to multiply by 2 and divide the result by 3. To apply the process of $\frac{2}{3}$ *of*, we perform familiar operations such as multiplication and division. The operations of multiplication and division may be viewed as individual operations or, when one is performed on the result of the other, may be regarded as a single operation. For example, the operator $\frac{2}{3}$ may be viewed as a single operation on a quantity $Q$, or it may be viewed as a multiplication performed on a division on a quantity $Q$, or it may be viewed as a division performed on a multiplication on quantity $Q$:

$$\frac{2}{3}(Q) = 2\left(\frac{Q}{3}\right) = \frac{2Q}{3}$$

- $\frac{2}{3}$ of 6 [ XXX ] [ XXX ] [ XXX ] [ XXX ] (2 copies of 6) ÷ 3 = 4

XX   XX                                    2 copies of (6 ÷ 3) = 4

Notice that you get the same result regardless of the order in which you carry out the operations. Sometimes it makes more sense to do one or the other of the operations first. For example, suppose in trig class, you are converting $\frac{5\pi}{6}$ radians to degrees. Most people reach for their calculator to multiply 5·180 and then they divide the result by 6. They could have done it in their heads if they had done the division first: 180 ÷ 6 = 30 and 5·30 = 150 degrees.

- Troy has $1\frac{2}{5}$ as many baseball cards as I have. I have 55 cards. How many does Troy have?

  $\frac{7}{5} \cdot 55 = ?$ It is harder to do 7·55 in your head than it is to do 5 into 55 and then 7 · 11.

- I canned 40 pounds of tomatoes last year. Jan did $\frac{5}{6}$ as many. How many pounds did Jan can?

  $\frac{5}{6} \cdot 40 = ?$ It is harder to divide 6 into 40 and then multiply by 5. It is easier to divide by 6 after multiplying 5·40 = 200.

Particularly when applying an operator to a set of discrete objects, it is easy to see and interpret the results. Suppose the following diagram shows the effects of an operator in two stages. Without regard to which operation was performed first or second, we want to decide what the operator was.

- We begin with a set of 4 objects and perform two operations. The result of the first operations is that 4 objects became 2, so we much have divided by 2.

After the application of the second operation, the set of 2 objects was enlarged to 18, so it must have been multiplied by 9. Composing the two operations, this is equivalent to operating on a set of 4 objects by multiplying by 9 and dividing by 2, so the operator is $\frac{9}{2}$. We can express this is in the following symbolic statement: $4\left(\frac{9}{2}\right) = 18.$

- We can show the effects of an operator in a single drawing as well. Consider a set of objects and write a symbolic statement expressing the operator that acted upon them, as well as the result.

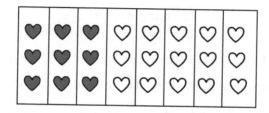

In this example, an operator acted upon a set of discrete objects. There are 24 hearts. They have been partitioned into 8 equal parts. 3 out of the 8 parts have been shaded. So $24\left(\dfrac{3}{8}\right) = 9.$

Here are an area and a length after different operators have acted upon them.

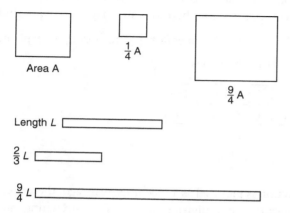

In the process of applying an operator, both shrinking and enlarging (contacting and expanding, enlarging and reducing) may take place. The end result of the process is shrinking or enlarging, depending on which has dominated the process: the end result of a $\dfrac{4}{3}$ *of* operator will be enlarging because it specifies more enlarging that reduction. It enlarges by a factor of 4 and reduces by a factor of 3. However, an operator of $\dfrac{3}{4}$ will have the effect of making the object it is acting upon smaller because it does more contracting than it does expanding.

The operator interpretation of rational numbers is very different from part—whole comparisons and quotients. In the operator interpretation, the significant relationship is the comparison between the quantity resulting from an operation and the quantity that is acted upon. The operator defines the relationship

$$\frac{\text{quantity out}}{\text{quantity in}}.$$

- 12 candies and 18 candies relate to each other in a two-to-three way when the operator $\frac{2}{3}$ of acts on a set of 18 candies to produce 12 candies.

- 35 candies relate to 20 candies in a seven-to-four way when the operator $1\frac{3}{4}$ of acts on a set of 20 candies to produce a set of 35 candies.

## EXCHANGE MODELS

The input–output relationship suggests the connection of the operator to functions. Another representation, the function table, situated either vertically or horizontally, may be used to list various input and output values. Then students may be asked to find the rule that relates the input and the output. The operator $\frac{2}{3}$ of, for example, explains the relationship between the sets given in the tables.

| Input | 6 | 9 | 60 | 150 |
|--------|---|---|----|-----|
| Output | 4 | 6 | 40 | 100 |

$$\text{output} = \frac{2}{3} \text{ input}$$

Sometimes the input–output function is pictured as a machine. Years ago, there were math programs that built multiplication and division ideas using stretching and shrinking machines. They operated on sticks of various lengths to lengthen or shorten them. A slightly different model is a machine that acts like an exchanger. For example, you put money into a machine to purchase bus tokens and, in exchange for some number of coins, you get a number of tokens.

In the case of the stick stretcher, the label on the front of the machine would identify that machine as a 1-for-2 machine, or a $\frac{1}{2}$ machine, because it proportionally reduces any length stick that is inserted to half its length. The label on the token machine will identify it as a 2-for-5 machine, or a $\frac{2}{5}$ machine, because the ratio of tokens it spits out to the number quarters deposited will always be 2 to 5.

It is not too difficult to determine the operator if you think of the fractions as multiplications and divisions.

Think of $\frac{7}{10}$ as $7 \cdot \frac{1}{10}$. think of $\frac{1}{2}$ as $1 \cdot \frac{1}{2}$.

Then you have $7 \cdot \frac{1}{10}( \ ) = 1 \cdot \frac{1}{2}$.

$7 \cdot \frac{1}{7} = 1$ and $\frac{1}{10} \cdot 5 = \frac{1}{2}$.

So the operator is $\frac{1}{7} \cdot 5 = \frac{5}{7}$.

Bartering situations and currency exchange problems also embody the concept of an operator as an exchanger.

- Harry and Dan agree that 3 chocolate bars for 4 (5-packs) of gum is a fair exchange. If Dan gives Harry 42 chocolate bars, how many packs of gum should Harry give Dan? What is the operator?

  The operator is the rate of exchange: 4-for-3 or $\frac{4}{3}$.

  The operator acts upon the input (the chocolate bars): $\frac{4}{3} \cdot 42 = 56$.
  Harry owes Dan 56 packs of gum.

- $1 US is worth 0.825 Euros today. If I give the bank $50, how many Euros will I get? (Let's ignore the fees for changing money.)

  I am putting US dollars into the machine and getting out Euros, so the operator acts upon the input (US dollars) and the machine gives out Euros. The operator is 0.825 for 1.

  $$0.825 (50) = 41.25 \text{ Euros.}$$

  I have 30 Euros and I exchange them for US dollars before coming back to the states. In machine language, Euros go in and dollars come out.

  $$\text{The operator is 1 for } 0.825 = \frac{1}{0.825} = 1.212.$$

  The operator acts upon Euros: $(1.212)(30) = \$36.36$.
  All unit conversions work on an input-output model as well.

- Convert 16,000 pounds to tons (1 ton = 2000 pounds).

  Input is pounds. Output is tons. So the operator is $\frac{1}{2000}$. $16000 \cdot \frac{1}{2000} = 8$ tons.

## COMPOSITION

Our airport has machines that perform two functions. They will allow you to buy bus tokens or train tickets. You can deposit quarters and choose to receive tokens or train tickets by pressing the appropriate buttons. You can also trade bus tokens for train tickets.

When you put in quarters and want train tickets, this machine can be seen as a system composed of two machines. The second machine operates on the output of the first. Although both machines perform operations and have their own ID tags that describe what they do, the *system* also has an ID.

The first machine performs a 2-for-3 exchange $\left(\dfrac{10}{15} = \dfrac{2}{3}\right)$.

The second machine performs a 1-for-5 exchange $\left(\dfrac{2}{10} = \dfrac{1}{5}\right)$.

The second machine operates on the output of the first $\dfrac{1}{5}\left(\dfrac{2}{3}\right) = \dfrac{2}{15}$ and the result of this multiplication is the system ID. The full system accomplishes a 2-for-15 exchange.

In mathematical terms, this system is a *composition*. When you perform some operation, then perform another operation on the result of the first operation, it is possible to *compose* operations, or do a single operation that is a combination of the two.

Part of what it means to understand operators is that you can name the system (the composition) and not merely its components. Also, given the system ID and the function of one of the machines, you should be able to discover what the other machine does. Compositions occur frequently in everyday applications that involve successive increasing and decreasing. We will look at department store discounting and at shrinking or enlarging on a copy machine. The second operation (increase or decrease) is always performed on the result of the first operation.

- From 1980 to 1990, there was a population decrease of 10% in a certain city. The next census covering the years from 1990 to 2000 reported that, due to economic recovery, the city's population increased by 10% since the last census. How does the population of the city in 2000 compare to the population in 1980?

| 1980 population | Decrease by | Increase by |
|---|---|---|
| $100\% = \dfrac{100}{100}$ | 10% of 100 = 10 | 10% of 90 = 9 |
| Result | 90% (of the 1980 pop.) | 99% (of the 1980 pop.) |

This means that after a decrease of 10% followed by an increase of 10%, we do not break even. The population is not back to the 1980 figure.

- Yesterday, our department store had a sale—30% off. Today, they advertised that they are taking 10% off their already-reduced prices. The store advertises sales this way because they can fool many people who think that they are going to get 40% off. They think they are getting a better deal than they really are!

    Yesterday, I would have paid 70% or 0.7 of the ticket price on an item I wanted. Today, they will take 10% off yesterday's price. So I would pay 0.9 of yesterday's price. 0.9 (0.7) = 0.63. If I pay 63% of the price, then the discount must be 100% − 63% = 37%.

- You reduced a picture to 80% of its original size and later learned that you were supposed to enlarge it by 20%, not reduce it by 20%. Unfortunately, you lost the original. What can you do to the 80% copy to obtain a copy that is 120% of the original size?

How can I operate on the 80% size to get 120% of the original size?

$$( ) \cdot \frac{4}{5} = \frac{6}{5}$$

Remember that you can split the shrinking part from the enlarging part of an operator and deal with one operation at a time. Let's look at the denominator first. What times 5 = 5?

$$\left(\frac{}{1}\right) \cdot \frac{4}{5} = \frac{6}{5}$$

Now look at the numerator. What times 4 gives 6? $4 \cdot \frac{6}{4} = 6$

$$\left(\frac{\frac{6}{4}}{1}\right) \cdot \frac{4}{5} = \frac{6}{5}$$

The operator is $\frac{6}{4} = 1\frac{1}{2}$.

You should put the picture into the copier and set it to 150%.

The copy machine problem solved by the children at the start of the chapter entails the composition of shrinking and enlarging functions. We have seen in the examples above that shrinking and enlarging are multiplicative processes, rather than additive ones. Elliot's solution, typical of many children's solutions, is an additive one. He thinks that shrinking the picture involved subtracting something from its size, so he proposes to "ellarge" by adding 25%. When he set the computer's scaling control at 125%, the computer produced a picture that was $\frac{3}{4} \cdot \frac{5}{4} = \frac{15}{16}$ of its original size. Brigid was very close. She proposed to enlarge the $\frac{3}{4}$-size picture to 400% then reduce that version to $\frac{1}{3}$ its size. When she entered 400%, the computer produced a version of the picture that was 3 times the original size, and when she entered 33%, she got a version that was $\frac{99}{100}$ of the original size. The small discrepancy is due to her failure to use a precise enough percentage for $\frac{1}{3}$ $\left(33\frac{1}{3}\% \text{ or } 33.33\%\right)$. Stella entered a more accurate figure, 133.33%, and the computer produced a figure that was virtually indistinguishable from the original.

This problem calls for an "undoing" of the original reduction. The opposite process to multiplying by $\frac{3}{4}$ is multiplying by $\frac{4}{3}$. Notice that $\frac{3}{4} \cdot \frac{4}{3} = 1$. This means that multiplying by $\frac{4}{3}$ is the opposite process of multiplying by $\frac{3}{4}$, and thus returns the unit, the full-size picture. $\frac{4}{3} = 1\frac{1}{3} = 133.33\%$.

## AREA MODEL FOR MULTIPLICATION

The composition of operators leads very naturally to fraction multiplication. For example, $\frac{2}{3}\left(\frac{3}{4}\right)$ means "take $\frac{2}{3}$ of $\frac{3}{4}$ of a unit" and it is equivalent to taking "$\frac{6}{12}$ or $\frac{1}{2}$ of the unit." An area model is a convenient way to illustrate these compositions.

• $\frac{2}{3} \cdot \frac{3}{4}$

Let ⬜ represent the unit area and shade $\frac{3}{4}$ of it.

Now the operator $\frac{2}{3}$ *of* will operate on the result obtained by applying the operator $\frac{3}{4}$ *of*. That is, we will take $\frac{2}{3}$ of ($\frac{3}{4}$ of 1). We used vertical divisions to show the first operator. Now use horizontal lines to divide the area into thirds. Shade $\frac{2}{3}$ of the first shading.

Notice that the unit consists of 12 small rectangles, so the double-shaded region is $\frac{6}{12}$. If you do some visual rearranging of the double-shaded pieces, you will see a way to rename the product. After moving the two pieces as the arrow indicates, the result can be "read" as $\frac{1}{2}$.

- $2\dfrac{1}{3} \times \dfrac{1}{2}$

 is 1, then $2\dfrac{1}{3}$ copies of 1 is

Now take $\dfrac{1}{2}$ of $\left(2\dfrac{1}{3} \text{ of } 1\right)$:

The unit is 6 squares and we have 7 double-shaded squares.

The result is $\dfrac{7}{6}$.

The double-shaded pieces may be visually reorganized to create a mixed number. Visually move them to these positions:

and then you can see that they are $1\dfrac{1}{6}$ of the unit.

This model is a good one, but models have their limits! This model wears out (that is, it becomes too difficult to be useful for children) when multiplying mixed numbers by mixed numbers.

- $1\dfrac{1}{2} \cdot 3\dfrac{1}{4}$

We need more than 3 copies of $1\dfrac{1}{2}$, so we begin with 4 copies.

Now shade $3\dfrac{1}{4}$ of these.

There are 78 double-shaded squares out of 16 in the unit. So we get $\frac{78}{16}$ and with a little visual regrouping, we can see that that is $4\frac{7}{8}$.

## AREA MODEL FOR DIVISION

Division may also be interpreted as the composition of two operators and may be modeled using an area model.

- $\frac{3}{4} \div \frac{2}{3}$

  The division answers the question: "How many $\frac{2}{3}$ s are there in $\frac{3}{4}$?"

  Let [ ] be the unit and shade $\frac{3}{4}$ of it.

  In the horizontal direction, divide the unit into thirds but DO NOT SHADE.

  How much is $\frac{2}{3}$ of 1? Notice that it is the area of 8 squares.

  So our division question becomes: How many times can we measure an area of $\frac{2}{3}$ (or 8 small squares) out of the shaded area representing $\frac{3}{4}$?

Out of the area $\frac{3}{4}$ we can measure the area $\frac{2}{3}$ once and then we have 1 small square out of the next 8. So the answer is $1\frac{1}{8}$ times.

Notice that the unit area was used to determine the area that corresponds to $\frac{3}{4}$ and $\frac{2}{3}$, but the divisor, $\frac{2}{3}$, became the new unit of measure and the remainder was written as part of that unit.

- $\frac{5}{7} \div \frac{1}{3}$

$\frac{1}{3}$ is equivalent to 7 small rectangles. So we ask: How many times can we measure $\frac{1}{3}$ (7 small rectangles) out of $\frac{5}{7}$ (the shaded region)?

We can do that twice with 1 rectangle remaining. So we get $2\frac{1}{7}$.

## COMPOSITIONS AND PAPER FOLDING

Paper folding activities also illustrate compositions.

Take an $8\frac{1}{2}''$ by $11''$ sheet of paper as your unit. Again you are using an area model. The unit area is the area of the sheet of paper. Fold it in half by bring the $8\frac{1}{2}''$ edges together. You have in front of you the result of taking $\frac{1}{2}$ of 1. We can write it this way:

Now fold in half again. With your second fold, you have taken $\frac{1}{2}$ of $\left(\frac{1}{2}$ of $1\right)$. Record the result this way:

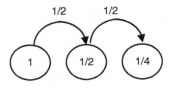

Think: I divided the half unit into 2 equal pieces and now each piece is called $\frac{1}{4}$.

Shade the rectangle that faces you. Now open up the paper and see what part of it is shaded. You should be able to see that the shaded region is $\frac{1}{4}$.

$$\frac{1}{2} \text{ of } \left( \frac{1}{2} \text{ of } 1 \right) = \frac{1}{4}$$

- Use paper folding to show this operation: $\frac{1}{4}$ of $\frac{2}{3}$

  First fold a paper into thirds. (Bend the paper into an S shape and make the edges even.) Open the paper, shade $\frac{2}{3}$, and refold it so that only the shaded area is facing you, like this:

You have done this:

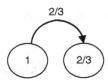

Now fold into fourths. With a different color, shade the area that is facing you. Open the paper and determine what part of the unit area your shaded area represents.

You should be able to see that it is $\frac{2}{12}$.

Paper folding helps to convey the sense that a composition is a rule describing the result of an action performed on the result of a previous action. It also helps build a base of understanding for fraction multiplication and is particularly effective in demonstrating that a product is not always larger than its factors. For example, it is quite clear to children that the result of taking $\frac{1}{4}$ of $\frac{2}{3}$ is not something larger than $\frac{2}{3}$.

The arrow notation helps children to keep track of the process and the written record helps them to see very quickly the algorithm for multiplication of fractions.

## UNDERSTANDING OPERATORS

To say that a student understands rational numbers as operators means that:

1.  the student can interpret a fractional multiplier in a variety of ways:

    a.  $\frac{3}{4}$ means $3 \cdot \left( \frac{1}{4} \text{ of a unit} \right)$;

    b.  $\frac{3}{4}$ means $\frac{1}{4}$ of (3 times a unit).

2.  when two operations (multiplication and division) are performed one on the result of the other, the student can name a single fraction to describe the composite operation:

    a.  multiplying the unit by $\frac{3}{4}$;

    b.  dividing a unit by 4 and then multiplying that result by 3 is the same as multiplying the unit by $\frac{3}{4}$.

3.  the student can identify the effect of an operator and can state a rule relating inputs and outputs:

    a.  an input of 9 and an output of 15 results from a 15-for-9 operator (an operator that enlarges), symbolized as $\frac{15}{9}$;

    b.  the output is $\frac{15}{9}$ of the input.

4.  the student can use models to identify a single composition that characterizes a composition of compositions:

$$\frac{2}{3} \text{ of } \left( \frac{3}{4} \text{ of a unit} \right) = \frac{1}{2} \text{ of a unit.}$$

## ACTIVITIES

1.  Taking $\frac{1}{3}$ of the result of taking $\frac{3}{4}$ of something is equivalent to multiplying your original amount by _____ .

2.    My company has 5 systems, each of which involves two machines hooked up so that the output from one immediately feeds into the next. We would like to have a name for each system. Using the given information, please come up with a name for each system.

| System | Input | Machine 1 | Output | Machine 2 | Output | System Name |
|--------|-------|-----------|--------|-----------|--------|-------------|
| 1 | 15 | 2-for-5 | | 5-for-2 | | |
| 2 | 20 | 2-for-5 | | 1-for-4 | | |
| 3 | 2 | 3-for-1 | | 3-for-2 | | |
| 4 | 9 | 2-for-3 | | 4-for-1 | | |
| 5 | 24 | 3-for-4 | | 2-for-3 | | |

3.  Fill in the missing information about this machine.

| Input | Output |
|-------|--------|
| 12 | |
| | 12 |
| 9 | |
| | 4 |
| 1 | |

4.  In a certain school, $\frac{5}{9}$ of the teachers are female, $\frac{3}{8}$ of the male teachers are single, and $\frac{1}{3}$ of the single males are over 50. What fraction of the teachers are single males under 50?

5.  Each of the following diagrams shows the effect of an operator. What was the operator? Write a complete statement showing the operator, the quantity it operated upon, and the result: (operator) • $(x) = y$

   a.

b.

c.

6. Use pictures to show two different ways to take $\frac{2}{3}$ of a set of 9 dots.

7. Are these machines performing different functions? Put the name of each machine on its label.

8. Write a complete multiplication statement ($a \cdot b = c$) based on each of these models.

a.

b.

c.

d.

9. Can you see $\frac{1}{4}$ of $\frac{1}{3}$ of $\frac{1}{2}$? Shade it. How many pieces of that size would it take to make the whole area? Name the product $\frac{1}{4} \cdot \frac{1}{3} \cdot \frac{1}{2}$.

10. Write the name of the shaded area as a product of fractions.

a.    b.    c.

11. Use an area model to do the following multiplications:

    a. $\dfrac{3}{4} \times \dfrac{1}{2}$    b. $1\dfrac{1}{3} \times \dfrac{3}{5}$    c. $1\dfrac{1}{2} \times \dfrac{1}{3}$

12. Use an area model to do the following divisions:

    a. $\dfrac{3}{5} \div \dfrac{1}{3}$    b. $\dfrac{2}{3} \div \dfrac{5}{8}$    c. $1\dfrac{3}{4} \div \dfrac{2}{5}$    d. $1\dfrac{5}{6} \div 1\dfrac{1}{3}$

13. The equivalent of 1 Israel New Shekel (ILS) is 0.2239 US dollars. How many ILS can I get for $50 US?

14. One South African Rand (ZAR) can be exchanged today for 0.161 US dollars. How many US dollars can I get for 50 ZAR?

15. Find the number of men and the number of women if you know that there are 16 children.

16. My cousin made me a poster by blowing up a picture from our vacation together to 360% of its original size. It looked too blurry, so we decided to make it only 220% of its original size. We took it to the copy store to get it reduced. What percent of its present size should we request?

17. Use an input–output machine to set up each calculation.

    a. 250 millimeters = _____ centimeters
    b. 224 ounces = _____ pounds
    c. 65 minutes = _____ seconds
    d. 22 gallons = _____ quarts
    e. 280 centimeters = _____ meters

18. Standard sizes for photographs are 4 × 6, 5 × 7, and 8 × 10. Can a photocopier be used to enlarge a 4 × 6 photo to one of the other standard sizes or not? Show how you can figure this out.

19. Name some sizes to which you could reduce an 8 × 10 photograph.

20. Yesterday I saved $15 on a blouse that was originally marked $65. My sister bought the same blouse today at the same store and got an additional 10% off of yesterday's prices. How much did she save?

21. You start with a certain quantity and successive increases and decreases are performed on the quantity. On the result of your first action, another increase or decrease is performed. What percent of the original quantity will result?

    a. A decrease of 10% is followed by an increase of 15%.
    b. An increase of 10% is followed by a decrease of 10%.
    c. A decrease of 50% is followed by an increase of 60%.
    d. An increase of 20% is followed by a decrease of 50%.
    e. A decrease of 30% is followed by an increase of 25%.

22. Fold a unit into sixths and shade $\frac{5}{6}$. Fold another unit into ninths and shade $\frac{4}{9}$. Refold both units. Continue the folding process on each unit until the denominators of the resulting units are the same.

    Rename $\frac{5}{6}$ and $\frac{4}{9}$ in terms of the new denominator.

23. Use paper folding to perform the following composition. Write the notation for two more compositions that also result in $\frac{1}{24}$, each having a different number of steps.

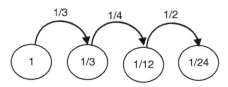

24. For each problem, (a) find the operator and (b) solve the problem.

    a. Manny and Penny agree that a fair exchange is $1\frac{1}{3}$ chocolate bars for 6 doughnuts. If Manny gives Penny 6 candy bars, how many doughnuts should she give him?

    b. Manny and Penny agree that a fair exchange is 6 sodas for $\frac{2}{3}$ of a pizza. If Penny gives Manny 21 sodas, how much pizza should he give her?

    c. Manny and Penny agree that a fair trade is 10 peanuts for $\frac{1}{4}$ of a chocolate bar. If Manny gives Penny 3 chocolate bars, how many peanuts should he give her?

    d. Manny and Penny agree that a fair trade is 2 peach pies for 5 apple pies. If Penny gives Manny 6 apple pies, how many peach pies should he give her?

25.    You have a photo that has been reduced to half the size of the original. At what % do you need to set a copying machine to copy this photo to produce an image that is 20% larger than the original?

26.    Bradley's had a sale yesterday and they advertised 30% off marked prices on all winter coats. Today they advertised that they would take off an additional 25%. If you buy a coat today, what percent will you save?

# CHAPTER 10

# Fractions as Measures

## STUDENT STRATEGIES: GRADE 4

Students were given this number line and their job was to use successive partitioning until they could name the point marked on it. Do this problem yourself, and compare your result to the points the students named.

## MEASURES OF DISTANCE

Rational numbers measure directed distances of certain points from zero in terms of some unit distance. (We say *directed* because rational numbers may be negative, as on a thermometer, and we say *certain* points because there are other points on a number line whose distance from zero cannot be measured with rational numbers.) The rational numbers become strongly associated with those points and we speak of them as if they are points, but they are, in fact, measures of distance. With this caveat, we continue to refer to rational numbers as points on the number line, and we restrict ourselves to the positive rational numbers.

Under the measure interpretation, a fraction is usually the measure assigned to some interval or region, depending on whether we are using a one- or two-dimensional model. In a one-dimensional space, a fraction measures the distance of a certain point on the number line from zero. The unit is always an interval of length $l$ if you are working on a number line. In a two-dimensional space, a fraction measures area. When an interval of length $l$, for example, is partitioned until there are b equal subintervals, then each of the subintervals is of length $\frac{1}{b}$. In this case, the measure interpretation of the fraction $\frac{a}{b}$ means *a intervals of length $\frac{l}{b}$*.

## STATIC AND DYNAMIC MEASUREMENT

A unit of measure can always be divided up into finer and finer subunits so that you may take as accurate a reading as you need. On a number line, on a graduated beaker, on a ruler or yardstick or meter stick, on a measuring cup, on a dial, or on a thermometer, some subdivisions of the unit are marked. The marks on these common measuring tools allow readings that are accurate enough for most general purposes, but if the amount of stuff that you are measuring does not exactly meet one of the provided hash marks, it certainly does not mean that it cannot be measured. Fractions provide us with a means to measure *any* amount of stuff. For example, if meters will not do, we can partition into decimeters; when decimeters will not do, we can partition into centimeters, or millimeters, and so on.

When we talk about fractions as measures, the focus is on successively partitioning the unit. Certainly partitioning plays an important role in the other models and interpretations that we have discussed, but there is a difference. There is a dynamic aspect to measurement that is not captured in most textbook exercises. Instead of comparing the number of equal parts you have to a fixed number of equal parts in a unit, the number of equal parts in the unit can vary, and what you name your fractional amount depends on how many times you are willing to keep up the partitioning process.

- Locate $\frac{3}{4}$ on this number line.

While this example is nominally a measure problem, it is essentially like a problem that asks children to shade $\frac{3}{4}$ of a pizza. The children are told to make 4 equal subintervals and to mark the end of the third interval.

- How far from the starting point is turtle?

This problem asks students to determine an appropriate fractional name for the turtle's position. The task requires successive partitioning until one of your hash marks falls on the turtle's point and it can then be given a name.

As students engage in successive acts of partitioning, they will become confused and lose track of how many subintervals they have. Therefore, it is helpful to use the arrow notation (previously used in paper folding) to record the number of equal parts into which each existing subinterval is partitioned and the resulting name of the new subintervals.

- Locate $\frac{17}{24}$ on the given number line.

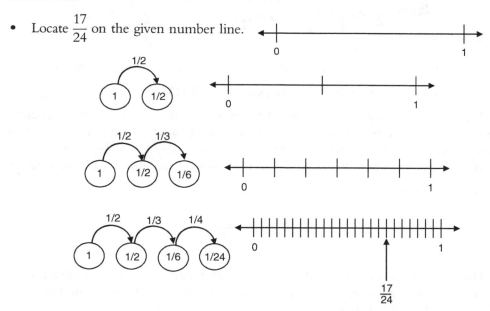

# THE GOALS OF SUCCESSIVE PARTITIONING

It is easy to construct problems that require successive partitioning. For example, draw a unit segment of length 10 cm and place a point at 29 mm, but do not reveal these measurements to the students. Later, this information can help you to provide feedback to let them know how close they came to the actual measurement. You can divide their fractions to see how close they come to 0.29.

Part of the goal in these activities is to have the students gain a sense of how fractional numbers relate to each other and where they are located in relation to $\frac{1}{2}$ and to the unit. To keep students focused on that goal and to make the partitioning process more reflective, it helps to have them comment on their location after each new step in the partitioning process. Barb's work on the turtle problem illustrates this commentary.

The turtle's actual distance from the starting mark was 33.5 out of 100 mm or 0.335. Barb's fraction shows that she was very close. $\frac{11}{32} = 0.34375$.

At first, students "equal" segments did not look so equal, but with more experience, they were able to partition much more accurately. They made a game of trying to get as close as possible to the actual measurement. At first, it should not be a concern that every subinterval is not of the same size. It is no worse than a third grader who draws this representation of $\frac{3}{4}$:

The idea is there. Similarly, in the successive partitioning process, the emphasis is on having students experience the relative positions of the fractions on the number line. The accuracy comes in time.

The student work shown at the beginning of the chapter illustrates what happens as human error and individual choice play out in a successive partitioning problem. The actual fraction was about 25 out of 89 mm, or $\frac{25}{89}$ or 0.28. Both children were close. Allan's fraction was about 0.29 and Paige's was 0.30. No matter. Both of them chose to carry out the partitioning process in different ways, and they ended up with subintervals of different lengths. Nevertheless, both carried out the process correctly and they correctly named their fractions.

# UNDERSTANDING FRACTIONS AS MEASURES

Experience with fractions as measures entails a dynamic movement among an infinite number of stopping-off places along the number line, and helps students to build a sense of the density of rational numbers, a sense of order and relative magnitudes of rational numbers, and a richer understanding of the degrees of accuracy in measurement. In short, this fluidity, flexibility, and comfort in navigating among fractions is what is referred to as *fraction sense*.

It is unlikely that any other fraction interpretation can come close to the power of the number line for building number sense. In a previous chapter, where we talked about reasoning with fractions, you saw the work of Martin and Alicia. Both of these students began their fraction instruction with the measure interpretation. Their comfort with fractions and their flexible thinking came from their fluid movement on the number line. As they moved back and forth on the number line during in their successive partitioning problems, they gained a superb sense of relative sizes, relative locations, and of fraction equivalence. The power of this interpretation cannot be over-emphasized! Martin and the group of students he worked with in class, abandoned the physical act of partitioning and were able to reason about size and order of fractions with ease by the time they were in fifth grade.

Simply stated, the *density property of rational numbers* says that between any two fractions there is an infinite number of fractions and that you can always get as close as you like to any point with a fraction. You will undoubtedly notice the remarkable likeness to the measurement principle that says we can make any measurement as accurate as we like by breaking down our unit of measure into smaller and smaller subunits. This closer and closer approximation is enabled by the density of the rational numbers.

- Name three fractions between $\frac{1}{4}$ and $\frac{1}{3}$.

  We know that when we have partitioned the unit interval into twelfths, $\frac{1}{4}$ is renamed as $\frac{3}{12}$, and $\frac{1}{3}$ is equivalent to $\frac{4}{12}$.

  If we partition the interval between $\frac{3}{12}$ and $\frac{4}{12}$ again, this time dividing it into two equal parts, then our new subunits will be twenty-fourths and $\frac{3}{12}$ and $\frac{4}{12}$ will be named $\frac{6}{24}$ and $\frac{8}{24}$, respectively.

  If we partitioned the interval between $\frac{3}{12}$ and $\frac{4}{12}$ again by dividing each subunit into three equal parts, then our subunits will each be $\frac{1}{36}$ of the units and our given fractions will be renamed $\frac{9}{36}$ and $\frac{12}{36}$. Then it is easy to see that $\frac{10}{36}$ and $\frac{11}{36}$ lie between them.

Commercially available products such as fraction strips, rods, and blocks (length and area models) provide students some experience with different units and subunits of measure, but they have severe limitations. They do not allow students the freedom to break down the unit into any number of subdivisions. The subdivisions available to the user are restricted by the size of the pieces supplied, while on the number line, a given unit can be divided into any number of congruent parts. After using certain predetermined subunits in manipulative products, most students fail to recognize the infinite number of subdivisions allowable on the number line. Often when they no longer have lengths or areas to provide visual means of making comparisons, we discover that they have not developed any reasoning or strategies or even any intuitions about how to compare two fractions in size.

In summary, it may be said that students understand fractions as measures when they (a) are comfortable with successive partitioning; (b) are able to find any number of fractions between two given fractions; and (c) are able to compare any two fractions.

## UNITS, EQUIVALENT FRACTIONS, AND COMPARISONS

Because we have choices as to the size of subunit we can use to measure a distance from zero, the compensatory principle and fraction equivalence also come into play. The smaller the subunit used to measure the distance, the more of those subunits will be needed; the larger the subunit, the fewer that will be needed to cover the distance. When two different subunits are used to cover the same distance, different fraction names result. There is only one rational number associated with a specific distance from zero, and the two fractions are equivalent names for that distance.

- The unit is invariant, and so is the distance of any point from zero, but because the unit may be subdivided into any number of congruent parts, a point may be identified by different names.

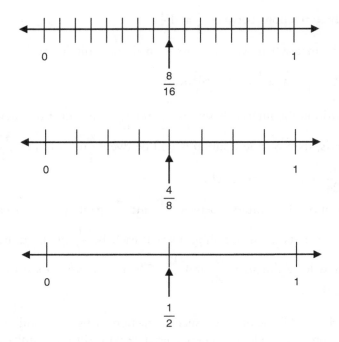

In part–whole comparisons, we are given the unit in a problem's context, (either implicitly or explicitly). If it is given implicitly, we can reason up or down to determine the unit. Likewise, when using fractions to measure distances on the number line, we must have the unit interval marked, or else we need information to tell us the size of the subintervals between the hash marks. Once we know the size of the subintervals, we can determine the unit interval.

- Given the point $\frac{2}{3}$, determine point x.

If $\frac{2}{3}$ consists of 10 subintervals, then $\frac{1}{3}$ must consist of 5. The unit, or $\frac{3}{3}$, must consist of 15. If each subinterval represents $\frac{1}{15}$, then the distance of $x$ from 0 must be $\frac{6}{15}$.

But if 1 is 15 subintervals in length, then $\frac{1}{5}$ must be 3, and $\frac{2}{5}$ must be 6. This means that $\frac{6}{15} = \frac{2}{5}$.

- Which fraction is larger, $\frac{2}{3}$ or $\frac{5}{7}$?

Grade 4

Grade 5

Grade 6

In addition to illustrating a comparison on the number line, this example of children's work shows the development of their thinking across grade levels. The fourth grader anticipated that twenty-firsts were going to be needed, but after getting 21 subintervals, didn't know how many of them would constitute $\frac{1}{7}$. His work is promising because it suggests that he knew he was going to need 21 as a common denominator, but he needed a reminder that he could have reasoned down to $\frac{1}{7}$ so that he could locate it on his number line.

21 spaces make 1 whole

3 spaces make $\frac{1}{7}$

The fifth grader was accurate with her partitioning, and clearly showed that $\frac{5}{7} > \frac{2}{3}$.

Her teacher pointed out that she could have gone one step farther and noted the equivalent fractions $\frac{5}{7} = \frac{15}{21}$ and $\frac{2}{3} = \frac{14}{21}$ to make her point. The sixth grader showed very little work, but seemed to realize that $\frac{5}{7}$ was just a little smaller than $\frac{5}{6}$, so $\frac{2}{3}$, which is $\frac{4}{6}$, had to be smaller than $\frac{5}{7}$. Knowing nothing about him, you might think that because his work is so sparse, that it was just a lucky guess. In reality, his work is typical of sixth graders whose fraction work had concentrated on measurement since the end of third grade. It shows curtailment, the shortening of a lengthier process, simply because it isn't necessary to go through it. By sixth grade, reasoning took over (remember Martin!) because the children had already developed such a good number sense and were comfortable working with fractions.

## FRACTION OPERATIONS

Obviously, partitioning plays a major role in the measurement interpretation of fractions, as does reasoning up and down. Through successive partitioning, children quickly learn about equivalence and common denominators. Aided by the arrow notation, multiplication and division are the first operations to develop.

Well before introducing any algorithms for addition and subtractions of fractions, rational numbers viewed as measure on a number line provide a good model for these operations. The fifth grade student, whose work is shown above, demonstrates this point. Once she knew how to write two fractions using twenty-firsts, it was an easy extension to ask her how she might add the two fractions. Addition in the measurement interpretation of fractions provides a conceptual basis for later work with vectors.

- What is the sum of $\frac{2}{3}$ and $\frac{1}{4}$?

Given two number lines with the same unit interval located on each, identify the points $\frac{2}{3}$ and $\frac{1}{4}$.

Place the lengths end-to-end and continue to partition until you can name the sum, or convert both lengths to twelfths and add by placing end-to-end.

Because the successive partitioning process is emulated in the use of fraction strips, as shown in Chapter 7, children whose instruction began with the measurement interpretation of fractions found it very easy to use fraction strips if they needed a physical model when they were learning the standard algorithms for addition and subtraction. In general, the most noteworthy characteristic of children who spent most of their initial fraction instruction studying fractions as measures was their fraction sense. They knew the relative sizes of fractions and when they got to middle school and began fraction computation, they were far less likely than other children to come up with far-out answers. Their powerful sense of the size of fractional numbers enabled them to predict the approximate size of an answer and they knew when an error produced a strange result.

## ACTIVITIES

1.  Complete the arrow notation and name the subdivision that would result after partitioning a foot (12 inches) according to the successive partitioning indicated by the arrow notation.

a.

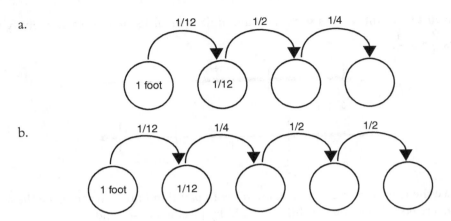

b.

2.  Here are two gas gauges. By successive partitioning, determine what part of a full tank of gas remains in each tank.

a.                                                          b.

3.  a.  Put an arrow on the following gas gauge to show how much gas you would have left in your tank if your filled it up and then took a drive that used 6 gallons. A full tank holds 16 gallons.

b.  Your gas tank was reading "empty," but you were low on cash. You used your last $10.00 to buy gas at a station where you paid $2.00 per gallon. If a full tank hold 14 gallons, put an arrow on the gas gauge to show how much gas you had in your tank after your purchase.

c.  You filled up your tank this morning and then took a drive in the country to enjoy the fall colors. Your odometer said that you had gone 340 miles and you have been averaging about 31 miles per gallon. If your gas gauge looked like this when you got home, how much does your gas tank hold when it is full?

4. I buy motor oil in plastic bottles that have a clear view strip in on side so that I can tell how much oil is in the container. There is a quart of oil in each bottle (32 ounces). What fraction of a bottle remains in each of these partially used bottles that I found in the garage?

a.

b.

5. If you paid to park for 25 minutes on the following meter, draw an arrow to show how your time would register on this meter.

6.  In each case, use a number line to order these fractions from smallest to largest.

a. $\dfrac{11}{12}, \dfrac{5}{6}, \dfrac{21}{24}$     b. $\dfrac{3}{9}, \dfrac{5}{6}, \dfrac{1}{2}$     c. $\dfrac{13}{14}, \dfrac{6}{7}, \dfrac{27}{28}$

7.  Use successive partitioning until you can name two fractions that lie between each pair of points.

a.

b.

8.  a.

This cup is full when the coffee level is up to the mark where the arrow points. Doug drank his coffee down to the fourth mark from the top. What part of a cup does he have left?

b.

Jenny likes to fill her cup to the rim. She drank some coffee and now the coffee level is between the fourth and fifth lines from the bottom. What part of a cup remains?

9.

Answer these questions about the short hand on a clock (the hour hand).
a.  What does one full rotation mean?
b.  What do the spaces between the longer hash marks represent?
c.  What do the spaces between the shorter hash marks represent?

10.  Answer these questions about the longer hand on a clock (the minute hand).

a.  What does one full rotation mean?
b.  What do the spaces between the longer hash marks represent?
c.  What do the spaces between the smaller hash marks represent?

11. Figure out what Annie is doing and then use her method to find 3 fractions between $\frac{7}{9}$ and $\frac{7}{8}$.

Annie

$\frac{7}{12}$    /   |   \    $\frac{7}{11}$

$\dfrac{7}{11\frac{1}{2}}$    $\dfrac{7}{-11\frac{1}{4}}$    $\dfrac{7}{11\frac{1}{5}}$

$\dfrac{7}{\frac{23}{2}}$    $\dfrac{7}{\frac{45}{4}}$    $\dfrac{7}{\frac{56}{5}}$

$\dfrac{14}{23}$    $\dfrac{28}{45}$    $\dfrac{35}{56}$

12. Jon also found three fractions between $\frac{7}{12}$ and $\frac{7}{11}$. Figure out his method and use it to find three fractions between $\frac{5}{9}$ and $\frac{5}{8}$.

Jon

$\dfrac{7}{11\frac{4}{4}}$    $\left(\dfrac{7}{11\frac{3}{4}} \quad \dfrac{7}{11\frac{2}{4}} \quad \dfrac{7}{11\frac{1}{4}}\right)$    $\dfrac{7}{11\frac{0}{4}}$

13. By successive partitioning, find out how much time is left on each 2-hour parking meter.

a.

b.

14.  Analyze the work of a fourth grader who answered the following problem. Is he competent in fraction computation?

A full bottle of oil has a view strip on the side. Originally, it contained 1 quart or 32 ounces, but someone used part of it. Figure out how many ounces remain.

15.  Locate $\frac{5}{8}$.

16.  Locate $\frac{7}{24}$.

17. Compare the given fractions using successive partitioning.

a. $\dfrac{7}{8}, \dfrac{3}{4}$

b. $\dfrac{4}{7}, \dfrac{9}{14}$

c. $\dfrac{7}{12}, \dfrac{15}{24}$

d. $\dfrac{1}{3}, \dfrac{7}{15}$

18. Draw both hands on the clock to show as precisely as possible, the following times.

a.  3:18                    b.  7:27                    c.  10:52

19. If you have a unit interval that is partitioned into 18 equal subintervals, what fractions will you be able to locate without further partitioning?

# CHAPTER 11

# Ratios and Rates

## STUDENT STRATEGIES: GRADE 6

First solve the problem for yourself and then analyze the student work given below.

Two bicyclists practice on the same course. Green does the course in 6 minutes, and Neuman does it in 4 minutes. They agree to race each other five times around the course. How soon after the start will Neuman overtake Green?

Monica

track : 2 miles long

   N : 20 minutes

   G : 30 minutes

whole race : 10 miles

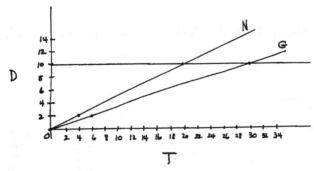

We can see by the graph that N is always ahead.

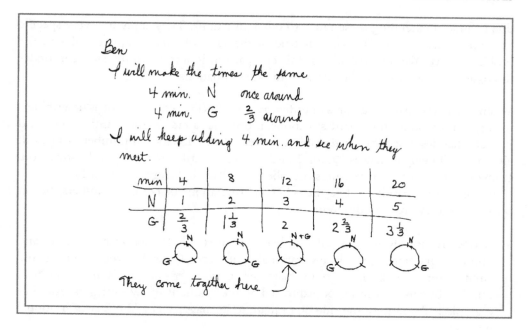

## WHAT IS A RATIO?

A *ratio* is a comparison of any two quantities. A ratio may be used to convey an idea that cannot be expressed as a single number. Consider this example:

> Harvest festivals in towns A and B drew visitors from all of the surrounding areas. Town A reported a ratio of 4,000 cars to its 3 square miles. Town B reported a ratio of 3,000 cars to its 2 square miles.

Why was the information reported in this way? By comparing the number of cars to the size of the town, we get a sense of how crowded each town was with cars, of how difficult it may have been to drive around, and to find parking. This information is different from either of the pieces of information that were combined to create it. It answers the question "Which town was more congested during the festival?"

In this situation, the ratio of cars to square miles compares measures of different types. Ratios sometimes compare measures of the same type. There are two types of ratio that compare measures of the same type: part–whole comparisons and part–part comparisons. Part–whole comparisons are ratios that compare the measure of part of a set to the measure of the whole set. Part–part comparisons compare the measure of part of a set to the measure of another part of the set. For example, in a carton of eggs containing 5 brown and 7 white eggs, all of the following ratios apply: 5 to 7 (brown to white part–part comparison), 7 to 5 (white to brown part–part comparison), 5 to 12 (brown part–whole comparison), 7 to 12 (white part–whole comparison). Usually we don't think of extending these ratios to other situations. They apply to a very specific case under discussion. The same is true of the ratio of cars to square miles in the problem above. We understand that this comparison is specific to the situation under discussion and we would not extend it to other situations.

When a ratio compares measures of different types AND is conceived of as describing a quality that is common to many situations, it becomes a rate. For example, $3 per yard is a rate that described the relationship between cost in dollars and number of yards in all of the following instances: $6 for 2 yard, $24 for 8 yard, $54 for 18 yards, and so on. It involves two different measures: number of dollars and number of yards.

In some ways, ratios are like the other interpretations of rational numbers, but in some ways, they are very different.

- Ratios are not always rational numbers, but part–whole, operator, measure, and quotient fractions are always rational numbers. Consider the ratio of the circumference of a circle to its diameter: $C:d = \pi$. Pi ($\pi$) is not a rational number because it cannot be expressed as the quotient of two integers. Another example is the ratio of the side of a square to its diagonal. $1:\sqrt{2}$. $\sqrt{2}$ is an irrational number.

- Ratios may have a zero as their second component, but fractions are not defined for a denominator of zero. For example, if you report the ratio of men to women at a meeting attended by 10 males and no females, you could write $10:0$.

- A fraction is an ordered pair; that is, if you reverse the order of $a$ and $b$ in the fraction $\frac{a}{b}$, you have written a completely different fraction. The same is true with ratios. 4 boys: 3 girls and 3 girls: 4 boys are different ratios and they may not be used as if they are interchangeable. However, the ratios 4 boys: 3 girls and 3 girls: 4 boys give you the same information about a situation.

- Ratios arithmetic can be very different from fraction arithmetic. Consider this problem: yesterday Mary had 3 hits in 5 turns at bat. Today she had 2 hits in 6 times at bat. How many hits did she have for a two-day total?

  Mary had $3:5 + 2:6 = 5:11$ or 5 hits in 11 times at bat. If we were adding fractions, we would never write $\frac{3}{5} + \frac{2}{6} = \frac{5}{11}$!

Researchers are still trying to capture the difference between ratios and rates; however, when we consider the many ways in which the words are used in both mathematical and nonmathematical circles, definitions can prove unsatisfactory. Part of the difficulty is that everyday language and usage of rates and ratio is out of control. The media have employed the language of ratios and rates in many different ways, sometimes inconsistently, sometimes interchangeably. Students are exposed to less-than-correct usage and terminology, and it is no easy task to reconcile precise mathematical ideas with informal, colloquial usage. In order to help children understand real contexts in which they encounter ratios and rates, teachers must be prepared to help children analyze each situation individually. In this chapter, we will look at some of the issues and nuances that require discussion in the classroom.

## NOTATION AND TERMINOLOGY

A ratio is sometimes written in a fraction form, but not always; part–whole comparisons, operators, measures, and quotients are usually written in the fraction form $\frac{a}{b}$.

The ratio of *a things to b things* may be written in several ways:

1.  $\frac{a}{b}$ or $a/b$
2.  $a \rightarrow b$
3.  $a : b$
4.  $@\, b$

In different countries different notations are favored. In the United States, we use the colon notation and fraction notation alternately, depending on which characteristics or ratios we wish to highlight. Fraction notation is used when referring to those aspects in which ratios behave like other interpretations of rational numbers written in fraction form (part–whole comparisons, operators, measures, and quotient), while the colon notation is favored by those who like to emphasize the ways in which ratios do not act like other fractions. If the fraction notation is used, care should be taken to use quantities, and not merely numbers. That is, a ratio of 5 girls to 7 boys should not be written as $\frac{5}{7}$, but rather as $\frac{5 \text{ girls}}{7 \text{ boys}}$. When people are not careful to label quantities and they write $\frac{5}{7}$ in the fraction form devoid of context, the conceptual and operational differences between ratios and part–whole fractions can become fuzzy or lost. When children are trying to build up meaning for fractions and ratios, it is probably a good idea to use different notations for each. To keep things straight, we will try to use the colon notation when we mean a ratio. There may be exceptions. For example, you will rarely see the miles per hour written with colon notation. Regardless of the notation used, any of the following may serve as a verbal interpretation of the symbols:

1.  *a* to *b*
2.  *a* per *b*

3.   *a* for *b*
4.   *a* for each *b*
5.   for every *b* there are *a*
6.   the ratio of *a* to *b*
7.   *a* is to *b*

Many statements may be translated into ratio language and symbolism. Often, ratio language is used as an alternate way of expressing a multiplicative relationship.

- There were $\frac{2}{3}$ as many men as women at the concert.

  This says that the number of men was $\frac{2}{3}$ the number of women. Let *m* represent the number of men and *w* represent the number of women. Then:

  $$m = \frac{2}{3}w \text{ or } \frac{m}{w} = \frac{2}{3}$$

  To distinguish this comparison from a part–whole comparison, we write $m : w = 2 : 3$ (the ratio of men to women is 2 to 3).

  Although most mathematics curricula introduce ratios late in the elementary years, for some children, from the beginning of fraction instruction, the ratio interpretation of rational numbers is more natural than the part–whole comparison. These children identify

 and

as $\frac{2}{3}$. Teachers frequently report that they see children using this interpretation.

There is some research evidence that when children prefer the ratio interpretation and classroom instruction builds on their intuitive knowledge of comparisons, they develop a richer understanding of rational numbers and employ proportional reasoning sooner than children whose curriculum used the part–whole comparison as the primary interpretation of rational numbers. These children favored discrete sets of coins or colored chips to represent ratios. Our discussion of equivalence and comparison uses strategies that these children developed to explain their thinking.

## EQUIVALENCE AND COMPARISON OF RATIOS

Chips or other discrete objects provide a useful way to talk about the difference between part–whole comparisons and ratios.

The part–whole comparison depicted here is $\frac{2}{3}$. The ratio interpretation is 2 : 1.

When testing two fractions for equivalence, we saw that unitizing was an important tool. The same is true when testing for equivalent ratios.

- Is 6 : 9 equivalent to 2 : 3?

By physically or just visually rearranging 6 : 9, we can see 2 columns shaded and 3 columns white, or 2 : 3. Thus, the ratios are equivalent.

Two of the methods we used to compare fractions were (a) SSP (creating same-sized parts or equalizing denominators), and (b) SNP (creating same number of parts or equalizing numerators). When comparing ratios, equalizing parts—either the first components of each ratio, or the second components in each ratio—are useful strategies. As you can see in the example above, when *both* parts are equalized, the ratios are equivalent.

- Compare 3 : 4 and 5 : 8.

Let's compare by equalizing the first components in these ratios.

We did this by copying or *cloning* the ratios until we had the same number of colored chips in each representation. A 5-clone of 3 : 4 and a 4-clone of 5 : 8 equalize the first components of the ratios. However, in the case of 3 : 4, there are 20 in the second component, while the 5 : 8 ratio has 24 in the second component.

- Compare the same ratios (3 : 4 and 5 : 8) by equalizing the second components of the ratios.

In this case, cloning the first ratio accomplished the goal. We have the same number of white chips in each of the second components.

How should we interpret these results? Ratios may be compared in several different ways, but it is the interpretation that is tricky. Think about the juice problems we studied earlier. We could not compare number of parts of juice in each pitcher. The strength of the juice depended also on how much water (the second component of the ratio) was mixed with the juice in each pitcher.

Ratios have a "for–against," positive–negative interpretation. Which is the better win–loss record, 5 wins and 6 losses, or 2 wins and 3 losses? We would never say 5 wins are better than 2 wins. Our interpretation has to take into account how many losses there were. This brings us back to absolute and relative comparisons. Ratios are relative comparisons. In other words, 5 wins can be a good season or a bad season, depending on the number of loses you are comparing to.

- 5 wins as compared to 150 losses is bad.
- 5 wins as compared to 6 losses is so-so.
- 5 wins as compared to 2 losses is a good record!

With this in mind, let's get back to interpreting the examples above.

If a team has 15 wins, would it have a better season if its losses numbered 20 or 32? Obviously, your wins look more impressive if there were only 20 losses, so $3:4$ is the better record.

If the first component is orange juice and the second component is water, which juice has a stronger orangey taste, that produced by the first ratio or the drink produced by the second ratio? If 15 cans of juice concentrate are diluted with only 20 cans of water, the juice will taste more orangey than if 15 cans of orange juice are diluted with 32 cans of water.

If 15 positives are each matched with a negative, in the first case, you have 5 extra negatives, while in the second case, you have 17 extra negatives. This means $3:4$ is more positive (or desirable); alternatively, $5:8$ is more negative (or undesirable).

If you and your friends (15 of you total) were playing a game, would you stand a better chance of winning if you had 20 opponents or 32 opponents?

If you bought 15 items for $20 and your friend bought the same 15 items for $32, who got the better deal?

- Which would be the better deal, 2 tickets for $3 or 5 tickets for $6?

  We can shorten the solution by noticing that after we have cloned both ratios until one of the components is equalized, we are really comparing the other components by subtraction to help us determine which is the better or more desirable or more economical scenario.

  Let's begin with the ratio $2:3$ and equalize first components (same number of tickets). Clone $2:3$ until its first component is a multiple of 5. Then you can see that have a 2-clone of $5:6$. Circle both copies of $5:6$.

(A)

A 5-clone of $(2:3)$ gave $10:15$ with which we can match 2 copies of $(5:6)$. But we are left with 3 white chips. What does this mean? (Remember that ratios require interpretation!)

We started with $2:3$, matched with $5:6$ and ended up with extra dollars, money left over. This must mean that 2 tickets for \$3 is more expensive than 5 tickets for \$6. 5 tickets for \$6 is the better deal.

Let's think about this in terms of positives and negatives. If you take a quantity A and subtract from it something that is smaller, you should have something in the positive component. However if you take quantity A and subtract from it something larger, then you have something in the negative component. This is why we conclude that 5 tickets for \$6 is the larger ticket-to-dollar ratio.

- Another way.

  Beginning with the $5:6$ ratio, we can see that we don't have to clone it to match with copies of $2:3$. After we circle 2 copies of $2:3$, there is one colored chip remaining (signifying a ticket).

  (B)

What does this mean? We started with 5 for \$6. We matched it against the other deal. At the rate of 2 tickets for \$3, we could get only 4 tickets for \$6. So 5 for \$6 gives us an extra ticket for the same price. In terms of positives and negatives, after we subtracted the second ratio from $5:6$, we ended up with a positive component. Thus, $5:6$ is the larger ticket-to-dollar ratio.

After drawing and manipulating bi-color chips to understand how to compare ratios, it becomes more convenient to use ratio arithmetic to represent the operations we are performing. For example, we can express the chip operations we just did in the ticket problem like this:

Solution A: $5(2:3) - 2(5:6) = (10:15) - (10:12) = (0:3)$
Solution B: $(5:6) - 2(2:3) = (5:6) - (4:6) = (1:0)$

The two chip solutions are different, but when we interpret the results, we reach the same conclusion. In fact, for any ratio comparison question, there are different solutions, depending on which ratio you start with, and which way you order the components (for example, tickets-to-dollars or dollars-to-tickets). The next example shows 4 different ways to set up and interpret the solution of a ratio comparison.

- The local theatres had bargain prices last weekend and both the Young family (all adults) and the Dyer family (all adults) went to the movies, but to different theaters. The 5 people from the Young family got into the Strand for $9 and the 4 people from the Dyer family got into the Majestic Theater for $7. Which theatre had the better prices last weekend?

  a. Begin with the Strand prices and use a ratio of people to dollars:

  $$4(5:9) - 5(4:7) = (20:36) - (20:35) = (0:1)$$

  The Strand has a greater ratio of dollars to people, and a smaller ratio of people to dollars. Therefore the Majestic has the better prices.

  b. Begin with the Majestic and use a ratio of people to dollars:

  $$5(4:7) - 4(5:9) = (20:35) - (20:36) = (0:-1)$$

  The Majestic has a smaller ratio of dollars to people, and a larger ratio of people to dollars. Therefore the Majestic has the better prices.

  c. Begin with the Strand prices and use a ratio of dollars to people:

  $$7(9:5) - 9(7:4) = (63:35) - (63:36) = (0:-1)$$

  The Strand has a smaller ratio of people to dollars, and a larger ratio of dollars to people. Therefore, the Majestic has better prices.

  d. Begin with the Majestic and use a ratio of dollars to people:

  $$9(7:4) - 7(9:5) = (63:36) - (63:35) = (1:0)$$

  The Majestic has a bigger ratio of people to dollars and a smaller ratio of dollars to people. Therefore the Majestic has better pieces.

## RATIOS AS AN INSTRUCTIONAL TASK

Ratios in contexts present a challenge in the classroom because of the many nuances that occur in their everyday usage. This means that when solving ratio problems, it is important to discuss each situation in detail. What is legitimate knowledge when information is reported using ratios—whether implicit or explicit? Interpreting ratio information has many implications for other topics and applications, for example, topics, such as sampling, statistics, and probability.

Classroom discussions of ratio situations should focus on these questions:

- In addition to the explicit facts, what else do I know about this situation?
- Does it make sense to reduce this ratio? Can this ratio be extended?
- If I extend or reduce this ratio, what information is gained or lost?
- If I choose a smaller or larger sample, will the ratio apply?
- What is the meaning of a divided ratio?

- You have a dozen eggs in which the ratio of brown to white eggs is $3:9$. The brown eggs comprise $\frac{3}{12}$ of the carton. The white eggs comprise $\frac{9}{12}$ of the carton.

  Now suppose that you were blindfolded and you took 4 eggs out of the carton. Could you predict how many of them are brown? No! Both the ratio $3:9$ and the fractions $\frac{3}{12}$ and $\frac{9}{12}$ refer only to the entire carton. They do not refer to any subset of the carton. If you grab 4 eggs at random, you have no guarantee of getting 1 brown and 3 white.

- If you are told that the ratio of girls to boys in a class is $3:4$, what can you tell about the class?

  The ratio tells us that for every three girls, there are 4 boys. In the whole class, there must be some multiple of 7 students. We cannot tell if there are 7, 14, 21, or more students in the whole class, but it we could put the total number of girls over the number of students in the whole class, that fraction would reduce to $\frac{3}{7}$. That is, the class is $\frac{3}{7}$ girls and $\frac{4}{7}$ boys.

- There is a ratio of 3 girls to 4 boys in a class. If you chose 7 students at random, will you get 3 girls and 4 boys?

  Not necessarily. The ratio (3 girls:4 boys) or, similarly, the fractions $\frac{3}{7}$ girls and $\frac{4}{7}$ boys, refer to the total number of girls and the total number of boys in the class.

  They do not apply to portions or samples of the class. So if I took 7 student names at random, I have no guarantee of getting 3 girls and 4 boys.

- You have a 30% concentration of alcohol in water. If a take a cup of the mixture, what percent will be alcohol?

  The amounts of the elements that compose this mixture exist in constant ratio to one another no matter what size sample we choose to inspect. This mixture is composed of 3 parts alcohol to 7 parts water. No matter what size sample is taken from the mixture—3 cups, 3 drops, or 3 gallons—it will consist of alcohol and water in a ratio of 3 parts to 7 parts.

- Oranges are sold 3 for \$0.69. Is this ratio extendible? That is, if you buy more than 3 oranges, will you pay at the rate of 3 for \$0.69?

  The ratio $3:69$ may be meaningfully extended to $6:138$.
  That is, if we saw the price of oranges advertised as 3 for \$0.69, we might reasonably assume that we could purchase 6 for \$1.38.

- John is 25 years old and his son is 5 years old. Is this ratio extendible?

  The ratio $\frac{25}{5} = \frac{5}{1}$ compared the father's age to the son's age right now. Next year, it will not be true that the father is five times as old as his son, nor will it be true at any time in the future. The ratio $\frac{5}{1}$ describes the age relationship only in the present situation. It is not extendible over any other years and has no predictive capacity.

- John is 25 years old and his son is 5 years old. What is the effect of reducing this ratio?

  The ratio $25:5$ is reducible to $5:1$. In reducing the ratio, the present ages of the boy and his father are lost, but the information that the father is five times as old as his son is retained.

- This season, our team had a record (ratio) of 4 wins:2 losses. What is the effect of reducing this ratio?

  A ratio of 2 wins : 1 loss is not the same as a ratio of 4 wins:2 losses. In reducing the ratio, information about the total number of games is lost. The given ratio, 4 wins:2 losses, a season record, tells us that the team played 6 games. The ratio 2 wins:1 loss no longer describes the team's season record because it refers to only 3 games. Furthermore, we cannot assume that the season record is a multiple of the ratio 2 wins : 1 loss. That ratio does not refer to either the first half or the second half of the team's season because there are many different ways in which they could have had a season of 4 wins and 2 losses.

- What does it mean to say that John's batting average is 0.368?

  The batting average is not an average in the sense of being an arithmetical mean, and unlike average speed, it is not reported as a comparison of two quantities. A batting average is the divided ratio of the number of hits to the total number of times at bat (where "hits" and "at bats" have technical definitions). A baseball batting average is an indicator of the ability of a batter.

  In other cases, interpretation may be complicated by the interaction of ratio properties, for example, extendibility and divisibility. Suppose John had a good day at bat and hit 5 times out of his 6 times at bat. As a divided ratio, his average could be reported as 0.833. It would be nearly impossible for John to extend such an exceptional record. He could not keep up such a performance over 60 times at bat, and yet, 5 out of 6 and 50 out of 60 are both 0.833. Thus, the divided ratio obscures the fact that 5:6 and 50:60 are very different phenomena.

- What is the meaning of these divided ratios?

    $\pi = 3.14159\ldots$ (approximately 3.14) is the ratio of the circumference of a circle to its diameter.

    $\sqrt{2}:1$ (approximately 1.4) is the ratio of the diagonal of a square to its side.

    $\Phi = 1.61803\ldots$ is the golden ratio.

    1.9 is the ratio of the length to the width of the American flag.

    These ratios are reported in their divided form rather than being reported as comparisons. This is because of their dual nature as descriptions and prescriptions. They describe very special properties of circles, squares, some rectangles, and the American flag. However, flags, rectangles, circles, and squares come in many different sizes. Reporting their special properties as divided ratios gives us a formula for reproducing them in many different sizes. For example, if $\pi$ were reported as $\frac{15.708}{5}$, then it would refer to the circumference and diameter of a specific circle, the one with a diameter of 5 units. However, $\pi = 3.14159$ identifies the special relationship of the circumference to the diameter in all circles.

- I have a ratio of 4 textbooks to 5 children. What does it mean if I divide that ratio? If we write 4:5 in fraction form, $\frac{4}{5}$, and obtain the indicated quotient, do we get something meaningful?

$$4 \div 5 = \frac{4}{5} \text{ book per child.}$$

    Taken at face value, this quotient is awkward. Nevertheless, you hear such things as 1.5 children per household—another divided ratio. These divided ratios convey information as averages. On the average, we have 0.8 books per child. Every child in the classroom does not have $\frac{4}{5}$ book. Rather, the information tells us how close a particular class is to having enough books to go around.

## WHAT IS A RATE?

We can think of a *rate* as an extended ratio, a ratio that applies not just to the situation at hand, but to a while range of situations in which two quantities are related in the same way.

- The rule of thumb for ordering pizza at Reggie's Pizza is "Order 2 medium pizzas per 5 people." The rule means to order 4 pizzas for 10 people, 6 pizzas for 15 people, 30 pizzas for 75 people, etc. Serving a party of 10 people 4 pizzas (4 pizzas:10 people) is a specific instance of the restaurant's general rule for how much pizza to order.

*Rates* can also be thought of as descriptions of the way quantities change with time. They are identified by the use of the word per in their names, and they can be reduced (or divided) to a relationship between one quantity and 1 unit of another quantity. This is called a *unit rate*.

- 30 miles per 5 hours can be expressed as 6 miles per 1 hour. In this case, the unit rate is 6 mph.

These examples do not begin to exhaust the nuances involved in understanding rates. Almost every rate context will require some discussion in the classroom to uncover contest-specific meaning. The following examples suggest some of the points that students need to think about as they encounter rates in various contexts.

- The soccer team has a ratio of 3 wins to 2 losses so far in the season. At this rate, what would be their record at the end of the 15-game season?

  Ordinarily, it makes no sense to extend a ratio of 3 wins to 2 losses, because as soon as the team plays another game, the ratio is different, no matter whether they win or lose. However, the words *at this rate* give us permission to imagine what the season might look like *if* the team were able extend their present record proportionally to a 15-game season. However, it does not help to determine the number of wins and losses at the end of, say, 8 games.

- Rates can be constant or varying.

  Conversion factors, such as 12 inches = 1 foot, 10 centimeters = 1 decimeter, are constant rates.
  International monetary exchange rates are constantly changing.
  The speed at which one is traveling in a car is constantly changing unless the cruise control is on.
  The rate at which the bathtub fills with water may be slow or fast, depending on how far you have opened the tap.

- It may be mathematically possible to extend a rate, but this does not mean that it always makes sense to do so in the real world. Suppose a track star runs 3 km in 25 minutes. It would not make sense to talk about running 300 km in 2500 minutes (over 41 hours).

- Some rates are reported as single numbers.

  Her heart rate was 68.
  The birthrate of country A is 12.4.
  The unemployment rate is 3.4%.
  The inflation rate is 4.6%.

In these examples, rates are implicit *per* quantities, but are more like divided ratios or quotients. To reconstruct the comparisons that any of them represent, additional information is needed about how they were computed. A heart rate is the comparison of the number of times a heart beats per minute, usually counted over 10 seconds and then extended by multiplying by 6. In other divided per quantities, where the division results in very small numbers, the result of the division is multiplied by 100 or by 1,000 and the rate is reported as a percentage or as some number per thousand. In some countries, the birth rate is defined at 1,000 times the ratio of the number of babies born alive to the total number in the population (the number of live births per thousand of the population). Similarly, the unemployment rate is expressed as a percentage. It is 100 times the ratio of the number of people who are unemployed to the number of people who are in the civilian labor force, as determined by sampling. Finally, the inflation rate is perhaps the most elusive of these rates. In actuality, many variables figure into its computation, and most people probably have only a sense of its meaning, without really knowing how it is computed.

## OPERATIONS WITH RATES AND RATIOS

As we have seen thus far, there are no rules for operating with ratios and rates, nor for interpreting results. In the classroom, it is important to discuss each problem that comes up because meanings and appropriate operations are situation-dependent. To put it simply, we get to know ratios and rates, what they mean, and how to operate with them, on a one-by-one basis. There is no substitute for experiencing ratios and rates in as many contexts as possible.

We have also seen that considering ratios and rates purely as mathematical objects, it is always possible to reduce them or to expand them to equivalent forms, but in the real world, such operations can be meaningless.

Ratios and rates often do not behave like part–whole fractions. For example, consider this example:

- Suppose a basketball player takes 6 free shots and makes 4 baskets. Later in his practice, he takes another 6 shots and makes 3 of them. How can we sum up his free shot performance for the day?

  Looking at the ratio of baskets to free shots, we get $(4:6) + (3:6) = (7:12)$.

  If we write those ratios in fraction form, we get $\frac{4}{6} + \frac{3}{6} = \frac{7}{12}$. Adding numerators and denominators certainly does not follow the conventional algorithm for adding fractions.

- When we solved the movie ticket problem above, we wrote $5(2:3) = (10:15)$. In conventional fraction multiplication, we would never write $5\left(\dfrac{2}{5}\right) = \dfrac{10}{15}$. However, this multiplication *does* correspond to writing equivalent fractions. When we write equivalent fractions, we are simply multiplying top and bottom of a fraction by 1:

$$\frac{2}{3} \cdot \frac{5}{5} = \frac{10}{15}$$

## LINEAR GRAPHS

As we have seen, in any particular context, a ratio may be extendible or reducible or not, depending on the sense it makes. As abstract mathematical objects, ratios are always extendible and reducible and, in fact, are divided into families or classes. Each class contains all of the extensions and reductions of a particular ratio and we call the whole class an *equivalence class*. In pre-algebra classes through high-school mathematics, as students' mathematical experience begins to move away from applications and becomes more abstract, equivalence classes, graphing, and slope become more important.

Suppose that the market has advertised 2 pounds of peanuts for $3.00 and there is no restriction on the amount I can purchase at that price. Then I can transform the multiplicative relationship between pounds of peanuts and dollars to get various pieces of useful information:

2 pounds costs $3

1 pound cost $\$\dfrac{3}{2}$ or $1.50

$1 buys $\dfrac{2}{3}$ pound.

With any number of pounds, I can associate a dollar amount by multiplying pounds by $\dfrac{3}{2}$. For example, 4 pounds will cost $6; $6\dfrac{2}{3}$ pounds will cost $10. Of course, many of these ordered pairs are possible, especially because we are not restricted to using whole numbers. Suppose we graph these pairs putting pounds on the horizontal axis and dollars on the vertical axis.

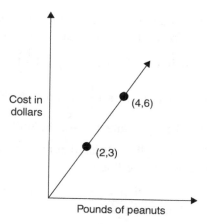

This graph shows two points, (2,3) and (4,6), corresponding to the ratios $3:2$ and $6:4$ of dollars to pounds and the line determined by those points. When we draw the line, we are imagining the extension of the advertised rate to all of the different amounts of peanuts we might buy, some less than 2 pounds, some more than 2 pounds, some whole numbers of pounds, and some fractional numbers of pounds.

Note that in proportional situations, the line graph will always go through the point (0,0). (The cost is $0 if you are not buying any peanuts.) Be careful about distinguishing point coordinates $(x,y)$ from the rate being represented graphically. The point (2,3) in usual Cartesian coordinates is not in the class {2,3}, but rather, in the class {3,2} when we are considering dollar-to-pounds rates.

These rates are in the same equivalence class because they represent the same relative comparisons. That is, 3 relates to 2 in the same way that 6 relates to 4 in the same way that 10 relates to $6\frac{2}{3}$. All rates in which the quantities share the same relationship belong to the same class and they reduce to the same ratio. None of them is preferred as *the* name of the equivalence class. We can write $\left\{\dfrac{3}{2}\right\}$ to refer to the equivalence class to which the rate $\dfrac{3}{2}$ belongs. Because $\dfrac{10}{6\frac{2}{3}}$ belongs to the same class, we could have called the equivalence class $\left\{\dfrac{10}{6\frac{2}{3}}\right\}$. Actually, the equivalence class may be designated by placing any one of the rates in the class inside brackets { }. For example $\left\{\dfrac{6}{4}\right\}$ or {6,4} refers to the entire equivalence class to which the rate $\dfrac{6}{4}$ belongs.

On the graph comparing cost to pounds of peanuts, the coordinates of *all* the points have the same relationship. For example, look at the points whose coordinate rectangles have been drawn. Their coordinates are $\left(3, 4\frac{1}{2}\right)$ and $(6,9)$. They represent the cost to pound ratios (*y*-to-*x* ratios) of $4\frac{1}{2} : 3$ and $9 : 6$. Notice that all of the rates in this class are equivalent and they reduce to $\frac{1.5}{1}$, the unit rate, the cost per 1 pound.

Now let's look at the slope of the line. Recall that for any 2 points $(x_1, y_1)$ and $(x_2, y_2)$ on a non-vertical line, the slope of the line is

$$\frac{\text{vertical change}}{\text{horizontal change}} = \frac{y_2 - y_1}{x_2 - x_1}$$

Therefore the slope of the line segment connecting the points $(2,3)$ and $(4,6)$ is

$$\frac{6-3}{4-2} = \frac{3}{2} = 1.5$$

On the graph, if you determine the slope between any two points, say, $(6,9)$ and $(2,3)$, you get $\frac{1.5}{1} = 1.5$. The divided ratio is the slope of the line!

We get the following connections:

- All rates in the same equivalence class are composed of different quantities, but they all reduce to the same unit rate.
- The slope of the line containing all of the rates in the same class is the unit rate.
- A constant—a number that does not change—is associated with each equivalence class. That constant is found by dividing any ratio from the class. If you know that constant, you may generate any of the members of the equivalence class. That constant is the slope of the line containing all of the ordered pairs in the equivalence class.
- That constant, the slope of the line, is the constant of proportionality.

## COMPARING RATIOS AND RATES GRAPHICALLY

The Flavorful Fruit Juice Company bottles various fruit juices. A small barrel of apple juice is mixed using 12 cans of apple concentrate and 30 cans of water. A large barrel of raspberry juice is mixed using 16 cans of raspberry concentrate and 36 cans of water. Which barrel will be fruitier?

This problem asks us to compare ratios, which we have done in other ways, but now we will see how the connections we have just discovered about equivalence classes, unit rates, slope, etc. can be helpful.

Let's graph each equivalence class. If both mixtures are equally fruity, we will get only one line. If each recipe belongs to a different class, we will get two lines and we will be able to compare their slopes.

If we put the amount of fruit concentrate on the vertical axis, and draw the line for each equivalence class by connecting (0,0) and any member of the class. $12:30 = 6:15$, so we may plot the line for the apple drinks using the points (0,0) and (15,6). $16:36 = 4:9$, so we may use the points (0.0) and (9,4) to plot the raspberry line. Note that the larger ratio of fruit to water will be the steeper line. In this case, we can see that the raspberry mixture is fruitier.

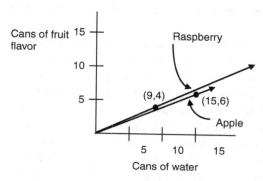

Let's check by calculating the slope of each line.

Raspberry line: $\dfrac{4-0}{9-0} = \dfrac{4}{9}$ or 0.44     Apple line: $\dfrac{6-0}{15-0} = \dfrac{6}{15}$ or 0.4

The slope is the change in fruit juice as compared to the change in water, so a greater slope represents more concentrate as compared to water. The raspberry mixture will taste fruitier.

Without graphing, we could check the constant associated with each equivalence class. For each class, this constant is given by a divided ratio from the class. The concentrate-to-water ratio for apple is $12:30 = 0.4$. The concentrate-to-water ratio for raspberry is $16:36 = 0.44$. Every ratio in $\{16:36\}$ is associated with the constant 0.44. For example, $\dfrac{16}{36} = 0.44$ and $\dfrac{4}{9} = 0.44$. Every ratio in $\{12,30\}$ is associated with the constant 0.4. For example, $\dfrac{2}{5} = 0.4$ and $\dfrac{6}{15} = 0.4$. This tells us that the ratio of concentrate to water is greater in the raspberry mixture.

If, instead, we had looked at the ratio of water to concentrate for each flavor, we would get:

$$30 \text{ water} : 12 \text{ apple} = 2.5$$
$$36 \text{ water} : 16 \text{ raspberry} = 2.25$$

These divided ratios indicate that there is more water in the apple mixture. Therefore the raspberry is less watery and will have the stronger fruity taste.

# SPEED: THE MOST IMPORTANT RATE

One of the most common rate situations is the distance–time–speed relationship. Although we all encounter this relationship in some way every day of our lives, research has shown that is it not well understood by most people. Most students have seen the formula

$$\text{distance} = \text{speed} \cdot \text{time}$$

and have mechanically substituted two numbers (without their labels) into the formula to solve for the third, but understanding this system of relationships takes a long time.

Children's early understanding of distance is usually based on their experience of how long it takes to get someplace by bicycle or by running. When asked what will happen if two cars start at the same time and place and one car moves at a speed of 30 mph and the other car moves at a speed of 40 mph, the most common answer is that the second car *will always be 10 miles ahead of the other one*. These ideas persist well into adulthood: distance is time and speed is distance. We hear these misconceptions from children all the time, and yet, distance–speed–time relationships get very little attention in the curriculum. In fact, the children's main contact with these quantities comes from experiences outside of school, in which incorrect ideas are reinforced repeatedly. They are very familiar with a car's speedometer and with each of those numbers—25, 55, etc.—they associate a certain physical experience of movement. The speedometer, however, reinforces the notion that speed can be measured directly. In addition, they hear adults answer distance questions with time. How far is it? Oh, about 10 minutes from here.

Students need to encounter the distance–speed–time system of relationships and to explicitly think about and discuss (a) ways to compare speeds of movement, (b) the characteristics of rate discussed so far, (c) the meaning of constant speed, (d) the meaning of average speed, and so on. It has been taken for granted that students understand these ideas, but in interviews, we discover that they understand very little. This is a handicap that can affect their conceptual understanding through high-school mathematics and even later. From my experience, even in calculus classes, students struggle with speed and all of the closely connected concepts: average rate, speed vs. velocity, distance vs. displacement, etc. In many situations, time is overlooked as an important changing quantity. A rather surprising admission by many calculus students is that they never really knew that speed is a rate. Sometimes teachers used the rule $D = R \cdot T$ and sometimes, $D = S \cdot T$, so they thought that speed and rate were different things.

Most beginning high-school students do not realize that speed is a composite quantity, the comparison of a distance to a time. Although students use the words *miles per hour*, they think the phrase is just a label for speed and have never thought about how speed is calculated. Ben and Monica, the sixth graders who solved the problems at the beginning of the chapter, are unusually bright, and they had been studying the distance–time–speed relationship for several weeks. Ben's solution was sophisticated.

He first determined how far around the track each man would bike in 4 minutes. Then, using a ratio table, he recorded minutes of cycling time against times around the track (rather than actual distance), and using his own notation system, noted the men's position on the track at 4-minute intervals. Monica assumed that the track was 2 miles long, and she used that fact to calculate the distance and the men's times in cycling five laps. However, when she graphed total distance against time, she ignored position on the track, as if the men rode their bikes on a country road. Monica interpreted her graph as saying that the men never met and that Neuman was always ahead. It is not clear from her statement whether or not she understands what her graph shows, and we would want to ask her for further explanation. Does she think steeper and "ahead" mean farther or faster?

What does it mean to understand the distance–time–speed quantity structure? The answer to that question is not a list of facts, nor it is the *rule* $D = R \cdot T$. Although the rule captures the relationships among the three quantities at some abstract level, there is a great deal of variation in the way this cluster of relationships plays out in real situations. Knowing the rule does not provide the level of comprehension needed to solve problems. We want students to develop an understanding of the structure of this set of relationships that comes from, but goes beyond, the investigation of specific situations. After sufficient experience, they should be able to make generalizations such as this: if distance doubles, time will have to double if speed remains the same, or speed has to double if time remains the same. In short, there is no substitute for gaining a deep understanding of the quantities and their relationships through analysis and problem-solving in a wide variety of situations.

## CHARACTERISTICS OF SPEED

Like other rates, speed has a domain. That is, it applies to some explicit portion of a trip, which may or may not be the entire trip under discussion. In addition, it is important to take into consideration whether or not a speed is constant over any particular portion of the trip. If you drive a certain distance with the cruise control on, then over that distance, it may be said that your speed was constant. (Technically, even when using a cruise control, your speed will not remain constant, but we agree that it is close enough to call speed constant.) Discussion of these nuances in real contexts is essential for helping children to develop a richer understanding of distance–speed–time relationships. It is important not to assume that these are obvious. Ask questions in every distance–speed–time situation: What information does this give us? What can I assume about this situation? What is constant? What quantities are changing? How are the changing quantities related?

- Tim drove half the distance to another city with his cruise control set at 55 mph and the rest of the distance with the cruise set at 50 mph. What do we know?

Tom's speed of 55 mph was constant for the first part of the trip, and his speed of 50 mph was constant over the second part of the trip. Because his speeds were different, each segment of his trip took a different amount of time.

- Jack set his cruise control at 65 mph. How far did he travel in 2 days?

  Although the cruise control may have kept his speed close to constant during Jack's actual driving times, in a 48-hour period, rest stops will be necessary and these will affect the nature of the trip. We cannot say how far he traveled in 2 days.

- Jack drove for 3 hours with his cruise control set at 65 mph. What does this information tell us?

  Because Jack's speed was constant with regard to the 3-hour trip, we can say that he traveled a total distance of 195 miles during that time. We can also determine the distance he had covered at any intermediate time. For example, after 1.5 hours, he must have gone 97.5 miles and in 2.25 hours, he must have covered 146.25 miles.

- Marcia drove 195 miles with her cruise set at 65 mph. What does this information tell us?

  Marcia must have driven for 3 hours.

## STUDENTS' MISCONCEPTIONS ABOUT SPEED

Students can have many misconceptions, and we always have to be on the lookout for them. However, there are some very common misconceptions that are worth mentioning. These misconceptions are part of the reason that discussing quantities and change is such an important aid to rational number understanding.

Students have a great deal of trouble whenever they are working with *chunked* quantities. Chunked quantities are those for which we have a special name that disguises their true nature as a ratio of two different quantities. For example, speed and density are both ratios. Students need to know that speed is not measured directly and that it is a measure of motion that comes about by comparing two other quantities.

Many students interchange numbers and labels on a ratio as if it doesn't matter where they are placed. This problem seems to be connected to their understanding of a ratio as ordered pair and simple lack of regard for quantities (bad habits of just manipulating numbers). 5 mph means 5 miles:1 hour or $\frac{5mi}{1hr}$. $\frac{5mi}{1hr}$ cannot be used interchangeably with the ratio $\frac{1mi}{5hr}$ nor with the ratio $\frac{5hr}{1mi}$.

Now for the biggest misconception of all! Students believe that to find average speed, you total the speeds of individual parts of a journey and divide by the number of segments in the journey. That is, they believe that finding average speed is like averaging test scores. Test scores are just whole numbers, but speed entails the comparison of two quantities, and when finding average speed, the length of time for each stage of a journey has to be taken into account. This problem and the others just mentioned are all related, so it is important that instruction address all of them explicitly.

## AVERAGE SPEED

In relation to speed, when we use the word *average*, it means *distributed proportionately*. It does not refer to an arithmetic mean. That is, it is not equivalent to the average of the speeds over the respective segments of the trip. Average speed is the total distance traveled as compared to the total time it took to travel that distance. The average speed is the speed you would have traveled *if you had* traveled the same distance in the same amount of time, using a constant speed.

• If a plane traveled for 3 hours at a constant speed of 500 mph, what was its average speed over the first two hours?

Because the speed was constant over the two-hour time period, 500 mph is also the average speed for the first two hours. It was the average speed for the entire 3-hour time period and for *any* portion of that time period.

• Suppose you took a road trip in which you drove for 1 hour at 60 mph, and then drove back the same distance on a scenic route at a leisurely 20 mph. What was your average speed? Hint: It is NOT 40 mph.

Look at the whole trip in equal time periods. The return distance of 60 miles will take 3 hours if you are driving at only 20 mph.

| Distance | 60 mi | 20 mi | 20 mi | 20 mi |
|---|---|---|---|---|
| Time | 1 hr | 1 hr | 1 hr | 1 hr |

When you look at this way, the total distance is 120 miles and it takes 4 hours. Therefore, the average speed is 30 mph.

• You drove a distance of 5 miles at 80 mph on the highway, then drove home 5 miles on the city streets at 40 mph. What was your average speed for the trip? *Hint*: It was NOT 60 mph. You spent different amounts of time traveling at each speed.

Analyze your trip in equal chunks of time. At 80 mph, you would go 5 miles in 3.75 minutes. Look at the trip in chunks of 3.75 minutes. At 40 mph, you could go only half as far in 3.75 minutes:

| Distance | 5 mi | 2.5 mi | 2.5 mi |
|---|---|---|---|
| Time | 3.75 min | 3.75 min | 3.75 min |

So the whole trip was 10 miles and it took 11.25 min. This would be a speed of $\frac{10}{11.25}$ mi per min or $\frac{10}{11.25} \cdot 60$ mph $= 55.33$ mph

- A biker went 10 mph for 30 minutes, got a flat tire, and had to walk the bike home at 4 mph. What was his average speed for the trip?

The average speed is NOT $\frac{10 + 4}{2} = 7$ mph. The reason is that the biker traveled at 10 mph for a much shorter time than he traveled at 4 mph.

The first part of the journey took 30 minutes. How long did the second part take? We know he went 5 miles before he got the flat tire, so he had to walk back 5 miles. At the rate of 4 mph, it would take him 1 hour and 15 minutes to walk back.

Now look at the total trip in chunks of 30 minutes. The first leg of the trip took 30 minutes, but the second took two 30-minute time periods plus another half of a 30-minute time period.

| Distance | 5 mi | 2 mi | 2 mi | 1 mi |
|---|---|---|---|---|
| Time | 30 min | 30 min | 30 min | 15 min |

This means that he traveled 10 miles in 1.75 hours. $\frac{10}{1.75} = 5.7$ mph

## DISTANCE–SPEED–TIME AND GRAPHS

Biker A traveled 40 miles in 3 hours. Biker B traveled 20 miles in 2 hours. Let's assume that they were each able to maintain a constant speed. The following distance–time graph reflects their trips.

Recall that distance = speed (or rate) × time or $d = st$. We know the time and distance for each biker, so we can find of their speeds.

$$s = \frac{d}{t}$$

A's speed is $\frac{40}{3} = 13.3$ mph. B's speed is $\frac{20}{2} = 10$ mph.

Now let's calculate the slope of each line on the graph.

A's slope $\frac{40 - 0}{3 - 0} = \frac{40}{3} = 13.3$. B's slope $= \frac{20 - 0}{2 - 0} = \frac{20}{2} = 10$

As you probably suspected, the slope of a line on a distance-time graph is speed. We could have known by looking at the graph that A was moving faster because his line was steeper.

My favorite graph story was this one, told by a middle school student. I told him that the following graph describes a trip that I took on Saturday. I asked him to tell me a story suggested by the graph.

*I think you went to the mountains and had a picnic then drove home a different way.*

Reading graphs is a problem for this student. He thinks that graphs are pictures. To read a graph, you must think about one variable *as compared to* the other. To help students read graphs correctly, it is useful to have them look at segments of this graph. Look at three rectangles that have been marked on the next graph.

Looking at the dotted rectangle farthest to the left, you can see that in 1 hour, the person traveled a distance of 6 miles. He must have had an average speed of 6 miles per hour. Where does that speed appear on the graph? Find the slope between the points

(0,0) (home) and the point (1,6) (the upper right corner of the rectangle). Slope is the vertical change over the horizontal change.

$$\text{slope} = \text{average speed} = \frac{\text{change in distance}}{\text{change in time}} = \frac{6-0}{1-0} = 6$$

The straight dotted line connecting the beginning point and the end point of that segment of the trip shows distance vs. time if the trip *had* been traveled at a constant speed. The average speed is the constant speed that characterizes that leg of the trip even though the traveler did not move at a constant speed; it is the slope of that straight segment.

Now look at the dotted rectangle that marks the second segment of the trip. Its width tells us that the time elapsed was 4 hours. The height of the rectangle tells us that the distance from home is still 6 miles. This means that for these 4 hours, the person was not moving. The average speed for this segment of the trip (from the point (1,6) to the point (5,6)) is 0.

For the final segment of the trip, the last 3 hours, the distance from home decreases until finally the person is home again. The time it took to the destination and the time it took to return home were different, even though the distance to and from the destination (6 miles) does not change. So the person must have traveled at a speed of 6 miles per 3 hours or 2 mph. The average speed for that segment of the trip, the slope of the dotted line from the point (5,6) to the point (8,0), is

$$\frac{\text{change in distance}}{\text{change in time}} = \frac{0-6}{8-5} = \frac{-6}{3} = -2\text{mph}$$

What could be the meaning of a negative speed? At this point, we begin to talk about velocity, rather than speed, and we introduce a new term so that we can talk about both the net distance from our starting point and the total distance traveled. Velocity is a vector composed of both speed and direction. In this problem, the velocity for the return trip was −2 mph, meaning that I traveled at a speed of 2 mph in a direction opposite to the way I first traveled. Displacement tells how far away I am from my starting point. My total distance traveled was 12 miles (6 mi there, 6 mi back), but the displacement for this journey was 0 because I ended up at my starting point.

## ACTIVITIES

1.  Translate these statements into ratio notation:

    a.  There are 2 boys for every 3 girls.

    b.  Farmer Jones has $\frac{4}{5}$ as many cows as pigs.

    c.  Mary is $\frac{2}{3}$ as tall as her mom.

    d.  Dan is $2\frac{1}{2}$ times as heavy as Becky.

2.  Interpret the following picture as (a) a part–whole comparison, and (b) a ratio.

3.  There are 100 seats in the theater, with 30 in the balcony and 70 on the main floor. 80 tickets were sold for the matinee performance, including all of the seats on the main floor.

    a.  What fraction of the seats were sold?
    b.  What is the ratio of balcony seats to seats on the floor?
    c.  What is the ratio of empty seats to occupied seats?
    d.  What is the ratio of empty seats to occupied seats in the balcony?

4.

    a.  If the larger gear makes one complete turn, how many turns will the smaller gear make?
    b.  If the small gear makes 5 turns, how many turns will the larger gear make?
    c.  How many teeth would the large gear need in order to make $1\frac{1}{3}$ turns in the time that the small gear makes 4 turns?
    d.  How many teeth would the smaller gear need in order to turn $3\frac{2}{3}$ times to 4 turns of the large gear?

5.  In a class of 27 students, the ratio of girls to boys is 3:6. Which of the following statements is (are) true?

    a.  We know exactly how many girls are in the class.
    b.  We can figure out how many boys there would be in a class of 36 students.
    c.  We know exactly how many boys are in the class.
    d.  If I randomly choose 9 students from the class, I can expect that 3 will be girls.
    e.  Half the class is female.
    f.  The ratio of boys to girls is 6:3.

6.  Kim compared $3:4$ and $5:9$ and her picture is shown here.

a.  What could she conclude?
b.  What do the 7 empty circles outside of the boxes mean?
c.  Reinterpret the picture in terms of a ratio subtraction and express symbolically.

7.  Make dot pictures comparing these ratios or fractions and write the operations symbolically:

a.  $5:6$ and $11:12$      b.  $12:16$ and $3:4$      c.  $5:8$ and $7:9$
d.  $\dfrac{7}{8}$ and $\dfrac{9}{10}$      e.  $7:8$ and $9:10$      f.  $\dfrac{4}{9}$ and $\dfrac{3}{10}$
g.  $4:5$ and $8:15$

8.  For each of the following situations, determine if the ratios are extendible to more general situations and reducible without loss of information.

a.  For every 3 adults in a theater there are 6 children.
b.  A small gear on a machine has 30 teeth and a large gear has 45 teeth.
c.  In a certain classroom, the ratio of children with pets to those without is $12:14$.
d.  The ratio of the perimeter to the area of a square is $12:9$.
e.  In a bag of candies, the ratio of red piece to green pieces is $3:6$.
f.  The ratio of my age to my mother's is $4:6$.
g.  Dave's height is 6 feet and his baby son is 24 inches long. The ratio of their heights is $6:2$.
h.  The Latte House sells coffee for $2.60 for 4 ounces.
i.  The Wilsons have 6 children. The ratio of boys to girls in the Wilson family is $4:2$.

9.  A school system reported that they had a student-teacher ratio of $30:1$. How many more teachers would they need to hire to reduce the ratio to $25:1$?

10. As children gain some facility with ratios, they begin to take shortcuts and to invent their own strategies for comparing. Sometimes they are good strategies; sometimes their strategies are flawed and need revision. Study the way each of these students reached his or her conclusion and determine which strategies are good ones.

Student A compares 3 : 4 and 5 : 8.

My picshure shows that 3:4 > 5:8.

Student B compares 3 : 4 and 5 : 6.

3:4 > 5:6 because there
are 5 copies of 3:4 and
only 3 copies of 5:6

11. Suppose the Sweet Shop sells Charles's favorite candy at 4 cents per gram. Charles bought it at a different store for $\frac{1}{4}$ gram per penny. Did he get a good deal or not?

12. Use ratio arithmetic to do these problems and fully interpret your results.

 a. Seven people paid $59 to get into the Golden Theatre. Three people paid $26 to get into the Starr Theatre. Which theatre has better ticket prices?
 b. Which is the better season record: 5 wins to 7 losses or 7 wins to 9 losses?
 c. Which is more crowded, a 6-seater car with 5 people in it, or a 14-seater van with 11 people in it?

13. The ratio of boys to girls in a class is 3 : 8. How many girls are in the class if there are 9 boys?

14. Several men share an office, Mr. A comes to work 2 days a week; Mr. B comes to work 4 days a week; Mr. C comes in 6 days a week. If the utility bill is $60 per week, how should they split the bill?

15. Solve this problem in your head. (Set up a "per" quantity.) $\frac{1}{2}$ liter of juice costs $1.89. At the same rate, what is the price per liter?

16. Solve this problem in your head. (Set up a "per" quantity.) John took a step that measured 0.75 meters long. Would it take more than 10 or fewer than 10 steps to measure a distance of 10 meters?

17. Two gears, A and B, are arranged so that their teeth mesh. Gear A turns clockwise and has 54 teeth. Gear B turns counterclockwise and has 36 teeth. If gear A makes 5.5 rotations, how many turns will gear B make?

18. What does each of these short stories tell you?

    a.  28 mi in 7 hr          b.  28 mph for 7 mi          c.  7 mi in 20 min
    d.  7 mi at 35 mph         e.  15 sec to go $\frac{1}{5}$ mi

19. Explain how you would compare drivers' speeds if you were the official:

    a.  in a 3-hour auto race
    b.  in a 50 km auto race

20. You decided to check the accuracy of the speedometer in your car by timing your travel between miles markers on the highway. If you found that it was 50 seconds between markers, what would you know?

21. If I drive to the mall on city streets, at 40 mph and it takes me 20 min to get there. I return the same distance at 50 mph on the highway. How long does the return trip take?

22. Jet Fighter 1 travels 75 miles in 225 seconds. Jet Fighter 2 travels 30 miles in 90 seconds. Their target is 110 miles away. Which will get there first?

23. A police helicopter clocked an automobile for 10 second over a stretch of highway $\frac{1}{5}$ mile long. At what rate was the auto traveling?

24. Jim cuts the lawn in 4 hours. His brother can cut the same lawn in 3 hours. If they work together, how long will it take to mow the lawn?

25. Mack and Tom are riding the train and trying to figure out the distance between the different stations. The only information they have is that it is 40 km between stations A and B. They use a watch to find the time between station A and B (16 minutes) and between station B and C (36 minutes). Assuming that the train ran at a constant speed, what is the distance between stations A and C?

26. Two workers working for 9 hours together made 243 parts. One of the workers makes 13 parts an hour. If the workers maintain a steady pace all day, how many parts does the second worker make in an hour?

27. Your salary rose $2.50 per hour in your first year with the company, then stayed the same for the next 2 years. What was your average salary increase for the first 3 years?

28. Suppose that while you were driving along, you noted the time at the following mile markers.

| Time | Mile Marker |
|------|-------------|
| 2:00 pm | 42 |
| 2:29 pm | 66 |
| 3:01 pm | 105 |

   a.  What is the average rate of change of distance between mile 42 and mile 66 in miles per hour?

   b.  What is the average rate of change of distance between mile 66 and mile 105 in miles per hour?

   c.  What is the average speed of your car between mile 42 and mile 105?

29.  On a 6-mile stretch of road, two people started running together as part of their daily exercise routine. You looked down from a helicopter and checked the position of each person every 10 minutes and made the following sketch of what you saw.

   a.  Who was moving faster?

   b.  How can you figure out exactly how fast each person was moving?

   c.  Was that an average speed or a steady pace? How can you tell?

30.  Jake went on a 60-kilometer bike ride. After 3 hours, he was 40 kilometers from the start, but he was tired and he slowed down. He did the remaining 20 kilometers in 2 hours.

   a.  What was his average speed on the first part of the trip?

   b.  What was his average speed on the second part of the trip?

   c.  What was his average speed for the whole journey?

31.  My friend and I exercise together and we are always looking for new scenery on our hikes, so we take a bus out into the country and then walk back. The bus travels at about 9 mph, and we walk at the rate of 3 mph. If we have only 8 hours for our trip on Saturday, how far can we go before we get off the bus?

32.  Troy and his older sister Tara run a race. Troy runs at an average of 3 meters every second and Terry runs at an average of 5 meters every second. In a 100-meter race,

Troy gets a head start of 40 meters because he runs at a slower pace. Who wins the race?

33. Maurice was driving his car and Jenny was following in her car right behind him. It took them 25 minutes to drive 50 kilometers to Maurice's home. Jenny continued for another 150 kilometers at the same speed until she reached her home.

   a. How much longer did it take Jenny to get home?
   b. Which quantities are proportional? Solve this problem using the constant of proportionality.

34. Information about two cars and the trips they took is contained in the following distance-time graphs. In each case, what can you tell about the cars?

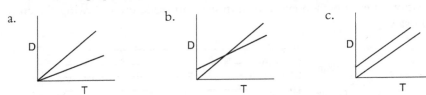

35. This graph relates the distance to the time elapsed on a trip in an experimental airplane. During which hour was the average speed of this airplane the greatest?

36. Dee and Mary are in a handicapped race. Dee runs at an average speed of 7 meters per second and is not given a head start. Mary runs at an average speed of 5 meters per second and is given a head start of 7 meters. Will they ever meet? If so, when?

# CHAPTER 12

# Changing Instruction

---

## STUDENT COMMENTS: GRADE 6

The math lady really makes us think. My brain is fried. I never thought so hard in my life.

Math class is so much fun I wish we could do it all day. The time goes by too fast.

I think I'll be some kind of career that uses math because I get good ideas in math class.

We talk about math every night at dinner time. My dad says the whole family is learning how to think.

---

## WHY CHANGE?

No one knows better than teachers who have had experience teaching fractions that current instruction is not serving many students. However, in addition to having a *need* to change, there must be a viable direction for change. Research has now gone beyond documenting student difficulties and has moved toward uncovering promising new activities and teaching methods. A few of the most compelling reasons to change fraction instruction are given here.

- Fraction, ratio, and other multiplicative ideas are psychologically and mathematically complex and interconnected. It is impossible to specify a linear ordering of topics (as in a scope and sequence chart) that can be used to plan instruction.

- A long-term learning process is required for understanding the web of ideas related to proportional reasoning. Current instruction that gives a brief introduction to part-whole fractions and then proceeds to introduce computation procedures does not give children the time they need to construct and become comfortable with important ideas and way of thinking.

- Students whose instruction has concentrated on part–whole fractions have an impoverished understanding of rational numbers. Although there are multiple different interpretations of a rational number, these are represented by a single fraction symbol $\left(\text{for example, } \dfrac{3}{4}\right)$. Instruction needs to provide children the opportunity to build a broad base of meaning for fraction symbols, to become flexible in moving back and forth among meanings, to establish connections among them, and to understand how the meanings influence the operations one is allowed to perform. It is simply not sufficient to use only part-whole fractions as a basis for building understanding of rational numbers.

- The fact that a large portion of the adult population does not reason proportionally suggests that certain kinds of thinking do not occur spontaneously and that instruction needs to take an active role in facilitating thinking that will lead to proportional reasoning.

- It is estimated that over 90% of students entering high school do not reason well enough to learn high school mathematics and science with understanding. This means that for most people, maturation and experience, even when they are supplemented by current instruction, are not sufficient to develop sophisticated mathematical reasoning.

- Long-term studies show that instruction and learning can be improved. Research in which children were given the time to develop their reasoning for 4 years without being taught the standard algorithms for operating with fractions and ratios produced a dramatic increase in students' reasoning abilities, including their proportional reasoning. The student work in the preceding chapters illustrates the powerful thinking that they produced.

- Even for students who will never pursue work in mathematics-related or science-related fields, reasoning in many everyday contexts can be greatly enhanced by the content and thinking methods you have studied in this book. It is virtually impossible to run a household or to understand magazine and newspaper articles without some facility in decimals, percents, probability, similarity, recipe conversions, gas consumption, map reading, inflation, scale drawings, slopes, fluid concentrations, speed, reducing and enlarging, density, comparison shopping, and monetary conversions.

## A SUMMARY OF FRACTION INTERPRETATIONS

In this book, we looked at 5 rational number interpretations and the ways that they might be approached in fraction instruction. In the chart on the next page, these interpretations are summarized using the fraction $\dfrac{3}{4}$ as an example.

The question naturally arises as to the kind of learning experiences that will result in a well-rounded understanding of the five interpretations. One way that question is asked is: Should we teach one interpretation in depth or should instruction include all of the interpretations? This is the wrong question. As we have seen, all of the interpretations do not provide equal access to a deep understanding and no single interpretation is a panacea. On the other hand, interpretations are tightly intertwined and with the proper attention to other components of instruction, we can help to facilitate the growth of other interpretations. Here is brief summary of each fraction personality and the connections that developed when it was used as the primary interpretation in fraction instruction in longitudinal studies.

| Interpretations of $\frac{3}{4}$ | Meaning | Selected Classroom Activities |
|---|---|---|
| Part-Whole Comparisons with Unitizing<br><br>"3 parts out of 4 equal parts" | $\frac{3}{4}$ means three parts out of four equal parts of the unit, with equivalent fractions found by thinking of the parts in terms of larger or smaller chunks.<br><br>$\frac{3}{4}$ pies $= \frac{12}{16}\left(\frac{1}{4}\text{-pies}\right) = \frac{1\frac{1}{2}}{2}$ (pair of pies) | Unitizing to produce equivalent fractions and to compare fractions |
| Measure<br><br>"$3\left(\frac{1}{4}-\text{units}\right)$" | $\frac{3}{4}$ means a distance of $3\left(\frac{1}{4}\text{-units}\right)$ from<br><br>0 on the number line or $3\left(\frac{1}{4}\text{-units}\right)$<br><br>of a given area. | Successive partitioning of a number line; reading meters and gauges |
| Operator<br><br>"$\frac{3}{4}$ of something" | $\frac{3}{4}$ gives a rule that tells how to operate on a unit (or on the result of a previous operation); multiply by 3 and divide your result by 4 or divide by 4 and multiply the result by 3. This results in multiple meanings for $\frac{3}{4}$: $3\left(\frac{1}{4}\text{-units}\right)$, $1\left(\frac{3}{4}\text{-units}\right)$ and $\frac{1}{4}$ (3-unit) | Machines, paper folding, Xeroxing, Discounting, Area Models for Multiplication and Division |
| Quotient<br>"3 divided by 4" | $\frac{3}{4}$ is the amount each person receives when 4 people share a 3-unit of something. | Partitioning, sharing |
| Ratios<br>"3 to 4" | $3:4$ is a relationship in which there are 3 A's compared, in a multiplicative rather than an additive sense, to 4 B's. | Bi-color chip activities |

## CENTRAL STRUCTURES

There are certain themes that are pervasive in mathematics. They run through a vast expanse of the curriculum, right into the college years when students study calculus. I think of them as *central* structures because they are so critical to mathematical thinking in general. They support a much bigger system than just rational number learning. These are overlapping—but different—ideas that have a symbiotic relationship. Growth in one of nodes of the following diagram has repercussions in the other nodes as well.

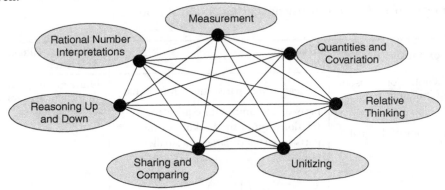

These ideas are central in yet another sense. They are critical to the way in which children's mathematical thinking develops. These nodes were identified not merely by studying abstract mathematics, but also through years of research that studied the way children think in real situations where that mathematics comes into play. Phenomenological research, as it is called, first identified the kinds of experiences and situations from which the mathematics naturally emerges, but then studied what children perceive about those situations and how they come to understand them.

When instruction focused on all of the nodes of this diagram simultaneously, children's understanding "grew" together and although they did not receive explicit instruction in other interpretations, by the end of grade 6, they were using multiple interpretations and they engaged in reasoning such as I have never seen from such young children. Their fraction operations were strong; they had developed the conventional algorithms for fractions operations, or some equally good alternative algorithms of their own invention. Finally, the elusive by-product of fraction instruction, proportional reasoning, was strong among these children.

## CHARACTERISTICS OF PROPORTIONAL THINKERS

When students reason proportionally, their thinking is marked by most of the following characteristics. You will recognize these characteristics in the kinds of reasoning that are encouraged throughout this book.

- Proportional thinkers do not think solely in terms of 1-units or unit rates, such as $\dfrac{13 \text{ miles}}{1 \text{ gallon of gas}}$ or $\dfrac{\$1.19}{1 \text{ pound}}$. They think in terms of complex units, such as 3-units or 10-units, and they use composite units, when possible. That is, instead of opening packs of gum and counting individual sticks, they can think in terms of packs. When possible, they reason with unreduced rates such as $\dfrac{26 \text{ miles}}{2 \text{ gallons of gas}}$ or $\dfrac{\$1.98}{3 \text{ pounds}}$.

- They exhibit greater efficiency in problem-solving. The ability to think in terms of composite units gives them this advantage. One example is in cases where unit pricing produces nonterminating decimals. If oranges are priced 3 for $0.68, it is more efficient to think of the price of 12 as $0.68 × (4 groups of three) = $2.72.

- They understand equivalence and the concept *same relative amount*.

- Proportional thinkers can look at a unit displayed in an array, such as the one shown here, and immediately see how many objects are in $\dfrac{1}{3}, \dfrac{1}{2}, \dfrac{1}{4}, \dfrac{1}{6}, \dfrac{1}{12}, \dfrac{2}{3}, \dfrac{3}{4}, \dfrac{5}{6}$, and so on.

- They can flexibly interpret quantities. For example, 3 apples for 24 cents can be interpreted as 8 cents per apple or as $\dfrac{1}{8}$ apple per 1 cent. They can unitize (mentally regroup) several times without losing track of the unit.

- Proportional thinkers are not afraid of decimals and fractions. Often, students replace the fractions and decimals with whole numbers (nice numbers) to help them think about a problem. They exhibit a kind of fraction and decimal avoidance, while proportional thinkers move around flexibly in the world of fractions and decimals.

- They have often developed strategies—sometimes unique strategies—for dealing with problems such as finding fractions between two given fractions.

- They are able to mentally use exact divisors to their best advantage and can quickly compute, say, $\dfrac{3}{8}$, if they know $\dfrac{1}{8}$, 80% if they know 10% or 20%, or add $\dfrac{1}{8} + \dfrac{1}{16}$ if they know $\dfrac{1}{2}$.

- They have a sense of co-variation. This means that they can analyze quantities that are changing together, talk about direction of change and rate of change, and determine relationships that remain unchanged.

- Proportional thinkers can identify everyday contexts in which proportions are or are not useful. Proportions are not just mathematical objects or situations to which they know how to apply an algorithm. They can distinguish proportional from nonproportional situations and will not blindly apply an algorithm if the situation does not involve proportional relationships.

- They have developed a vocabulary for explaining their thinking in proportional situations.
- Proportional thinkers are adept at using scaling strategies. For example, they are able to reason up and down in both missing value and comparison problems, whether quantities are expressed using fractions, decimals, or percents.
- By seventh or eighth grade, they understand the relationships in simple proportional and inversely proportional situations so well that they have discovered for themselves the cross-multiply-and-divide algorithm.

## OBSTACLES TO CHANGE

It is important to emphasize the difference between *changing* instruction and *adding* to the mathematics curriculum. Teachers argue that there is no room in the curriculum for additional topics; they can barely "cover" everything as it is. The research on which this book is based was carried out in real classrooms, fully integrated with multicultural students and disabled students, by teachers who had a full syllabus in their mathematics classes. For these teachers, changing their mathematics instruction meant engaging children in reasoning about fractions and ratios, instead of drilling year after year on fraction computation algorithms. The operating theory was that if you can teach children to reason and to solve problems, their ability to think mathematically will pay off in the long run and will have consequences in all of the mathematics they will study in the future. In other words, teaching kids to use their heads replaced all the time that would have been spent drilling on algorithms. In addition, the teacher who is really committed to changing kids' encounter with fractions, uses study hall time, homework, projects, group work, work stations, and other means to incorporate good reasoning activities.

The second big issue raised by teachers is that they have to prepare their students for standardized state-mandated exams. My response is that conventional fraction instruction continues to result in poor performance on fractions year after year. If you keep doing the same thing, how realistic is it to expect different results? It is true that at the end of third and fourth grade, the students in my study could not yet carry out fraction computation, so their scores on standardized test questions requiring computation were also poor. However, the big differences showed up by the end of grade 6. While other children continued to do poorly on the fraction components of the exam, the children in the study far exceeded them on both computation, conceptual, and problem-solving questions. The moral of the story is: take time to lay a good foundation or you will persist in the teach/re-teach activities that are currently used with very low success.

## SEQUENCING TOPICS

In short, decision-making always involves trade-offs. Scope and sequence charts result from an author's decisions to create chapters that convey a simple and sequential ordering of the content. There is nothing scared about the order. Other arrangements might work equally well. Because there is not sufficient research to suggest how learners psychologize a topic, sequencing decisions are made in the interest of neatly packaging mathematical topics, with little consideration of the way in which children meet the topics in their everyday experience and little consideration of the way in which children's minds work.

The reality is that adults make decisions about what to teach based on what they *think* children of a certain age can handle. We have to wonder how many of these decisions are limiting achievement rather than encouraging it. We are often amazed by children's multitasking abilities, yet instruction is built to deal with one little topic at a time. Life experience is complicated, yet in mathematics class, we deem certain topics too difficult and put them off until middle school, as if protecting children from complexity. We have to wonder if artificially forcing children to think inside our little packages is teaching them that mathematics has nothing to do with real life.

Take, for example, the topic of ratios. We have seen that it is practically impossible to keep part—whole and part—part comparisons separated in real life situations. Ratio thinking is pervasive in daily applications, and we move back and forth between the two modes of thinking all the time. Children have been exposed to both kinds of comparisons in their everyday living for 7 or 8 years and then, at the start of fraction instruction, someone makes the decision to protect them from ratios until late middle school. How badly does this decision curtail the achievement of children who have a propensity for ratios by limiting them to part—whole thinking?

It is clear that the central structures chart above is not sequential. After many years of research on children's thinking, we know that learning does not occur in a lock-step manner, no matter how hard we might channel our students into a specific scope-and-sequence regimen. In addition, when we move from whole numbers to fractions, the mathematics takes a giant leap in complexity, and there is a dramatic increase in the types of everyday phenomena that nuance our fraction understanding.

## DIRECTIONS FOR CHANGE

Over the last 10 years, textbook authors have gradually incorporated these new approaches to fraction instruction. But change is always a long-term process. It is still up to teachers to commit to change that is recognizable in their teaching methods and in the general culture within their mathematics classes. The teacher needs to be able to handle an unspecified, nonsequential treatment of topics to make change happen. People who have read this book already have the first and most important requirement for change: dissatisfaction with what their students are learning under current fraction instruction. To whatever degree you are comfortable and confident in incorporating changes, I encourage you to do so. Of course, to achieve a radical make-over of fraction instruction will require a commitment from all of the teachers your students will meet over several years of fraction instruction. If you want to improve your instruction and such a large commitment is not forthcoming, there is still a great deal you can do as an individual.

As you read the chapters, you probably came across some activities or some ideas that you liked and with which you felt comfortable. Incorporate these into your current fraction instruction.

- Assign problems from this book to your students for homework. Ask them to discuss the problems at home with parents or older brothers and sisters.
- Use the activities as a warm-up activity every day. Have the students discuss them in class.
- Have problems available for students to do during study periods or free time.

# Index